EDUCATION, TRAINING
and ECONOMIC PERFORMANCE

EDUCATION, TRAINING
and
ECONOMIC PERFORMANCE
1944 to 1990

Derek H. Aldcroft

MANCHESTER UNIVERSITY PRESS
MANCHESTER AND NEW YORK

distributed exclusively in the USA and Canada by St. Martin's Press

Copyright © Derek H. Aldcroft 1992

Published by Manchester University Press
Oxford Road, Manchester M13 9PL, UK
and Room 400, 175 Fifth Avenue, New York,
NY 10010, USA

British Library Cataloguing-in-Publication Data
A catalogue record for this book is available from the British Library

Library of Congress cataloging in publication data
Aldcroft, Derek Howard.
    Education, training, and economic performance, 1944 to 1990 /
Derek H. Aldcroft
        p.   cm.
    Includes bibliographical references (p.   ) and index.
    ISBN 0–7190–3460–4
    1. Economic development—Effect of education on.   2. Education—
Great Britain.   3. Vocational education—Great Britain.   I. Title.
HD75.7.A43   1992
331.11′4—dc20   91–39719

Photoset in Linotron Janson
by Northern Phototypesetting Co., Ltd, Bolton

Printed in Great Britain
by Billings of Worcester

CONTENTS

PREFACE

This book is not a history of postwar education and training as such since there are already plenty of institutional and policy discussions in print. Rather its specific aim is to illustrate some of the main shortcomings in educational provision which are particularly relevant to Britain's economy. The period covered spans the two major Education Acts of 1944 and 1988, popularly known as the Butler and Baker Acts.

Not every aspect of education and training is covered. Attention is focused on the major sectors: compulsory education; vocational education and training; higher education; and the education and training of managers. These subjects comprise Chapters 3–6. Chapter 2 discusses the general relationships between education and economic growth and development and examines the postwar British experience in aggregate terms. Chapter 7 looks at some of the ways in which educational and training deficiences have affected economic performance. The final chapter considers some of the reasons for Britain's poor showing in this field.

This volume grew out of a larger study of the British economy in the postwar period and a preliminary paper was presented to the Tenth International Economic History Congress held in Leuven in August 1990. At a preparatory meeting in Valencia in the previous year led by Professor Tortella, I benefited from the stimulus and comments of several scholars working in the field of education and economic development.

I should like to thank Steven Morewood, Research Associate in Economic History in the University of Leicester, for invaluable help in supplying references and taking an interest in a subject well removed from his own field of study, and Roy Kirk, Librarian of the School of Education Library in the University of Leicester, for his unfailing good humour when faced with my persistent bibliographical inquiries. Gillian Austen of the Department of Economic and Social History very kindly prepared the large tables. I am also grateful to Christopher Pollock who loaned me his word processor during the summer vacation.

Derek H. Aldcroft
University of Leicester

1
INTRODUCTION

The relevance of education and training to the economy has long been recognised. So too have the criticisms of the state of English education in this respect. As far back as 1690 an anonymous writer in *A Discourse of the Necessity of Encouraging Mechanick Industry*, expatiated on a now all too familiar theme: a weakness in mechanicks and finer arts compared with other countries such that we were 'now supplied from foreign parts with divers Commodities which, if the kingdom were replenished with Artizans they would furnish us with here at home'. Foreigners were more adept at acquiring mechanical skills: German apprentices, it was stated, took only four years in their training, whereas the British required seven largely because they were poorly educated before they embarked on their apprenticeship training (quoted in Evans and Wiseman 1984 129–30). As we shall see, by all accounts things have not changed much today.

Nearly a century later Adam Smith in his *Wealth of Nations* (1776 Book V Article II) echoed a similar theme. He was concerned that the 'common people' should receive at least the most essential parts of a basic education, especially in the elementary parts of geometry and mechanicks, before undertaking any employment. However, he expressed dissatisfaction with what was being taught on the grounds that it did not provide for life-time needs. 'if, instead of a little smattering of Latin; which the children of the common people are sometimes taught . . ., and which can scarce ever be any use to them: they were instructed in the elementary parts of geometry and mech-anicks, the literary education of this rank of people would perhaps be as complete as it can be.' He also criticised education of a more advanced type as being unsuitable for the needs of business: 'The greater part of what is taught in schools and universities . . . does not seem to be the most proper preparation for that business . . . which is to employ them (men) during the remainder of their days.'

During the nineteenth century criticisms of Britain's lagging educational system came thick and fast. In a lecture to the School of Mines

in 1851, Lyon Playfair argued that scientific skills would be the asset
of the future and that success on the industrial front would depend on
how efficiently these were exploited. Playfair subsequently toured the
continent to get a first-hand view of technical and scientific education
abroad. He found a much greater measure of state support for education generally on the continent, especially in Germany, whereas
England had no proper organised system of general education, let
alone technical instruction (Roderick and Stephens 1978 3–4;
Roderick and Stephens 1981 6). He continued to press the case for
better provision since he believed the poor quality of education was
'impoverishing the land'. (Mathieson and Bernbaum 1988 157).

The debate was taken up by *The Economist* in 1862 (19 April 423,
quoted in Musgrave 1967 258) when it argued that the low state of
intelligence and education among the population was resulting in 'the
want of pliability and flexibility' and inhibiting adaptation to new
circumstances. The message was rammed home even more forcibly a
few years later when the Schools Inquiry Commission (Taunton
Report 1868 79–80), in a wide-ranging investigation into the state of
the country's education, found that:

> our industrial classes have not even that basis of sound general educa-
> tion on which alone technical instruction can rest. It would not be
> difficult, if our artizans were otherwise well educated, to establish
> schools for technical instruction of whatever kind might be needed. But
> even if such schools were generally established among us, there is
> reason to fear that they would fail to produce any valuable results for
> want of the essential material, namely, disciplined faculties and sound
> elementary knowledge in the learners. In fact, our deficiency is not
> merely a deficiency in technical instruction, but . . . in general intelli-
> gence, and unless we remedy this want we shall gradually but surely find
> that our undeniable superiority in wealth and perhaps in energy will not
> save us from decline.

What was all the more remarkable about the Inquiry was its per-
ceptive insight as to future needs and its emphasis on the expediency
of devising a basic curriculum of useful subjects backed up by efficient
testing. While classical studies should not be sacrificed, they would
have to make room for more relevant subjects such as mathematics,
practical mechanics, modern languages and natural sciences, along
the lines of the *Realschulen* in Prussia. The Commission laid great
stress on the importance of raising the standard of attainment in
mathematical skills. Pupils should receive sound instruction in arith-

metic which should never be dropped since 'There can be little doubt that the inefficient teaching of arithmetic to little boys is at present a great obstacle to good instruction in mathematics and natural science in all our schools. . . . The aim should be to reconcile the cultivation of the faculties with the requirements needed for business and for professions' (Taunton 1868 82–6).

Some of the Commission's observations and suggestions have a very familiar modern ring to them. Would that their recommendations had been heeded Britain might today have a more efficient educational system. Needless to say, though considerable progress was made in developing the state education system in the latter half of the nineteenth century it was rarely free from criticism. The Royal Commission on Technical Instruction of the early 1880s (Samuelson Reports 1882–4), for example, could still find cause to complain that the neglect of education and training was a major factor in Britain's declining competitiveness, while a decade later the Bryce Commission (Bryce Report 1895) compared Britain's secondary education unfavourably with that on the continent. Shortly after the turn of the century Shadwell (1906 407), in a comparative survey of industrial efficiency, felt that British state education presented a sorry spectacle compared with the American or German: 'it has neither the inspiring idea of the one, nor the methodical completeness of the other, and it cannot be doubted that the country has suffered in comparison.'

The educational system continued to come in for criticism following the 1914–18 war. In contrast to that of the nineteenth century, it was centred less on the economic handicap arising from inadequate provision than on the social inequalities and wastage of talent as a result of the narrow opportunities available to the bulk of the nation's youth. The Hadow Committee, reporting in December 1926 (Hadow Report 1926 51–2), were distressed to find so few youngsters over the age of 11 had any chance of receiving advanced instruction either in elementary schools or in secondary schools. Only about 7.5 per cent of the age cohort of 11–15 were in secondary schools of one sort or another, while some two-thirds of the children over the age of 11 in elementary schools were not receiving any advanced instruction. Most children in fact abandoned their studies at the age of 14 so that the numbers staying on even to the age of 15 or 16 were very small indeed. In the same year, Kenneth Lindsay in *Social Progress and Educational Waste* (1926 7, 23–4) deplored the fact that a large segment of the nation's children of proven ability were denied the opportunity of expression. He estimated that of the 2.8 million adolescents in England and Wales no less than 80 per cent were not in full-time attendance at any school, and that at least 50 per cent of the pupils in elementary schools could stand to profit from some form of post-primary education up to the age of 16. Two years later the Liberal Industrial Inquiry (1928 393) argued strongly in favour of a system of universal education for 14–18-year-olds:

> We believe that no system of Education can be satisfactory if it does not provide for the age of adolescence; that the present lack of physical, mental, moral, and social training during the 14–18-year period prejudices our future as a nation, and that it is as much to the interest of employers that the educational needs of their juvenile workers should be met, as it is to that of the nation to meet the rightful demands which industry makes on the schools.

The plain fact was that though Britain by this time had an educational ladder it was a very narrow one. Only a small élite, principally those in the public schools and grammar schools, enjoyed the benefits of advanced secondary education with the opportunity to proceed to higher education. For the vast majority of children the only alternative was the elementary school which they left with little qualification at the age of 14. The chances of an elementary school child getting to the university were very slim indeed, only one in a thousand making the grade (Lindsay 1926 7). After elementary school there was little prospect of further education and training while in employment except for part-time evening study on a voluntary basis. Few firms, apart from those with formal apprenticeship schemes, regarded it their duty to educate and train their young workers and so the vast majority received no further instruction. Possibly some 15 per cent of youngsters, according to one sample inquiry, continued their education by attending classes at evening schools (Liberal Industrial Inquiry 1928 384).

Yet during the brief postwar reconstruction phase there had been high hopes of progress in the educational field, as in so many other areas of social policy. The Education Act of 1918 (Fisher's Act) held out promise of a better future. Compulsory schooling was made universal to the age of 14 and the local education authorities (LEAs) had the option of raising it to 15 if they so wished. The Board of Education and the LEAs were empowered to provide a comprehensive system of education from nursery school to evening classes. In addition, provision was made for the creation of continuation schools where young people between the ages of 14 and 18 were to carry on their education on a part-time basis for one day a week. The Act also expressed the pious hope that no child of proven ability should be debarred from receiving instruction through want of the ability to pay fees.

Many of the noble aspirations of this period, including those for education, were destined to be frustrated in the subsequent economy campaigns of the early 1920s when public expenditure was cut back sharply. This doomed the continuation schools and effectively put paid to the raising of the school leaving age to 15 which was an essential step towards a viable system of universal secondary education. However, all was not lost in this respect. The Hadow inquiry of 1926, whose recommendations were to form the basis of the future structure of education, proposed the scrapping of the all-age elementary system of education and its replacement by a universal system of post-primary education to be carried out preferably in separate establishments. The break would occur at the age of 11 and all normal children between the ages of 11 and 14, and as soon as possible 11 to 15, 'should go forward to some form of post-primary education' (Hadow Report 1926 172–3). Several types of school, with curricula and examinations suited to the differing abilities of pupils, were envisaged: the existing grammar schools were to cater for academic pupils and likewise the junior technical and trade schools for the vocationally orientated; the proposed modern schools, both selective and non-selective, would have 'a realistic or practical trend'; and finally, senior departments within the existing elementary schools were for children not going to any of the above schools.

The reorganisation along Hadow lines was the major feature of interwar educational history, though it was by no means complete by the end of the period. By 1938 the majority of children over the age of 11 were in reorganised modern schools or in senior departments of all-age schools, though few could claim to have a standard of instruction comparable to that in the grammar schools. In fact many of the reorganisations were often little more than window-dressing, since the separation of junior and senior departments took place without any effort being made to provide an education in senior schools or departments which differed radically from the previous elementary type (Cole 1937 306). The secondary schools (mainly the grammar) still only absorbed a small minority of the age group – no more than 14 per cent, either fee-paying or scholarship pupils – while trade schools of one sort or another were insignificant in terms of numbers.

Though the window of educational opportunity had been widened a little by the end of the interwar period, it was still a very restricted one. The vast majority of youngsters left elementary school at the age of 14 having received limited advanced instruction and with very few qualifications to show for their years at school (Simon 1991 26). Only a small minority of non-secondary school pupils, about 15 per cent, continued schooling beyond the age of 14 and most of those who went on to higher education originated in the public schools and, to a lesser extent, the grammar schools. The free place or scholarship, the numbers of which varied enormously from one area to another, was the only means open to children from lower income families of gaining access to proper secondary education. Even then free places were not always taken up because of the financial circumstances of the parents (Branson and Heinemann 1971 169). The prospects of an elementary school child reaching the university had only increased marginally.

Furthermore, for the majority of early school leavers the prospects for further education and training while in employment were very limited indeed. Plans for continuing education under the 1918 Act proved abortive and for the most part employers were not interested in promoting the instruction of their charges. Day-release facilities to attend external instruction were almost non-existent and, in any case, many who had left school at 14 were simply not sufficiently qualified to benefit from technical education, a problem which is still with us today. Ambitious and intelligent youngsters had little option therefore but to study part-time in their leisure. Judging by the large numbers enrolled in part-time classes at technical colleges or evening institutes, the age of self-help had not yet passed away. Over two million annually were on the registers in the 1930s, though since many students enrolled for more than one subject while others enrolled at the start of the term without attending regularly, the effective number of students was probably about half this total (Stevenson 1984 253; Cole 1937 296). Nevertheless, judging by the courses taken the great majority were studying utilitarian or vocational subjects which would be of benefit to them in their employment. 'The "black-coated" proletariat consists to an ever-increasing extent of these qualified workers, who have laboured away in the evenings to advance themselves, and by that means have in most cases raised themselves up the social ladder' (Cole 1937 297–9).

Thus by the end of the 1930s the educational system was still one dominated by class and money. The ability to pay determined in large part the quality of education received. Estimates suggest that almost as much talent was going to waste for lack of opportunity as had been the case at the beginning of the interwar years (Cole 1937 278, 318). It was with the intention of remedying this loss to the community that the educational planning of the war years leading to the Act of 1944 was aimed. Universal free secondary education at last became a reality, and the school leaving age was finally raised to 15 to make that reality effective.

In the decades after the second world war therefore, educational opportunity widened considerably, but it continued to retain some of its former exclusive characteristics with the result that class inequalities remained significant throughout the period (Sked 1987 75). Yet the expansion in facilities and opportunities did not quell the volume of criticism of the shortcomings of the educational system which, if anything, increased over time. The latest and most scathing indictment by an American management consultant (Porter 1990 497) sums up much of the past record:

The British educational system has badly lagged behind that of virtually all the nations we studied. Access to top-quality education has been limited to a few, and a smaller percentage of students go on to higher education than in most other advanced nations. Education for the elite has stressed humanities and pure science in favor of more practical pursuits, and many talented people in Britain have avoided practical disciplines such as engineering. Consequently, the proportion of university students in technical areas is lower than in other advanced nations. Even engineering has been treated in a theortical way at the leading universities.

The more serious problem is the education of the average student. British children are taught by teachers less qualified than those in many nations, receive less training in math(s) and science, put in fewer hours, and drop out more. The thrust of educational reform until the Thatcher years was to make the system more egalitarian rather than competitive. Standards have fallen and the performance of British children with them. . . . Moreover, once they are out of secondary school the alternatives are thin. Technical colleges still have a low status, and there is no well-developed apprenticeship system as in

Germany. The government-sponsored Youth Training Scheme, still poorly linked to the needs of industry, has not compensated.

In the chapters which follow we shall seek to determine the extent and substance of these allegations.

2
EDUCATION AND
THE ECONOMY

Education and economic growth

How do education and training affect the economy? Do greater inputs produce a better economic performance, and if so should lagging countries strive to pour more resources into these areas? Unfortunately there is no clear consensus on this matter. About the only point of agreement in the continuing debate on education and economic growth is that it is a big and complex subject the links between which are anything but clear-cut (Fagerlind and Saha 1989 91).

In very general terms one might plausibly expect that countries which spend heavily on education and training would do better economically than those which spend proportionately less. Taken to the extreme there is obviously a world of difference in terms of acquisitive instincts and skills and abilities between pre-literate or semi-literate societies and those which have an extensive system of formal education. In the former case it has been argued that some threshold level of literacy and education needs to be attained before modernisation and industrialisation can take place since to take advantage of economic opportunities a country requires a flexible, mobile and acquisitive workforce and such characteristics are only likely to emerge through investment in human capital development (Sandberg 1982 681–2; Easterlin 1981 7–14). On the other hand, some of the threshold levels of educational attainment specified as prerequisites for the early stages of modern economic growth have been questioned by other writers (Mitch in Tortella 1990 29–41).

In broad terms one can demonstrate a systematic relationship between income levels and educational endowment. A cross-section analysis of various countries shows that low income nations tend to have high rates of illiteracy, notably in Africa and Asia, and to a lesser extent in Latin America, whereas at the other extreme, highly literate nations have the highest per capita incomes (World Bank 1990 178–9). Kindleberger's graph (Fig. 2.1) depicts illiteracy rates at

Fig. 2.1 Literacy and income levels

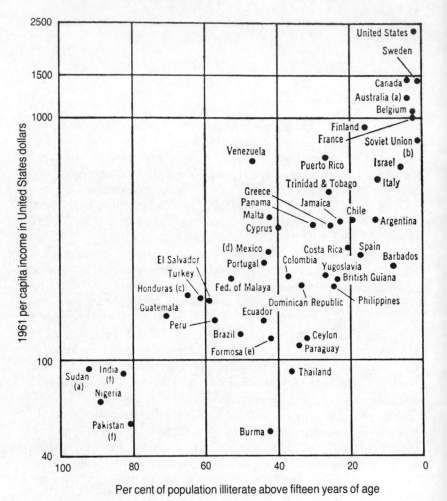

(a) For five years of age and older
(b) For ages nine–forty nine
(c) For ten years and older
(d) For six years and older
(e) For twelve years of age and older
(f) Data for population of all ages

Source: Kindleberger (1965 31)

various dates between 1945 and 1960 and per capita incomes in 1961 for a range of countries, and shows a fairly positive relationship between the two (Kindleberger 1965 31). Especially significant are the very low levels of literacy in many Asian and African countries – averaging around 70 per cent in the 1950s – in which the lowest incomes are to be found (Bairoch 1975 137). Of course the relationship is by no means perfect, nor can one necessarily infer any strong causal link between the two variables. Low income countries may have limited human resource endowments simply because they cannot afford anything better, while some countries with low rates of literacy, for example Middle East oil exporters, have relatively high incomes. Moreover, as Sandberg (1982 687) noted in his study of nineteenth-century European economies, relative literacy is not necessarily a reliable indicator of relative income at any one point in time. Several of today's developed countries, notably Denmark, Norway, Sweden, Finland and Germany, ranked highly in terms of literacy in 1850 yet their per capita incomes were still quite low compared with those of England and Wales, Belgium and Switzerland.

When we turn to the more mature economies which currently spend a fairly high proportion of their income on education and training, the differences in performance may be less readily apparent. Different levels of resource input into human capital improvement may not necessarily be reflected in differential economic pay-offs. For one thing there may be a point at which increased educational expenditure runs into diminishing returns, possibly as a result of the inflation of educational credentials (Dore 1976). There is moreover the qualitative factor to be taken into consideration. For example, two countries with virtually identical spending on education (that is per head or as a proportion of GNP) may not derive identical economic benefit from the outlay since one country may concentrate its spending on more productive activities such as vocational training and technological studies, while the other devotes the major share of its educational spending to areas with only a marginal relevance to economic growth, for example drama, music, historical studies and the humanities. Furthermore, even if the structural mix of their spending is very similar, the quality of the respective inputs may vary enormously in aggregate and between sectors owing to differences in the calibre of teachers and methods of instruction, the syllabi taught and even the quality of the candidates receiving instruction. Cultural and religious factors may also adversely affect both the quantity and quality of the final output. Spain in the nineteenth century experienced rapid educational growth but its content was so dominated by the narrow and restrictive influence of the Roman Catholic Church that as late as 1900 some two-thirds of the population remained illiterate (Easterlin 1981 10). Perhaps it is not surprising therefore that the Central Policy Review Staff in one of their reports (CPRS 1980 3) found it difficult, if not impossible, to prove that particular features of a country's education are associated with high or low growth.

If the relationship between education and economic growth is perforce a nebulous one it has not prevented much effort being devoted to trying to demonstrate that the two are associated in some way and that human capital improvement has been an important factor in the process of economic development. For some years after the war the question of investment in human capital attracted almost as much attention as that in fixed assets especially in connection with the progress of less developed countries, while cross-country comparisons, rates of return calculations and growth accounting exercises sought to provide some empirical support for the claims of the human capital theorists.

According to Blaug (1985 17) the high point came in the 1960s, 'the golden years of the economics of education when no self-respecting Minister of Education would have dreamed of making educational decisions without an economist sitting at his right hand'. It was a time when nearly everyone was proclaiming the virtues of manpower planning and educational improvement in terms of economic expansion as as well as for purposes of opening a window of opportunity for the nation's youth. A Conference on Economic Growth and Investment in Education held in Washington in October 1961 expressed the strong belief that educational expansion was a powerful agent of economic growth and a means of providing equality of opportunity (OECD 1985a 26). At this time there was a growing body of educational economists who supported the notion that investment in human capital was on par with that in fixed assets (Schultz 1961; Becker 1964). Schultz (1961 1, 11, 13, 16) for example, maintained that the most distinctive feature of the American economic system was the growth in human capital which he said was responsible for much of the rise in real income per head in the first half of the twentieth century.

Empirical backing was not long in forthcoming. Harbison and Myers (1964 40–1, 44) in a cross-section analysis of 75 countries found a high positive correlation between the level of gross national product per caput and a composite index of human resource development. However the authors were careful to warn about attributing any causality to the relationship. Moreover, their results showed little or no significant correlation between the percentage of students enrolled in scientific and technological faculties in higher education and GNP, nor between public expenditure on education as a percentage of national income and GNP per caput. On the other hand, Layard and Saigal (1966 12) found quite a strong relationship at the whole economy level between output per worker and the proportion of educated workers, though the association was less strong at the sectoral level. Mace (1987 24) however appears to draw the opposite conclusions from Layard and Saigal's study and is highly sceptical of the alleged links between education and economic growth.

Some of the more eclectic studies incorporating long-run development in both the nineteenth and twentieth centuries tend to stress the importance of educational inputs. McClelland (1966), in comparing aggregate data for a diverse range of countries, came to the conclusion that education mattered. Countries investing heavily in education tended to develop more rapidly than those where education was given a lower priority, while returns on educational investment might be as high as 12 per cent compounded under average conditions. His results encouraged him to prescribe optimal educational goals – in the range of twenty students in secondary education and two students in higher education for every 1000 inhabitants – for those underdeveloped countries intent on economic development. But he did also stress that it takes more than a highly educated populace to produce rapid economic development since knowledge must be combined with motivation to achieve the desired results. 'The people have got to *want* to achieve, to care about putting their knowledge to productive uses' (cf. Krueger 1968).

Yet according to Easterlin (1981 10–14), it is the spread of education that stimulates the motivational response. Using primary school enrolments for diverse groups of countries he presented a persuasive case for the importance of education as a modernising force. The spread of mass education of a secular and rationalistic type helps to foster attitudes and attributes which are conducive to the acquisition of new technology and the adoption of modern methods of production which lie at the basis of modern economic growth. A commitment to mass education moreover often heralds a shift in political power together with a break with traditional values and cultures which allows greater scope for ambition for a wider segment of the population. In this way education becomes the crucial link between modern economic growth and a society's cultural characteristics (Easterlin 1981 10–14; cf. Anderson and Bowman 1976). In very broad terms Easterlin's case is supported by the facts. By mid nineteenth century almost the whole population of the world outside North America and north-west Europe had had very little exposure to formal schooling. Literacy levels were therefore very low and well below the 40 per cent threshold considered by some development economists as essential to achieve a breakthrough in development. Nearly a century later this was still largely true in Africa, much of Asia and large parts of Latin America. By contrast, in the high income areas of North America and north-west Europe, which together accounted for the major share of world income, literacy levels were already high by 1850, formal schooling in one form or another was quite extensive and in some cases, for example Germany and North America, it had preceded modern economic growth. During the course of the next half century mass education and high literacy rates had become general in these countries. It is perhaps significant that outside these two regions only Japan had made considerable progress in educating its populace. One should point out of course that the relationship between educational levels and development may not be a direct causal one. Richer countries can obviously afford to devote more resources to education than poorer nations so that if there is a link between education and growth the former countries are in a better position to support it.

Sandberg (1982 686–97) has also explored the longer term relationships between education and income. In a heuristic analysis of European countries he argues that literacy levels in 1850 provide 'an amazingly good predictor of per capita income in the 1970s'. Using adult literacy rates as a proxy for human resource stocks, he finds that countries which were highly literate at the start of the period, even though poor, were generally the ones that eventually attained high per capita income levels. By contrast, the lower the initial per capita stock of human resource development, the slower the rate of economic modernisation was likely to be, as was the case with the poor and illiterate countries in the third panel of Table 2.1 (cf. Cipolla 1969

102). On the other hand, high initial income combined with high rates of literacy, as in the case of England and Wales, Scotland, Switzerland and Belgium, were not necessarily a decided advantage in maintaining original relative income rankings at a later date. Overall the results do suggest that early educational attainment may have been an important prerequisite for achieving modern economic growth. The reasoning is based on propositions similar to those of Easterlin: that to exploit new opportunities countries require a highly mobile labour force, an elastic supply of financial services, the ability to develop and utilise new technology, a ready supply of entrepreneurs, and 'a more rational and more receptive approach to life on the part of the population' (Cipolla 1969 102). All these attributes, it is argued, are very much dependent on the improvement in the educational stock of the population.

Other studies have sought to demonstrate that rates of return to education were postive and often quite high. especially at the private level (Layard 1971; Morris 1973; Morris and Ziderman 1971). More ambitious still was Denison's (1967, 300–18) attempt to allocate growth attributable to educational improvement for the United States and north-west Europe in the period 1950–62. Using a composite quality index based on the number of years in schooling embodied in the labour force and weighted by US earnings differentials attributable to differing levels of education, he found that education's contribution to national income growth varied from a low of 2 per cent in the case of Germany to as much as 15–22 per cent for the United States, while for the whole of north-west Europe it averaged around 5 per cent.

Despite such studies many remained sceptical of the relationship between education and growth. The main problem is that few of the studies could claim to establish convincingly the causality of education in the growth process. Moreover, the fragile nature of many of the calculations and the heroic assumptions involved in making them did little to win over the sceptics. Mark Blaug (1970), an agnostic from the beginning, felt that the relationship between education and economic growth could scarcely be other than tenuous given that countries traverse a variety of manpower growth paths which are dictated by a complex set of factors including social attitudes, political systems and the quality of inputs. Furthermore, the empirical studies were not without their measurement problems. Some of them only included part of the educational inputs, for example those of Easterlin

Table 2.1 Literacy and income levels in Europe

		GNP per capita (US dollars at 1960 prices)	
Literacy level and income ranking c.1850			
Literacy above 70%	Income ranking	1913	1970
Sweden	very low	680	3,411
Denmark	low	862	2,716
Norway	low	749	3,495
Switzerland	high	964	2,661
Germany	medium to low	743	2,873
Scotland	high	965	2,284
Finland	very low	520	2,797
Holland	high	754	3,334
Literacy above 50%			
England and Wales	very high	965	2,284
Belgium	high	894	2,654
France	medium	689	3,029
Austria	medium	498	2,168
Literacy below 50%			
Spain	medium to low	367	1,179
Italy	low	441	1,694
Hungary	low	498	1,851
Romania	very low	336	1,360
Portugal	low	292	1,247
Serbia	very low	284	1,182
Greece	very low	322	1,769
Bulgaria	very low	263	1,755
Russia	very low	326	1,887

Source: Sandberg (1982 687).

and McClelland, while most found great difficulty in incorporating a satisfactory measure of qualitative factors. As Daly (1982) noted, the qualitative element in education is very difficult to encapsulate in cross-country studies with any degree of accuracy.

Blaug (1970) also drew attention to the measurement distortions engendered by the conspicuous consumption of education. More education may well raise the earning power of those benefiting from it but it does not follow that they are more productive to the economy at large. Enhancement of this type may be due the snob value of employing educated manpower on the part of employers, resulting in a spurious association between education and earnings, which could lead to a deceleration rather than improvement in growth. This point was developed further by Arrow (1973), Berg (1973) and Dore (1976) who argued that a process of creeping credentialism had enabled employers to raise their entry requirements and use these as a selection or screening device irrespective of whether the superior qualifications made the candidates any better fitted for the jobs in question.

Even in the underdeveloped countries, which might have been expected to gain most from improvements to the human capital stock, the big educational strategies of the 1960s and early 1970s proved 'expensive, inefficient and inequitable', and failed to promote the well-being of the majority of the world's deprived population (Simmons 1979). This was not because of any inherent defect in education *per se*, but because the educational reforms were ill-conceived in terms of the specific needs of the countries in question and were often frustrated by political and social opposition and subversion. As with capital investment, the character of the educational changes were all too frequently modelled along western lines by planners incapable of appreciating the requirements of local conditions, which meant that the content of educational provision was often unsuited to specific needs with the result that drop-out rates were high (Bairoch 1975 140). Yet the politicians and policy makers in the underdeveloped countries were only too ready to accept the style of the West, without due thought for the consequences, since it appeared to them to signify modernisation. As Simmons (1979 1005) observes: 'Education may be the key to change, but it sometimes appears to be locked on the other side of the development door.'

Such criticisms were partly responsible for the disenchantment which set in during the 1970s when the euphoria over manpower planning and educational expansion of the previous decade began to wane. Not surprisingly of course since growth faltered in most advanced countries in the 1970s and early 1980s just at a time when they should have been reaping the benefits of the earlier educational expansion, which only served to undermine the credibility of the theories of the first-generation economists of education. Later studies (Blaug 1976; Lindley 1981; Glover and Kelley 1987) also helped to cast further doubt on the existence of a systematic relationship across countries between the education of workers and income per head or the rate of growth, as well as questioning the reliabilty of rates of return analysis. Nor had the expansion of educational facilities done much to reduce social inequalities in society. In fact the higher socio-economic groups continued to reap the main benefits from education, especially at the higher levels, so that the lower classes were still at a relative disadvantage as far as opportunities were concerned (Le Grand 1982).

Thus in the face of growing doubts and an increasingly uncongenial economic climate, indiscriminate quantitative expansion of education became a thing of the past as governments took the opportunity to prune educational budgets, particularly at the higher levels where the inflation of credentials appeared to be at its worst. Cost-effectiveness, efficiency and value for money therefore became the key considerations, especially in determining the supply of higher education. Within these parameters the British government subsequently acknowledged the need to provide access to higher education to all those capable of benefiting from it provided this involved no major additional resources from public funds. Inevitably this was to entail a considerable shake-up in the way higher educational institutions conducted their business in the expectation that they would thereby become more efficient and cost-effective and at the same time respond more readily to changing economic needs (Command Papers 9524 1985, 114 1987; Fulton 1990 152).

In other words, both policymakers and educational economists were changing their stance at much the same time. The belief in demand-driven educational opportunity no longer seemed tenable at a time when both for society and the individual 'the costs of education appear to be outstripping the apparent benefits' (Fagerlind and Saha 1989 85). It was felt that the indiscriminate expansion of educational facilities to cope with potential demand had not only delivered the wrong products – too few production engineers and too many arts graduates – but it had more generally produced too many over-educated young people which had helped to escalate the entry requirements for jobs on the part of employers. Moreover, at a time of fairly rapid structural and technological change, partly as a result of the oil crises, there was even greater need for the right education and training which would equip young people for the jobs of the future. This also in turn meant that the traditional and widely held distinction between general education, mainly to develop knowledge and aptitudes, and vocational education and training primarily designed for the development of specific skills, was becoming increasingly untenable since all learning, knowledge and skill formation could be deemed to be relevant to both life experience and the world of work (OECD 1980; OECD 1983b).

This did not of course undermine the value of education to modern society. 'On the contrary' observed one OECD report (OECD 1985a 28), 'education and training are more than ever central to modern economies that are based on rapidly changing knowledge and skills, many of them highly complex.' What it did do however was to focus closer attention on 'the sheer complexity of education's economic role' in providing the right balance of knowledge and cognitive skills in the modern world. As the report (OECD 1985a 106) continued:

> Education has to prepare people for a rapid and complex world of change and is itself a powerful vehicle that facilitates and guides this change. A central role for education and training derives from the fact that modern economies depend upon advanced knowledge and skills that are in a state of rapid evolution, hence generating the constant need for learning throughout the economically active population and a new balance between physical and human capital.

Thus in recent years much more emphasis has been given to the qualitative aspects of education as opposed to mere quantitative expansion. The shift itself has engendered considerable debate among radical economists and sociologists as to the precise function of education and its relationship to the economy. On the one hand, there is concern among policymakers about ensuring that education provides value for money for society as a whole. On the other hand, there is the question as to whether education should be designed to provide youngsters (and adults for that matter) with the skills and aptitudes to equip them for the world of work, along Smithian lines, or whether it should be more concerned with developing the whole personality of the child to cope with lifetime's experience.

This debate has a long history and harks back to the days when education and training were even more distinctly segmented than they are today. Despite a trend towards a greater fusion between the two some writers remain sceptical as to the utility of using the education service as a vehicle for teaching cognate skills. Blaug (1985 27) expresses doubts about this approach on the grounds that many skills can be learned on the job and that skill obsolescence is a very real danger in a rapidly changing technological world. As he remarks:

> No method of educational planning can keep pace with this kaleidoscope and in this sense there is a real economic merit in general,

academic education as a hedge against technical dynamism. The old battle cry for vocational job-specific education, which at first glance might seem to be the rallying grounds for economists, is actually the very opposite of what is implied by the 'new' economics of education.

This then raises the issue once again as to the precise purpose of education and its contribution to the economy. If prior cognate skills are less crucial to the world of work than learning by doing and the development of personality traits and socialisation, then the role of education in society can be seen in a quite different light. As Blaug (1985 26) concludes:

> In short, educational policies may be fitted to literally any level or rate of economic growth and cannot be justified in terms of these patterns of economic growth. Education does make a contribution to economic growth, not as an indispensable input into the growth process, as first-generation economists of education used to argue, but simply as a framework which willy-nilly accommodates the growth process.

In other words, the main thrust of the debate in recent years suggests a more modified role for education's contribution to the economy. Because of different growth trajectories, differences in the quality of educational inputs, not to mention the tricky problems of measurement, one would not expect to find a very strong cross-country relationship between education and economic growth, at least among advanced countries. On the other hand, the marginal gains from educational spending are likely to vary enormously depending on the level of a country's development. Countries with low incomes and low rates of literacy are likely to be very responsive to additional education and training. For example, in sub-Saharan Africa, with an average literacy rate of 47 per cent, the returns to investment in human capital, even at the primary stage of education, have been shown to be very high (McCarthy 1990 16, 29; Chisholm 1982 49).

In the more advanced countries the marginal gains from additional educational inputs are likely to be much smaller partly because of the much greater stock of educated human capital, and partly because at some stage there may be the problem of diminishing returns to further investment in human resources. Education and skill formation may still play a postive role but the impact will be more muted than in low income countries and, as Maddison (1989 77–8) notes, any estimates as to its contribution to economic growth must of necessity be very rough. Nevertheless, Hanna (1962 2–3) rightly points out that if a country continually falls behind in the provision of knowledge and skills of its populace compared with its nearest competitors, then it can expect in time to lag behind in economic performance. And as we shall see in the following chapters, much of the applied work in this field points to a problem in this respect for the British economy over the postwar period.

The British position

Britain has frequently been criticised for its underinvestment in human capital and for an educational system that fails to cater for the needs of an advanced industrial economy (Barnett 1986; Davies and Caves 1987). The most obvious question therefore is to ask whether this can be attributed to a sheer deficiency in educational resource inputs.

Before the war and shortly afterwards a shortage of resources may well have been an important factor since educational spending and provision were poor by the standards set by some of Britain's main competitors, for example the United States and Germany. Later this argument is of less significance since the shortfall seems to have been repaired subsequently. Public expenditure on all types of education has grown enormously in the postwar period, at a rate far faster than total output, so that by the middle of the 1970s it accounted for around 6½ per cent of gross national product, that is more than double what it had been in the early 1950s (UNESCO, *Statistical Yearbooks*). Anne Daly (1982 48) suggests that by the late 1970s it had reached a peak of about 8 per cent, compared with 3½ per cent some twenty years earlier, though we would have doubts about the later estimate which seems rather on the high side. Cottrell's series for total educational expenditure of central and local authorities as a pro-portion of gross domestic product show a steadily rising trend after the early 1950s, from just over 3 per cent to a peak of of more than 6 per cent by the mid 1970s, after which it declined to around 5–5½ per cent (Simon 1991 599).

These figures leave no doubt that education was a major growth area in the boom years of the postwar period. Along with defence and health and social services, education was one of the largest sectors of public activity, accounting for around 14–15 per cent of state expenditure. By the early 1980s some one-fifth of the total population was occupied as pupils or students in full-time education and about 1.8 million persons were employed in educational services of one type or another (including about 700,000 teachers at all levels) which was equivalent to 7½ per cent of the employed workforce (Landymore 1985 691–2).

In real terms public expenditure on education expanded steadily until level funding and cash limits began to bite from the later 1970s onwards. In nominal terms general government expenditure on education rose from £284 million to £6,626 million between 1948 and 1975, representing a more than threefold increase in real terms. The fastest expansion occurred in the 1960s and early 1970s. By the early 1980s it had risen to over £15,000 million, but most of this represented price inflation and in real values there was little further growth. (Page 1991 463; Landymore 1985 691–2). On a per capita basis the biggest gains were in primary education between the mid 1960s and the early 1980s; in secondary education funding tended to stagnate in real terms after the mid 1970s, while for university education there was a fairly consistent decline in real terms after the burst of expansion in the 1960s. These trends scarcely warrant the claim therefore that primary education has been starved of resources (Ryan 1987 100–2). However, because of a flattening out and then a decline in school enrolments after the 1970s, aggregate real expenditure per head held up fairly well following the imposition of tighter public spending controls. In fact, according to Cottrell's painstaking calculations educational expenditure per pupil and student combined was higher by the mid 1980s than it had been in the early 1970s (Simon 1991 602).

How does this compare with the experience of other advanced countries? For this purpose a most useful preliminary measure is the proportion of national income spent on education. Table 2.2 therefore provides cross-country comparisons of public expenditure on education as a percentage of GNP for selected years. Britain is certainly not the largest spender, being overshadowed by the high spending Scandinavian countries. However what is significant is that the British ratio compares favourably with that of several advanced countries including notably Japan, West Germany, France and Switzerland, all of which are often cited as having superior educational systems. Moreover, in terms of educational spending per head Britain has not compared unfavourably with its European Community partners. In 1978 general government expenditure on education and training per head of the population aged 5–64 years of age was very similar to the average for the EC countries and quite close to the German and French levels (NEDC 1983 15).

Table 2.2 Public expenditure on education as a percentage of GNP

	1965	1975	1986/7
Austria	3.6	5.7	5.9
Belgium	4.2	6.2	5.1
Denmark	5.7	7.8	7.9
France	4.1	5.2	5.7
West Germany	3.4	5.1	4.4
Ireland	3.9	6.1	7.1
Italy	5.2	4.5	4.0
Netherlands	6.3	8.2	–
Norway	5.3	7.1	6.8
Sweden	7.0	7.0	7.4
Switzerland	4.2	5.1	4.8
UK	5.1	6.6	5.0
Australia	3.6	6.5	5.8
Japan	4.4	5.5	5.0
US	5.3	6.8	–
Canada	6.3	7.6	7.2

Source: UNESCO, *Statistical Yearbooks.*

Physical indicators would also appear to support the contention that Britain has not fared too badly in terms of the quantity of regular education received by the population. In fact at the compulsory stage of education the average years of schooling have tended to be slightly higher than the European average though a little less than the American. This is to be explained by the fact that in many European countries the average age of entry into compulsory schooling is later than in Britain, while the age of exit is in some cases earlier. Taking all levels of education into account, we find that the average duration of education in Britain was quite similar to that in many European countries in the early 1970s, even though the average age of exit tended to be earlier than elsewhere. The average years of full-time education received between the ages of 3 and 25 works out at 12.3, which is very close to the average for the group of countries listed in Table 2.3. If moreover pre-compulsory or nursery education is excluded from the calculations, on the grounds that its provision is far less formalised and often of variable quality, and take the compulsory entry age as the starting point, then in terms of the average duration of regular education received Britain compares favourably with other countries as the figures in column 5 of Table 2.3 indicate. Turning to the stock of educational experience for the total population aged between 25 and 64, it can be seen from the data in Table 2.4 that Britain was far from lagging behind her competitors (cf. Maddison 1989 78, 136).

Table 2.3 Average age of entry into and exit from education and average years of education received, c.1970

	1	2	3	4	5
Austria	5.2	6	16.8	11.6	10.8
Belgium	3.2	6	17.7	14.5	11.7
Canada	5.7	6	18.5	12.8	12.5
Denmark	6.4	7	17.8	11.4	10.8
Finland	6.7	7	18.1	11.4	11.1
France	3.5	6	17.8	14.3	11.8
Germany	5.2	6	16.6	11.4	10.6
Italy	5.5	6	15.6	10.1	9.6
Japan	5.0	6	18.2	13.2	12.2
Netherlands	4.2	6	17.7	13.5	11.7
Norway	6.8	7	18.9	12.1	11.9
Sweden	5.8	7	18.7	12.9	11.7
Switzerland	5.4	6/7	17.5	12.1	11.5
UK	4.7	5	17.0	12.3	12.0
US	4.7	7	19.5	14.8	12.5
Average	5.2		17.8	12.6	11.5

Key: Col.1 average age of entry into schooling; Col.2: compulsory school age; Col.3: average age of exit from regular education; Col.4: average years of full-time education received between ages of 3 and 25; Col.5: average years of education received excluding pre-compulsory education.
Source: OECD (1974b 12–14).

Where the main difference occurs is at the post-compulsory stage, particularly in higher education, where British enrolment rates are very much lower than in most other OECD countries. In terms of the relevant age group Britain had a participation rate in higher education of about a half to two-thirds of that of many OECD countries during the 1970s (NEDC 1983 15–17). However, these figures are somewhat misleading as an indicator of the final delivery system because of the

Table 2.4 Average years of formal educational experience of the total population aged 25–64 in the 1970s

	1970/1	1976
Belgium	9.9	10.3
Canada	9.9	10.5
Denmark	9.4	9.7
France	9.1	9.9
Germany	9.2	9.4
Italy	6.4	6.9
Japan	10.0	10.4
Netherlands	8.6	9.1
Norway	8.7	9.3
Sweden	8.3	9.3
UK	10.2	10.4
US	11.1	11.6
Average	9.2	9.7

Sources: OECD (1974b 57); Maddison (1982 110).

much higher drop-out rates in European countries. As we shall see later, the final output of the higher education system bears little resemblance to the enrolment data.

Thus the aggregate data do not appear to suggest that there has been a serious input deficiency into British education compared with the experience in other countries. In which case the answer to Britain's educational problem may not lie simply in throwing more financial resources at it. Indeed, if Lynn (1988 142) is correct in asserting that greater expenditure is not necessarily accompanied by higher educational standards, then this conclusion is strengthened. In further support we might quote the examples of Japan, Germany and Switzerland with their high educational standards at moderate cost, and by contrast that of the United States, with deteriorating standards at high cost, which would seem to signal caution in advocating more spending in the British case. Of course one should be wary of drawing hasty judgements from the aggregate data at this stage since the latter tell us very little about the type and quality of education provided, about the allocation of resources between different sectors of education, nor do they fully take account of the resources devoted to vocational training. Until we look more closely at these aspects of the subject final judgement must be suspended.

As far as the estimated returns from increased educational provision are concerned, Britain's spending spree does not appear to have been very positive even though some of the private rates of return have been quite high. The big postwar increase in educational inputs seems to have had remarkably little impact on the economy. Landymore (1985 691–2), for instance, claimed that education had not delivered the goods as far the economy and the needs of industry were concerned. It is as if most of the extra inputs that were pumped into society seeped away without being commuted into productive use, rather in the way that much of the increase in consumption leaked abroad through rising imports. It is true that educational inputs made a greater contribution to economic growth than other qualitative improvements to the labour force, for example greater intensity of work or changes in labour force structure, or for that matter than actual quantitative changes in labour inputs measured in man-hours, but then the latter contributed very little anyway. However, what is revealing is that there was little trend change in the growth of labour force quality improvement due to education in the postwar period. As the figures in Table 5 indicate, the growth in labour quality associated with education was 0.5–0.6 percentage points between 1951–73, or almost identical to the long-term trend, the main difference being the slightly better showing from university and technical education compared with earlier years. Denison's (1967 315) estimates for the period 1950–62 show a similar order of magnitude but he gives no figures for earlier periods.

One should not draw too jaundiced a view of the role of education in the economy from these figures. For one thing the estimates are very approximate as the authors are at pains to point out: 'it would not

Table 2.5 Growth in labour quality derived from improvements in education (annual percentage growth rates)

	Formal education	Technical education	University education	Total
1856–1873	0.2	0.1	0.00	0.30
1873–1937	0.4	0.1	0.00	0.50
1937–1964	0.4	0.2	<0.05	0.65
1964–1973	0.3	0.2	<0.05	0.55

Source: Matthews, Feinstein and Odling-Smee (1982 111).

be surprising if they were subject to errors of 50 per cent or more'
(Matthews, Feinstein and Odling-Smee 1982 111). Secondly, the lag
between increased spending on education and its subsequent
economic impact is inevitably a long one since additions to educational inputs in any one year have only a very small effect on the total
educational stock. Any improvements in educational provision tend to
impact mainly on new entrants to the labour force so that the quality
of the total stock will change only very slowly. Thus the educational
standard or skill level of the total labour force will depend on the
average standard of educational provision over a very long period of
time, in fact up to half a century.

A further possibilty is that by the time the benefits from increased
educational provision might have been expected to be showing
through, their effect was swamped by other adverse factors which
dragged down the rate of growth of the economy. We refer here to the
uncongenial British economic climate after the early 1970s which was
far less conducive to rapid expansion than the boom years of the
previous two decades. It is conceivable that education may have been
improving its contribution to the economy in more recent years, but
circumstantial evidence does not lend strong support to this hypo-
thesis as the discussion in later chapters will demonstrate.

A final possibility for the seemingly poor showing of education may
be the fact that the increased educational spending was used in-
efficiently or misallocated with the result that it had little impact on
the economy. There are two main points to consider here. It could be
for instance that the educational system as a whole, or parts of it, had a
poor delivery system so that it produced inferior output or products
compared to those in other countries. To anticipate, an obvious
example would be the poor credentials of school leavers in mathematical skills or in languages. Alternatively, the distribution of resources between different sectors of education or even within specific
sectors may have been at fault.

In the British context several possibilities suggest themselves for
investigation. It could be argued for example that too large a share of
resources went into formal or compulsory education up to the age of
15/16, and possibly into some branches of higher education, while far
too little was devoted to technical education and vocational training.
The neglect of the latter has been one of the most frequently debated
topics in education in more recent years. Secondly, one might argue
that the quality and product mix in each sector of education left room

for improvement. In general terms the main argument here would be that at all levels of education too much emphasis was placed on academic or theoretical education to the neglect of applied studies and technical subjects. This bias towards academic, liberal and humanistic studies reflects in large part a hangover from nineteenth-century patterns of educational development which were designed primarily to satisfy the gentlemanly aspirations of the middle and upper classes. Thirdly, methods of instruction and training, the structure of curricula and the content of syllabi may come in for criticism, for in the final analysis it is these which determine the quality of the final product of the educational system. Finally, an issue of somewhat wider relevance and related to the previous points is that educational provision in Britain has never by any stretch of the imagination been geared to the world of work and the needs of industry, as it has been in some other countries. General rather than specific instruction has been the underlying theme. As the National Economic Development Council noted in one of its reports (1983 1): 'There is clear evidence that over a very long period industry's needs have remained a very low priority. Repeated attempts have been made to make education in the UK more appropriate to people's working lives. Despite this its character remains predominantly that of a filtering system for identifying the academically most able.'

The list of criticisms of the British education system is a long one and most of them have a lengthy heritage (Barnett 1977, 1985). Despite considerable changes and improvements during the postwar period many of the deficiences remain with us today. Indeed, the seemingly rather drastic upheavals in the education system in more recent years are in part a belated response to past mistakes and neglect.

In subsequent chapters we shall examine some of the major shortcomings in the context of the main branches of education and training, that is formal or compulsory education through to school leaving, intermediate or vocational education and training, and higher education to graduate level. This is then followed by a chapter on management education and training. The next chapter assesses the implications of Britain's education and training system in terms of the economy, while the final chapter offers some explanations for the failure to adapt the system to the needs of a modern economy.

3
THE FAILURE OF COMPULSORY EDUCATION

'The education of the common people', wrote Adam Smith in 1776, 'requires, perhaps, in a civilized and commercial society, the attention of the publick more than that of people of some rank and fortune' (Smith 1776 Book V Ch. 1). In this field Smith was conscious of the need for 'publick' intervention to provide a universal system of utilitarian education for the populace. Yet it was not until the 1944 Education Act that a general system of education for the 'common people' became a reality. Whether or not its application accorded fully with Smith's sentiments on useful and practical education, as opposed to what he regarded as the useless smattering of Latin which the schools in his day provided, is quite another matter.

Prior to the second world war both the quantity and quality of school provision was poor in Britain compared to the best international standards in for example Germany and United States. In fact Britain did not acquire a worthwhile system of formal education until the turn of the century, and even then only a small minority of elementary school children went on to some form of secondary school or higher education. Despite considerable changes through to 1939, together with innumerable reports bewailing Britain's continuing deficiency in the educational sphere, the backlog remained almost as great as ever. Correlli Barnett (1977; 1986 203) on several occasions has severely castigated the whole system of education in Britain, both before and after 1939, arguing that it was effectively turning out a nation of 'coolies' or at best 'white babus'. Apart from the lucky minority who went on to better things, young Britons were, he says, dumped out of school to look for work in obsolete, failing industries in decrepit and depressed areas, in striking contrast to most youngsters in Germany who were learning a trade and continuing their education at the same time (Barnett 1986 203).

Barnett's strictures may appear somewhat dramatic but they have more than a grain of truth in them. In essence they point to a qualitative deficiency rather than a quantitative one. As far as compulsory education is concerned, the volume of resources devoted to the school sector has been more than adequate. The main problem has been the delivery system: the structure and format of compulsory schooling, and for that matter secondary education as a whole, has been such that it has favoured a minority of academically gifted pupils to the neglect of the mass of the nation's youngsters and their needs for lifetime employment.

Structural changes in education

With a view to repairing the educational lag the wartime Coalition Government passed the 1944 Education Act. Though much of the wartime educational planning has been frequently criticised for its failure to lay adequate foundations for educating and training the nation's youth for their place in an industrial and commercial society, the 1944 legislation was seen to be something of a landmark at the time, its concepts only to be challenged in the more egalitarian climate of the 1960s.

The main provisions of the Act included the raising of the school leaving age to 15, which was implemented in 1947, the creation of a tripartite system of secondary education and the provision of compulsory further education for all youngsters between the ages of 15 and 18 who were at work.

Ironically in the light of later events, many of the provisions followed logically from the criticisms of earlier reports which had deplored the dominance of academic curricula in secondary education and the paucity of good practical and technical training for young persons. Thus continuation education for school leavers was a step in the right direction as too was the tripartite approach. This originally envisaged three types of secondary schools each with parity of esteem. These were to be grammar, technical and secondary modern schools which were to cater for different aptitudes on the basis of selective testing at the age of 11. Each sector had a specifically designed purpose and the intention was to have separate examinations to cater for the differing needs and talents of the respective pupils. The grammar schools were for the academically gifted pupils many of whom would no doubt aspire to some form of higher education; technical schools were for those with a more practical bent who more likely than not would enter some kind of industrial work and continue their education and training on a part-time basis at a further education college; while secondary modern schools were for those requiring a less formal but none the less useful and stimulating education.

In principle the objectives of the legislation were sound enough and had they been fully implemented Britain's education system would have borne a striking resemblance to that of Germany. Unfortunately, for one reason or another, many of the intentions of the Act were never realised, and it was this failure which was partly responsible for bringing the whole system into disrepute.

One of the main reasons for the failure to implement it properly was the lack of firm central control. Unlike some other countries, most notably France, Britain has had a long tradition of decentralised administration in educational matters, and this has made it extremely difficult to develop a coherent and unified policy for the country as a whole. Thus much of the detailed decision-making about what is done in education is effectively taken by the local authorities in conjunction with the schools themselves which means that there is a great diversity on offer from one authority to another. There were in fact clauses in the 1944 legislation empowering the Secretary of State for Education to exercise greater control over what took place at grass roots level but these were rarely used. Instead due deference was paid to the tradition of local autonomy which meant that the execution of the changes were left in the hands of some 155 local education authorities (LEAs) who, for want of both inclination and resources, failed to implement their side of the bargain. Thus the technical schools, on which great hopes had originally been placed, proved virtually a non-starter. Only half the authorities deigned to provide such schools and at the peak their coverage was but a mere 3–5 per cent of the school population. Nor did the programme for compulsory continuation education after school materialise which had been intended to further the education of those not proceeding to more advanced academic studies. In short therefore, an integrated system of education and training through to the age of 18 designed to serve the needs of the bulk of the nation's youngsters never transpired.

The failure to develop the technical schools as a strong third force at the compulsory stage was particularly unfortunate since it meant in practice that the bulk of the pupils eventually ended up in the secondary modern schools, having tried and failed to gain entry into the grammar schools through the 11 plus selection test. To put it bluntly, the secondary 'mods' were seen to be the dumping ground for for the majority of the school population who failed to surmount the

11 plus hurdle. Had the technical strand of education been developed properly this problem would probably not have arisen, or at least in not such an acute form as it was to do later. Moreover, had the role of the secondary modern schools been clearly defined then their place in the system of education might have gained greater respect. Unfortunately, almost from the start they were regarded, by teachers, parents and pupils alike, as second-rate institutions compared with the prestigious grammar schools. The latter, which absorbed around 20 per cent of the school population, came to be seen as the cream of the educational system, not simply because they were regarded as inherently better though that was often the case, but also because they tended to be better resourced, and of course they provided the main, indeed virtually the only, route into higher education. They provided a continuous ladder of educational opportunity for those fortunate enough to gain entry, which was not available to those who were relegated to the secondary moderns. Not surprisingly therefore they were regarded as the goal to aim for by any self-respecting parent.

The situation was made worse by the fact that there was very little facility to transfer from one sector to another. There were a few instances of transfer from secondary moderns to grammar school in deserving cases, but given the great imbalance in numbers between the two sectors any significant shift would have been logistically impossible. The reverse move, from grammar to secondary modern or technical school, would also have been impractical on political and social grounds since it would have been regarded as an ignominious demotion given the strong snob appeal of the grammar school.

A further divisive factor which accentuated the disparity between the different sectors was the examination system, or rather the lack of it. Neither the technical schools nor the secondary moderns were accorded a separate system of examinations to suit their specific needs, as had been originally intended. In fact until the middle of the 1960s the only public examination on offer was the General Certificate of Education (GCE) which replaced the former School Certificate (the 'Matric') in 1947. The new examination was more flexible than the former School Certificate in that subjects could be taken singly at 'O' level instead of the five required to matriculate under the old system. In time, too, a greater range of subjects and options was offered under the new system. But there the benefits ended. As with its previous counterpart the new examinations were very much in the traditional mold; the subjects offered and their format had a strong academic orientation, hardly surprising since they were set and examined by boards dominated by academia. Essentially therefore they were designed to suit the needs and abilities of the top 20 per cent academic range of pupils most of whom were located in the grammar schools and would go on to higher education. It is true that the GCE examinations could be taken by pupils from other types of school or even by candidates outwith the formal school system, but for the majority of pupils in these schools they were patently unsuitable. Nevertheless, for want of an alternative the GCE became a vehicle for the more academically able pupils in the secondary modern schools to acquire a leaving certificate. This consequently influenced the pattern of teaching in the modern schools which took on a more academic slant in order to give preference to the few high-flyers and and as a way of improving the prestige of these schools. As one report observed (NEDC 1983 5) 'It therefore came about that the academic values of a university-orientated examination, previously confined to the narrowly selective grammar schools for which it was intended, came to dominate the entire domain of the enlarged secondary system.' Yet despite the subsequent dismemberment of the tripartite system and the introduction of new examinations in later years little progress was made in removing this bias.

In theory there is much to commend the tripartite system. Germany has had, and still has, a perfectly satisfactory system which caters for pupils of different scholastic aptitudes. The main problem with the English system was its mode of application and the lack of follow-through courses post-school for the majority of the school population. Most youngsters and their parents felt that their children had been relegated to a dead-end stream from the start since the opportunities open to them were so inferior to those available to grammar school children. The selection process in particular was regarded as being divisive and unfair and it was probably instituted at too early an age in the school career. Thus the whole system was open to criticism on the grounds of equity and equality of opportunity and in the increasingly egalitarian climate of the 1960s strong pressure was exerted to replace the system by comprehensive schools. Thus from the mid 1960s the tripartite system was steadily eroded and by the early 1980s the majority (some 90 per cent) of secondary school pupils were in comprehensive schools. This was a dramatic change from the complex structure prevailing in 1965 when 26 per cent of secondary school pupils in England and Wales were in grammar schools (including direct grant), 49 per cent were in secondary moderns, 12 per cent were in comprehensives or multilateral schools, 8 per cent in private schools and the remaining 5 per cent in technical and selective central schools (Prais and Wagner 1985 56). Coinciding with the start of comprehensive education a new leaving certificate – the Certificate of Secondary Education (CSE) – was introduced in 1965 for pupils in the 40–80 per cent ability range, together with an experimental Certificate of Extended Education (CEE) for those staying on at school beyond the age of 15. Finally, in 1973 the school leaving age was raised to 16. This more or less completed the structural reforms until the major upheavals of the 1980s culminating in the Education Reform Act of 1988.

Quantitative provision

Before looking at some of the more qualitative aspects of the schooling system it might be instructive to glance at some of the main quantitative indicators to see how well British children fared compared with their counterparts in other countries. Here there is little evidence to suggest that Britain suffered from a shortfall in compulsory schooling. Indeed, because of the early age (5) of entry into compulsory schooling compared with that in some continental countries, and following the raising of the school leaving age to 16, a later exit date than some countries, Britain's educational input, measured in terms of full-time compulsory school years, compares favourably with most other countries except for the United States (OECD 1974b 12–14; 1981 22). As the figures in Table 3.1 indicate, the average years of primary and secondary school educational experience per employee have been consistently above the average in Britain's main competitor countries.

In a more limited study of three countries (the UK, US and Germany) Anne Daly (1982 51, 56) concluded that quantitative differences in educational input at the compulsory school level, measured in years of full-time schooling, did little to explain differences in productivity levels between countries or different rates of productivity growth, and that any addition to measured educational input at this level would not necessarily have a marked effect on productivity. This of course would not preclude some gain to be had from qualitative improvement of the delivery system through say better instruction. On the quantitative side however one could argue

Table 3.1 Average years of primary and secondary school experience
           per employee

	1950	1980
France	8.1	9.6
Germany	8.3	9.3
Japan	8.0	10.3
Netherlands	7.5	9.0
UK	9.3	10.3
US	8.9	10.7
Average	8.4	9.9

Source: Maddison (1986 18).

that too large a share of resources has been devoted to formal or
compulsory schooling especially in the latter half of the period. The
raising of the school leaving age to 16 made Britain almost unique
among OECD countries in the length of the compulsory schooling
period. And, as Landymore (1985 701–2) points out, the opportunity
costs of the extra year at school may be quite high since not only is
there a loss in production from the labour forgone, but for many
youngsters the additional year at school could no doubt have been
more profitably utilised in some form of vocational training in preparation for an industrial career. Strength is added to this point when
one reflects that both teachers and pupils, and in many instances
parents too, were ambivalent about the value of what, for many pupils,
amounted to one more year in academic subjects.

Other indicators suggest a trend improvement at the compulsory
schooling stage. Pupil–teacher ratios and the size of classes have
improved significantly during the postwar period. The number of
pupils per teacher in primary schools fell from 32.5:1 to 21.8:1
between 1946 and 1987, and from 21:4 to 15.4:1 in secondary schools.
Class sizes were steadily reduced. By the late 1980s very few primary
schools had classes in excess of 40 pupils as against 30 per cent in 1950,
while the proportion with classes between 30 and 40 pupils fell from
40 to 22.7 per cent over the period. Similar improvements were
recorded in the size of secondary school classes (Page 1991 468).
Cross-country data on class sizes do not suggest that Britain has been
at a serious disadvantage in this respect compared with say Germany,
Japan or France. In any case there is no very close association between
class size and cognitive performance. Japan, for example, has the

largest classes yet one of the best educational records, though hours of
instruction per year tend to be higher than in most other countries
(OECD 1983a 49–50; Lynn 1988 110–13).

The steady upward trend in the number of school leavers obtaining
accredited passes in public examinations would also appear to point in
the direction of a general improvement in performance. We express a
note of caution here however since later qualitative evidence suggests
that mere quantitative indicators of performance are not necessarily
an accurate guide to actual scholastic proficiency. As late as 1961–2
some 73 per cent of pupils in England and Wales left school without
ever having attempted a school-leaving examination. This is probably
not surprising given the fact that the only public examination then
available was the GCE. The introducion of the CSE led to a big rise in
accreditation; by 1973–4 only 20 per cent of pupils left school without
some graded GCE/CSE result and by 1980–1 the proportion had
fallen to 11 per cent (Dale 1985 12). There was also a slow but steady
improvement in the proportion of 16-year-olds securing higher
grades in first level examinations and in the numbers of 'A' level passes
(*Financial Times*, 13 March 1990; Sanderson 1987 2).

The improvement is less spectacular than it might appear at first
sight, however. The striking increase in accreditation is partly
explained by the fact that it includes many candidates securing the
lowest attainments, that is low grade passes in single subjects at either
GCE or more often at CSE level, which scarcely provided glowing
testimonials to prospective employers. No fewer than 47 per cent of
pupils still left school without a single 'O' level or its equivalent while
75 per cent of leavers failed to attain the notional equivalent of the old
School Certificate, that is five 'O' levels (Landymore 1985 700;
NEDC 1983 12). Moreover, as we shall later, the content of public
examinations was not suited to many pupils' needs while the quality of
performance in key subjects left much to be desired.

Qualitative deficiences

Although in quantitative terms formal schooling has fared quite well,
this has not been reflected at the final delivery level. Virtually every
aspect of compulsory schooling, whether it be the examination
system, the structure of the curricula, the syllabi taught or the preparation of youngsters for the world of work, can be criicised for one
reason or another. There have of course been changes and improve-

ments to the system, especially in the 1980s, but many of them have been partial in scope and they have done little to remedy many of the basic defects which have existed since the war. As a consequence a large part of the nation's youth has suffered from poor education and training for the world of work.

The first problem area to be discussed is the examination system. Though modified and enlarged over time it has retained a strong academic orientation which has been patently unsuitable for a large number of pupils (Hough 1987 25). Subjects tended to be measured by their academic status rather than by their utilitarian value so that in time as the system was extended pupils were effectively offered one choice (Dale 1985 15). Until 1965 of course the only public examination available was the GCE 'O' level and this was designed primarily for the top 20 per cent of the ability range. The introduction of the CSE in 1965 was designed to plug part of the examination gap, since it catered for pupils in the 40–80 per cent ability range. The new examination was aimed to be both flexible and liberal in that subjects could be taken singly, there was no specific pass/fail standard and there was a wider range of subjects offered than under the GCE system, each one of which could be taken in one of three different modes. New examination boards (fourteen) were set up, giving greater influence and control to teachers as compared with the university-dominated boards administering the GCE examinations.

The new examination was far from being an unqualified success. From the start it failed to inspire confidence among pupils, teachers, parents and employers alike, who regarded it as academically inferior to the GCE, which of course it was! More specifically, the format of the syllabi and the mix of subjects offered still had a distinct academic slant, a fact confirmed to some extent by the number of pupils sitting both the CSE and GCE examinations. Nor did it cater for the lower end of the ability spectrum, with the result that some 40 per cent or more of school leavers had very little to show for their eleven years of compulsory schooling. Few other countries automatically disqualified such a large proportion of their school population (Dixon 1987 25). In Germany for example only about one-tenth (and the same proportion in France) of all pupils fail to obtain certification 'attesting to the satisfactory completion of their studies covering a broad range of basic subjects' (Prais and Wagner 1985 69; Adonis 1991).

Thus despite the introduction of new examinations the public examination system since the war has been effectively dominated by the GCE whose prestige, along with that of the grammar schools and subsequently the top stream of the comprehensives, has been out of all proportion to their contribution to the education and training of the nation's future workforce. These examinations continued to be administered by university-dominated examining boards or by academically inclined teachers, with almost complete autonomy from influences outwith the education sector (Hough 1987 25). This meant that the curricula and syllabi were determined largely by the requirements and priorities set by the higher education authorities. It was not simply a case that these exclusive priorities drove out the more utilitarian subjects such as technological and vocational studies, for the fact was that, apart from economics and commerce, they rarely featured in the examination system in the first place. Despite repeated calls, in reports and white papers, for the introduction of more vocational subjects together with a validated accreditation system and a vocational stream within the comprehensives, very little was done to implement such proposals. When reforms did eventually come, as with the Technical and Vocational Educational Initiative (TVEI) and the merging of the GCE and CSE in the 1980s, they tended to be cosmetic rather than radical (see below). In effect therefore the educational establishment has managed to block any revolutionary change; it has set the standards and patterns for the schools catering for the top ability range and in so doing it has helped to perpetuate the academic bent of the nation's entire teaching force and with it the pattern of educational provision in most of the country's schools. It is somewhat ironic, given the egalitarian motives of those in favour of comprehensive schools, and in the light of one of the main objectives of the 1944 Act 'to afford all pupils such variety of instruction and training as may be desirable in view of their different ages, abilities and aptitudes', that so little was done under the comprehensive system to ensure the equality of opportunity for the bottom half of the ability range (Clare 1986 5).

The academic bias of the education service might not have been so serious had it managed to produce a satisfactory output. At one level it did of course. For the academically-gifted pupils there was no real problem. They could perform well at 'O' level, pass through to 'A' level with little difficulty and then proceed to some form of further or higher education. But not so for the vast majority of school leavers who could never aspire to the type of education offered beyond school. They more than likely would enter paid employment but they were ill-prepared for the transition. The most serious deficiency was in their knowledge of core subjects: mathematics, science/technology, English, foreign languages and commercial studies – subjects identified by the Central Policy Review Staff (CPRS 1980 3) as providing a firm foundation for those moving on to vocational training. Yet many pupils left school 'barely literate or numerate, with no skills and only the most limited aspirations' and with almost no facility in a foreign language. The most serious deficiency was in mathematics which is one reason why so many industrial trainees have found difficulty in coping with vocational training courses. Even by the 1980s only one-third of school children achieved the equivalent of an 'O' level pass in mathematics, one-third of all leavers failed to attain any useful standard in the subject at all, while nearly a fifth failed to sit any examination in mathematics at all (Prais and Wagner 1985 63; Prowse 1989 23).

The main problem in this respect was the lack of central control over what was taught in schools and how it was taught. This is in sharp contrast to the practice in many continental countries and Japan where core subjects are compulsory, often beyond the age of 16 as in the case of mathematics, and where one-half or more of school time is devoted to such subjects (Wilkinson 1977 64–5). Until recently the devolution of responsibility in Britain gave the LEAs and head teachers almost complete discretion as to what was taught in schools. There was no basic or core curriculum and no defined syllabi common to all schools, and the only compulsory subject was religious instruction. Thus it was a matter of chance whether or not pupils received a firm grounding in core subjects, especially in cases where they were allowed to drop subjects before they reached the examination stage, and where head teachers sometimes had little idea as to what was being taught by the teachers in their classrooms (Lynn 1988 132).

Worse still have been the repeated criticisms by the schools inspectorate and by other observers of the quality of teaching in schools. Many schools until the mid 1960s and beyond 'adhered doggedly to unimaginative curricula' which were boring and out of touch with the interests and abilities of many of the recipients. According to Carter (1966 18):

The fascinations of science are made mundane by the repetition of uncomprehended formulae; history is churned out in the form of dates and mixed with improbable stories; English is reduced to verbs and antonyms; and literature is debased as children are called upon to chant sonnets in unison or do some compulsory reading of classics that abbreviation has rendered meaningless.

Little wonder that pupils became frustrated and impatient in their last year of schooling when they were fed an educational diet that was boring and had scant relevance to their interest and needs. This was even more the case when the school leaving age was raised to 16.

Unfortunately when and where the teaching system was relaxed or liberalised it often lurched to the other extreme; pupils were given freedom to be creative and 'to do their own thing' with the result that there was even less prospect of them securing a firm grounding in basic subjects (Clare 1986 4–5).

Sub-standard teaching and lack of good leadership and management in schools have frequently been voiced by Her Majesty's Inspectors in their annual reports, as well as by numerous outside observers. This problem is a combination of several factors. Many teachers are unqualified in the subjects they teach partly because of staff shortages in key subject areas such as mathematics, physics and languages. The Cockcroft Committee in 1982 reported that 21 per cent of mathematics teaching was carried out by teachers with no qualifications in the subject (Prowse 1989 23). Yet even in English the Kingman report (1988) found that 28 per cent of the teachers had no qualifications in the subject beyond 'O' level, so that English lessons in some schools had become little more than a setting for a 'vigorous moral and social discussion' (*Financial Times*, 3 May 1988). Moreover, in the boom years of expansion in the 1960s and early 1970s many poor teachers were recruited at a time when the profession was regarded as a last resort by students unable to find employment elsewhere. Since then the status of the profession has steadily declined, pay and conditions of service have deteriorated, not least in recent years due to the increasing amount of bureaucratic paperwork, and this has led to a growing disillusionment among teachers which is no doubt reflected in their performance. British teachers also tend to have a shorter training period and devote less time to lesson preparation than their continental counterparts (Wilkinson 1977 83). Dixon (1987) also infers that teacher training colleges have done little to ensure that their entrants have the abilities to motivate children to learn.

Whatever the reasons, the defects of the compulsory school system show through in the final results and by international standards these have been poor. Sanderson (1988 45) maintains that more poorly educated pupils emerge out of of British schools than out of those of most of our competitors. The proportion of school leavers securing accreditation in public examinations has been low by international standards, while the proportion gaining recognised passes in core subjects has been even less. As we have already seen, there has been an improvement in the numbers gaining certificates on leaving school but one should bear in mind that the figures include many pupils who only manage to secure the lowest grade at CSE in a single subject. Even more significant is the large number of pupils with few worthwhile qualifications and the low proportion who manage to achieve a respectable result. By the first half of the 1980s some 60 per cent of German school leavers achieved the equivalent of 5 or more 'O' level passes compared with only 27 per cent in England and Wales (Sanderson 1988 45). At the other end of the spectrum only 10 per cent of German pupils left school without the equivalent of 5 CSE passes or better, whereas in this country over one-third left with only one or two CSE passes and 47 per cent without one 'O' level (Prais and Wagner 1985 55; Sanderson 1988 45).

Worse still has been the very poor showing in core subjects where Britain tends to fall seriously behind other countries. For three core subjects – English, mathematics and science – two-thirds of all school leavers in 1977 could not manage to attain CSE grade 5 in all three. Mathematics has been one of the most glaring blackspots, though no doubt foreign languages would run it a close second. International tests of matched pupils indicate that mathematical attainments are far lower than in almost any other major country (Sanderson 1988 46–7). Even by the late 1980s only about one-third of 16-year-olds in Britain secured the equivalent of an 'O' level pass in mathematics, as against twice that proportion in Germany and even higher attainments in France and Japan. The gap is particularly critical in the lower half of the ability range where, according to Prais and Wagner (1985 68), attainment levels lag the German by the equivalent of two years. Other selective testing of British and German pupils shows that some two-thirds of school leavers cannot work out simple decimal multiplications and divisions or the addition and multiplication of fractions, while only 12 per cent could calculate a simple interest on a capital sum. The German scores were often twice those of the British even though the pupils were a year younger (*The*

Independent, 22 August 1987).

Such low performance standards in core subjects mean that many school leavers are at a disadvantage when it comes to the point of securing employment and even more so when there is a question of training involved. Not only that, but there is also the question as to how far pupils are prepared in more general terms to face the world of work on leaving school. It is to these issues that we now turn.

Schooling and the preparation for work

Whether the formal system of education achieved the aim of producing an all-round liberal education to develop the personality of the 'whole child' as the Crowther report of 1959 put it, is very much debatable. What it certainly did not do was to prepare children for the world of work. Little was done to develop a separate stream of vocational education and training either in specific schools designed for the purpose as enshrined in the 1944 Act, or within the comprehensive system itself. The Newsom Committee's (1963) stress on the importance of practical and vocational subjects in the school curriculum was largely ignored. Thus apart from the minority of academically gifted pupils in the former grammar schools and subsequently in the top streams of the comprehensives, the bulk of the nation's youngsters remained poorly educated, with very little competence in core subjects of relevance to their future careers and with very limited guidance and preparation for the world of work. The most that many could aspire to might be a CSE low graded result in one of the traditional practical subjects of woodwork, metalwork or needlework.

This is one reason why it has proved difficult to develop further education for vocational purposes on the same scale as in some continental countries since many school leavers lack adequate training and motivation in subjects which form the basis of later work. The deficiency in mathematics in particular has been a handicap to those wishing to take up vocational studies. The limited preparation for the world of work and further training at the compulsory school stage contrasts sharply with the position in many other countries. Germany for example retained the selective tripartite system of schools in which most children are chanelled into either academic, vocational/technical or modern schools between the ages of 10 and 12, each with parity of esteem. Formal examination assessments appropriate to each type of school are available so that some nine-tenths of the pupils manage to secure a school leaving certificate with at least minimum attainments in core subjects. German schools also provide a much greater element of pre-vocational instruction and career training in their curricula, going well beyond the traditional subjects of woodwork and needlework in the typical British school. This means that the modal German school leaver is far better prepared than his English counterpart to enter the world of work and vocational training (Prais and Wagner 1985; Prais 1986).

Until relatively recently the majority of school leavers in Britain received little worthwhile guidance about career prospects and the world of work opportunities, least of all about those available in the technological and engineering dimensions. For many years careers guidance in school was often minimal; more than half the schools had no such thing as a careers teacher, and those who were assigned to this function were usually ill-equipped and uninterested in this capacity. For many the post of careers officer betokened 'Little more than the routine filling in of the appropriate forms for the Youth Employment Service, and holding the key of the cupboard where the careers literature is stored', together with the offer of 'vague and platitudinous advice', if required (Carter 1966 72, 78). A survey by the Department of Education and Science in 1973 found that many schools provided no careers guidance at all for pupils of 14 and upwards, and that the majority of schools did not even take the trouble to liaise with the local careers service (Taylor 1980 266). Consequently, it was only by matter of chance that school leavers secured employment which suited their needs and abilities.

The reasons for the reluctance of schools to prepare children for the world of work and society are complex. In part it stemmed from the difficulty of appointing teachers qualified in this capacity and those seconded to the task from normal teaching duties felt that it jeopardised their career prospects. But perhaps more important was the general ethos among teachers as to the purpose of schooling and their attitude to the outside world. The academic bias of the whole school system, fostered and perpetuated by the public examination system, tended to inculcate an anti-industry and anti-vocational bias in the schools. Brennan (1977 100) believes that this can largely be explained by the fact that the intellectual running in the debate was made by the educational philosophers and the sociologists who were highly critical of Newsom-type curricula. Their belief that vocational education and guidance were rather base and should be resisted at all costs had a powerful influence on teachers' perceptions of what the primary aim of schooling should be. Hence they rejected the idea that schools should have any part in the task of preparimg children for entry into work, and successfully resisted the encroachment of their traditional functions of preparing young people for further studies. Teachers could also draw support from the fact that the sociologists argued that many youngsters were already prepared for the transition from school to work by virtue of part-time work experience, family relationships and cultural contacts with the adult employment scene (Bates 1984 54, 59). Their case was further strengthened by industry's assertion that it could soon make what it wanted from 'unqualified' school leavers through minimal instruction on the job. Moreover, there were those who doubted whether the schools were really competent or equipped to take on what might be regarded as the role of employment advisers. Even such an august body as the OECD was questioning, as late as 1985 (1985a 132), the wisdom of such a step and argued strongly in defence of the status quo:

> It seems an incongruous and self-defeating enterprise to require schools to substitute for the family, the community or the workplace in preparing for adult life, tasks for which they are inadequately equipped, particularly as one of their main recognised missions is precisely to teach what other institutions or life experiences cannot or do not usually provide.

Ironically, it was just about this time that moves were being made to break down the artificial divide between schools and the workplace and to improve the facilities in schools for career guidance and work preparation. The drive to improve the contact between the two was inaugurated by Lord Young at the Manpower Services Commission in the early 1980s. On the surface at least it seems to have met with somewhat greater success than many of the other educational and training reforms of the 1980s. By the end of the decade some 70 per cent of 15–16-year-olds had the opportunity to gain some work experience compared with only about 15 per cent in the mid 1970s. In fact the majority of schools had become involved in work experience schemes of one sort or another and had some industrial contacts (Walford 1988 8–10). Around 90 per cent of secondary schools and over one-half of primary schools had links with local companies and nearly one-quarter of the secondary schools had seconded staff to gain direct experience in industry (*Financial Times*, 17 July 1990). It is doubtful however whether pre-work preparation was as rigorous and as thorough as in German schools. Clare (1986) suggests that many schools were doing little more than playing at preparing their charges for the world of work, a little unfair perhaps in view of the effort that has been made in recent years to make up for past neglect in this field.

Attempts at reform in the 1980s

The decade of the 1980s has probably seen more extensive change and reform in education and training than in any other similar period during the present century. Floods of government reports and papers heralded intense activity seemingly in an attempt to repair some of the past deficiences. No sector was left untouched. The main objectives behind the reforming zeal were to improve the standard of educational performance and to upgrade the provision of vocational training. In addition, educational bodies at all levels were to be subject to a greater degree of accountability and assessment.

As far as compulsory schooling is concerned there were several features of significance. Changes included a reorganisation of the examinations structure at least at the first level, the establishment of a national curriculum, the introduction of a greater vocational element for pupils through to the age of 16 and beyond, and changes in the structure of control of schools. Unfortunately there was no clear and coherent plan of reform which incorporated changes elsewhere in the educational system into a rational and integrated whole. Thus the results lacked in quality what they aspired to in quantity.

In chronological order the vocational side was the first to receive attention. In addition to the pre-vocational work preparation and school-industry links dicussed in the previous section, there were two major initiatives. In 1983, after very little consultation with interested parties, the government launched the Technical and Vocational Educational Initiative (TVEI) along with a Certificate of Pre-Vocational Education (CPVE) on an experimental basis. The main objective of this initiative was to offer pupils from 14 upwards a more vocationally-orientated curriculum, though much of the basic curriculum had to be retained in order to prepare pupils for the first level public examinations at 16. The pilot scheme eventually covered some 83,500 pupils with plans to extend it to all schools by the late 1990s.

A more ambitious move was the plan to establish a network of industry-funded City Technology Colleges (CTCs) in the inner city areas. These cut across the school system proper since they were designed to provide an integrated system of education and vocational training from 11 through to 18 for those pupils who were more suited to a broader curriculum than offered in the traditional schools. They were designated as 'beacons of culture', perhaps an unfortunate phrase in view of the association with our past record. Only a few have so far been established since they have run into funding difficulties.

The most far-reaching and controversial changes were those relating to the examinations system and the curriculum in schools. A new common examination, the General Certificate of Secondary Education (GCSE) replaced the former GCE and CSE for pupils of 16 plus and was first taken in 1988. Along with the new examination came the establishment of a common or core curriculum. The Department of Education and Science had been pressing strongly for a common curriculum on the continental model since the early 1980s and their efforts finally bore fruit later in the decade with the passage of the Education Reform Act (1988). Provision was made for a new national curriculum of around ten subjects for all school pupils up to the age of 16, with nationally defined syllabi and the testing of attainment at specified ages, the original proposals being for tests at 7, 11, 14, and 16.

It is too early as yet to make a proper assessment of the impact of these radical changes. They have been seen as a move to raise educational standards and to improve the vocational element of school provision and the main intent is laudable enough. However, there have been profound misgivings about the whole exercise, not least among the teachers themselves who have been remarkably reluctant to promote the improvement of school education. Some of this reluctance may be explained by the haste with which so many of the changes were instituted and the large increase in paperwork which they entailed for those concerned. Early results of the new system seem at best contradictory. Pupils under the TVEI scheme appear to have produced worse examination results than might have been expected, whereas first returns from the GCSE examinations appear to indicate some overall improvement in performance (*The Independent*, 24 June 1988).

However, there are several reasons for suspecting that the new policies will not really solve Britain's long-standing problems in this sector of education. For one thing there has been a distinct lack of co-ordination in the respective strands of policy. The TVEI scheme, though due to be extended, has not been linked satisfactorily to the changes in the national examination system. The new GCSE examination, while broader in its subject format, in some respects replicates the former GCE 'O' level and fails to provide a satisfactory core for non-academic students. Indeed, the government have recently recognised the absence of a proper vocational track by suggesting modifications to the number of subjects studied to GCSE level – possibly to mathematics, science and English – to make room for a vocational stream from the age 14 onwards for those pupils opting for this mode (*Financial Times*, 5 February 1991). Yet little provision has so far been made for pupils at the lower end of the ability range who are little better off than in the past.

Whether the new system will raise standards generally, in both core and non-core subjects, is a matter for some debate. It could be argued, in so far as pupils are expected to study a common core of some ten subjects with the addition of optional extras, that this is far too heavy a load for many of the less able candidates. Professor Prais favours a broad-based curriculum along the lines of the continental models, but this could defeat the aim of raising the standards of literacy and numeracy of weaker candidates (Prais 1990).

Specification of the contents of core curricula subjects to be taught in schools is to be welcomed wholeheartedly since for far too long has the 'secret garden' of what goes on in the classrooms prevailed (Thomas 1989). Regrettably this has proved to be one of the major bones of contention. Devising the curricula contents has not only led to a great deal of friction among educational interests which dominate the committees, but it has produced an unbelievably complex set of course criteria which has not gone down well with the teachers. Instead of concentrating on essential core skills within each subject group, the planners have devised broad-based courses covering almost everything that children of all abilities should study in ten subjects. The resulting documents are long, tedious and complex. The draft document for science ran to 82 pages specifying hundreds of goals that children should achieve, without laying down any clear priorities. When it came to subjects such as history there was a long and heated debate among the historians as to the correct way in which history should be taught.

In some subjects, mathematics, science and languages in particular, the average standards expected in key skills under the new curricula, are too low, partly because of the wide spread of the courses laid down. Professor Prais has severely critcised the mathematics syllabus and conludes that pupils will still lag seriously behind their continental counterparts (Prais 1990). Moreover, though course contents are specified, in deferencc to thc egalitarians there is to be no attempt to instruct teachers on how to teach the new courses. Modern educational theory lays great emphasis on group work and creative activity, and while this may be all very laudable in principle, experience suggests that it lacks sufficient disciplinary conduct to ensure that pupils, especially the weaker ones, achieve basic levels of attainment throughout their school careers. Moreover, the objectivity of the exercise at the final examination stage, that is GCSE, is weakened by the fact that part of the final grading is based on course work done at home and assessed by the pupils' own teachers. This, Prais argues, 'probably has the opposite effect to what was intended; that is it discriminates against pupils whose parents are intellectually or otherwise unable to help them at home' (Prais 1990).

In a recent report calling for a dramatic improvement in the stock of the nation's skills, the CBI (1989 17) highlighted some of the weaknesses of the compulsory school system in terms of the final product. It maintained that on average children leaving school at 16 were well behind other countries in basic mathematical skills – up to two years compared with Germany and Japan; that they were less likely to develop competent skills in a foreign language compared with pupils in continental countries; they showed a low level of economic awareness; and in general they had fewer and lower level educational qualifications than most European counterparts. It seems very unlikely that these gaps will be repaired by the educational reforms of the late 1980s. The standards set are generally too low, the curricula are too broad, and the objectives of the system ill-defined. Low achievers are still going to be at a disadvantage under the new examination system, and there is still no clearly defined vocational track for those who aspire to a less academic education. Perhaps as John Black suggested, the Education Reform Act like the 1870 Elementary Education Act 'is geared to train a nation of young people for a declining industrial nation' (Letter to *Financial Times*, 28 November 1990).

Equally critical of the deficiences of the educational record of the schools, Professor Hans Eysenck, the distinguished educational psychologist, in a recent Radio 4 broadcast (6 November 1991 8.15 pm), claimed, not without some justification that:

> Everybody should emerge from school able to read and write, do arithmetic, have some knowledge of history and geography, know some science. At the moment we turn out a high proportion of illiterate and innumerate adolescents, ignorant of their country's history or of world events. They are also two years behind comparable German and French children, and even more compared with Japanese children. Surely that can't be right?

In his opinion the mixed ability teaching of the modern school has proved to be an educational nightmare because the absence of streaming, selection and testing has led to a fall in standards in schools. IQ diagnostic testing, he argues, should be employed regularly in schools so that the results can be used to adapt teaching provision to ability needs through selection and streaming which are considered essential for good educational performance. Eysenck's proposals will no doubt appear abhorrent to the progressive egalitarians but as yet they have provided no alternative remedy to counter Britain's lagging educational attainments. They should be concerned about the matter however, if for no other reason than that the failure of the state system drives the well-endowed high achievers into the private sector of education thereby increasing inequality.

Assessment

In overall terms compulsory schooling has not been a success story in the postwar period. The high hopes of the 1944 Act were not realised and subsequent attempts to reform the system have not, by and large, been met with any greater success. As noted earlier, we do not feel that a deficiency of resources has been the problem, rather the main defect has been with the quality of output. This has been reflected in two main areas: a low level of attainment in core subjects, especially in the lower ability ranges, and the failure to devise a satisfactory system of pre-vocational education for the many pupils who leave school at the age of 16. It is the latter, rather than the minority of academically-gifted children, who have been the main losers. Sanderson (1988 38) regards the failure to develop technical education for teenagers of school age, through junior and secondary technical schools, as one of the greatest lost opportunities of twentieth-century education. This lapse not only deprived the country of a whole stratum of education normally found in most other countries, but it was an important factor behind the continued skill shortages in the postwar period. The *Financial Times* (9 May 1990), in a recent leader column on the subject, came to much the same conclusion: 'The absence of a tier of technical schools comparable with those found on the Continent and in Japan is the single biggest failure of British postwar educational policy.'

The proximate cause of the failure can be attributed in large part to the lack of a clearly defined educational policy: as one teacher once remarked, we have no educational system, we have only schools, together with an excessively fragmented and decentralised pattern of educational management. This would explain the failure to develop the technical schools under the 1944 legislation, as well as the continuation schools for further education and training. Even more inexcusable was the neglect of pre-vocational training and guidance under the comprehensive system and the continued academic orientation of the curricula and the examinations system. In the climate of the 1960s the educational needs of the majority of pupils and also the economy appear to have been sacrificed to the unlikely combination of the socio-political aspirations of the egalitarians and the goals of the academic elitists, though there is no reason to suppose that the two are mutually incompatible. As Prais and Wagner (1985 70) take stock of the position:

> The compromise on educational values reached in English schools in general continues to be heavily weighted by the requirements of the minority of university entrants, rather than by the requirements for their life-tasks of average pupils in an era of 'universal secondary schooling'. The development in the second quarter of this century in England of Technical, and Central (commercial) schools – which might have provided a remedy – proved only a brief interlude, and left an inadequate legacy of applied or 'practical' educational ideals for the ensuing Comprehensive system.

Efforts to rescue the system in the 1980s reforms only served to muddy the waters.

The implications are serious. Barnett's strictures, quoted at the beginning of this chapter, do have substance. With one of the longest compulsory school periods by international standards, we have managed to produce lower standards of attainment among school leavers than our main competitors. This is especially the case in the lower ability range of pupils many of whom have emerged from school in a semi-literate and semi-numerate state, such that they have found it difficult, if not impossible, to take advantage of further education and training when at work. The long-standing deficiency in mathematics and science attainments has serious implications for the quality of subsequent training and ultimately for work performance, not only in manufacturing but also in many service trades. Delivery delays, poor stock control, quality appraisal and the like, which are frequently cited as important causes of Britain's poor competitive performance, may be traced back to inadequate instruction at the formal stage of education.

But if school performance has been weak, it bears little comparison with post-school training and education for the majority of youngsters who entered the world of work at the age of 15 or 16. This forms the subject of the next chapter.

4
VOCATIONAL EDUCATION AND TRAINING

Britain has a poor record of long standing with respect to the education and training of school leavers and it did not improve all that much in the postwar period (Sanderson 1987). There has never been any coherent and comprehensive system for the education and training of those entering the labour market after completing compulsory schooling. Thus for most of the postwar period vocational training policy in Britain has been little short of 'appalling', writes David Lomax (1989 2). Both in quantity and quality provision has consistently fallen short of the standards set by other countries. It is this sector of education that has been the most neglected with the result that Britain has had one of the most poorly educated workforces amomg the advanced industrial nations.

This is a very serious matter both for the nation and for the individuals concerned since until recently enrolments in education beyond the formal school stage have been very low by international standards (OECD 1974b 29). The majority of youngsters – some 70 per cent or more – have left the education service after completing formal schooling and have entered the labour market or become unemployed. Until recently most of these youngsters received little or no vocational training or guidance while at school, and it was a matter of luck whether in subsequent years they received any proper education and training while at work. There was no effective programme for training the nation's youth, rather a patchwork of facilities on 'a make do and mend basis'. Initially the main route to acquiring skills and further education (mostly for boys) was through apprenticeships and on-the-job training, coupled with a modicum of part-time tuition at a local technical or commercial college.

No vocational track

The failure to develop the technical schools or to implement the compulsory further education provisions, under the 1944 Act, for those aged 15–18 in work, meant that Britain never had a recognised second educational track for the majority of youngsters who did not continue with their academic education. For at least two decades after the war the facilities for educating and training school leavers were still limited and patchy despite considerable growth in further education and the number of apprenticeships. Numbers of daytime students in further education tripled between 1946–7 and 1963–4 (Peters 1967 276), while the proportion of male school leavers aged between 15 and 17 entering apprenticeships was around 35 per cent by the mid 1960s compared with an estimated 20 per cent prewar (Matthews, Feinstein and Odling-Smee, 1982 109). The number of workers in England securing recognised technical qualifications also rose quite strongly from the early 1950s as the figures in Table 4.1 indicate. The figures may look impressive but what should be borne in mind is that the development was from a very low base so that even by the mid 1960s only a small proportion of boys and girls entered jobs which had prospects of leading to a recognised vocational qualification, while even fewer actually achieved that goal. Data for the earlier period are somewhat incomplete but it is posible to make an approximate tally of the diffusion of training among school leavers. Table 4.2 provides a breakdown for those entering employment straight from school at the age of 15 in 1964 which constituted two-thirds of the total of 608,000, the remainder being aged 16 or 17.

Table 4.1 Number of workers acquiring technical qualifications (000s)

	City and Guilds Institute		Ordinary National Certificate	Higher National Certificate
	Craft Certificate	Technicians Certificate		
1951	18.6	9.0	11.0	5.6
1964	47.7	37.0	23.0	12.8
1973	183.2	131.0	21.6	15.1

Source: Mathhews, Feinstein and Odling-Smee (1982 634).

Around one-half of all youngsters went into employment in which no significant training was provided. Moreover, the incidence of training was less favourable than the figures suggest because of the poor facilities for training at many places of employment and the limitations of the apprenticeship system (see below). Provision for instruction outside the workplace was also very limited, covering only about one-third of boys and less than 10 per cent of girls on the basis of one day a week or on block release from work for periods ranging from one week to three months. Many of those receiving tuition at local colleges were of course apprentices whose instruction was orientated towards their vocational needs, often in preparation for the examinations of the City and Guilds of London Institute. Over one-quarter of girl school leavers went into clerical employment which might or might not include some formal training.

Taking all factors into account and allowing for some double counting probably fewer than 40 per cent of all youngsters between the ages of 15 and 17 received some form of vocational training and further education, while even fewer, possibly around one-quarter, eventually secured a recognised vocational qualification of one form or another. There are no accurate figures for the qualifications of the labour stock as a whole, but on the basis of later estimates and the low annual stream of qualifiers before 1960, it is very unlikely that more than about one-fifth of the labour force had vocational qualifications of any significance at this time.

Table 4.2 Type of employment entered into by 15-year-olds in 1964 in Britain (%)

	Boys	Girls
Apprenticeship or learnership to skill occupations	35.2	6.5
Employment leading to recognised professional qualifications	0.1	0.2
Clerical employment	4.2	27.0
Employment with planned training not covered above	16.3	15.3
Other employment	44.1	51.0
Total numbers (000s)	218.5	207.2

Source: Carter (1966 135).

The apprenticeship system

Until the 1970s the apprenticeship system was the main route for the training of skilled male manual workers. At its peak in the mid 1960s it accounted for some 35 per cent of male school leavers aged 15–17 and

around 5–6 per cent of girls. In May 1964 the total numbers apprenticed in manufacturing were 240,000 while there were 149,000
recorded as other trainees (*Training Statistics 1990* 27). The system
had several defects and in many respects it epitomised Britain's traditional and somewhat rigid institutional structure. According to the
Central Policy Review Staff (1980 7), it embodied a system of training
which was 'rigid, conservative and slow to respond to the new industrial requirements'. Gertrude Williams, in an earlier study (1957 177),
was highly critical of the system of recruiting and training which, she
argued, 'in all essential points . . . is exactly the same as the method
introduced more than 800 years ago for an entirely different
economy. When this system was formalised by the Statute of Arti-
ficers in 1562 it was already old in practice.'

This time-honoured system was informally consolidated, through
collusive action between employers and the trade unions, during the
nineteenth century as a means of providing industrial training in a
narrow range of skilled craft occupations to the exclusion of workers
in less skilled activities. Not only were the entry and service qualifications extremely rigid and restrictive, but the system of training
itself was often far from satisfactory. Apprentices were recruited
direct from school, they normally had to serve a five-year indenture,
they learned one trade or skill only, and most of the training was done
on-the-job. Effectively therefore, the system excluded late entrants,
the retraining of adults and most women (Donovan 1968 85–7).

Some of the larger industrial concerns did run very good training
schemes both for apprentices and for non-apprentices. These
included firms such as ICI, Courtaulds, English Electric, Rolls Royce,
Babcock and Wilcox, Unilever, Dunlop and AEI. But there were
probably not more than about two hundred concerns, and these
mostly the larger ones, which had systematic training programmes of
any reasonable standard. Most firms in fact had very little provision
for training new recruits, or if they did it often tended to border on the
farcical. More often than not apprenticeship was seen as a condition of
employment rather than as a system of effective training in skills.
There was no obligation on the part of employers to provide formal
training or release facilities for purposes of external instruction; nor
was there any proper supervision of training under apprenticeship by
any recognised outside authority. Thus unless an apprentice had
taken and passed some external examination there was no way of
determining whether or not new recruits had reached a satisfactory

level of competence. Since skilled worker status or the 'craft badge' was automatically attained at the end of the indenture period irrespective of the competence of the individual apprentice, there was thefore no strong incentive for apprentices to take externally assessed examinations. In fact most of the knowledge and skills required were picked up on the job by watching others at work since the majority of employers provided little in the way of systematic instruction by trained personnel and they took only a passing interest in the progress of their charges. Since day or block release to enable apprentices to attend classes outside the firm was not legally compulsory only 30 per cent of male operatives and 19 per cent of female operatives were fortunate to secure it; in some occupations, for example the distributive trades, leather products, the textile industries, building materials, clothing and footwear and insurance and banking, it was almost unknown (Peters 1967 109). The proportion of recruits taking and passing the City and Guilds examinations or some near equivalent was even less (Williams 1963 8).

It is not surprising therefore that the Royal Commission on Trade Unions and Employers' Associations, reporting in 1968 (Donovan 1968 85–7), should be highly critical of the limited and patchy nature of Britain's system of industrial training at all levels and about the apathetic response on the part of employers to the needs of the individual and the economy. They were particularly critical of the restrictive and inflexible nature of the traditional craft apprenticeship system which, they argued, was very prejudicial to efficiency and to the needs of workers in a rapidly changing technological society, as well as to those outwith the craft trades. They also deplored the discriminatory nature of the craft training system which effectively excluded adults and women. But they reserved their most caustic observations for the way in which the training system operated in practice:

An apprenticeship served in the trade concerned is the normal badge of a craftsman. Whether the apprenticeship course was a good course is of secondary importance. Those run by the best industrial concerns are very good. On the other hand in very many cases training plays only a secondary part in an apprenticeship. What happens in practice is that those engaged as apprentices are put on to 'skilled' work after a few weeks' elementary training, and from then on they are doing 'skilled' work just as much as any other skilled worker. In such cases apprenticeship is a farce and provides less training than a properly constituted course lasting only a few months. There are cases also where a reasonably diligent apprentice could learn the skills involved in a few months but is prevented from actually performing skilled work while an apprentice, with the result that he is compelled, at the most formative period of his life, to spend up to five years under-employed and under-occupied in order to comply with the formal requirements of an apprenticeship.

The fact that a man has completed an apprenticeship does not therefore of itself guarantee that he has acquired any particular level of skills, or that he has passed any form of test of ability. It is perhaps because of the emphasis on the period of apprenticeship as the qualifying factor that there has so far been a failure to develop objective standards; and as a result there is no accepted way of judging the claims of a person who has not been apprenticed but who says that he is capable of skilled work (Donovan 1968 87).

The apprenticeship system seemed curiously resistant to change and adaptation to meet the needs of a changing industrial society. It was neither reformed or modernised as in the case of France and Germany, nor was it replaced by other forms of in-service training as happened in Japan. The unions blocked any attempt at reform and thus perpetuated a system of privilege and craft demarcation that was increasingly anachronistic in a modern society (Williams 1963 204; Political and Economic Planning 1965 222). One of the problems which the new Industrial Training Boards (ITBs), set up in the 1960s, had to contend with initially was the difficulty in shifting the traditional structure of apprenticeship which had become so firmly entrenched through the collective bargaining process. In many of the older sectors of industrial activity the time-honoured system remained firmly in place with little modification. Prais (1981a 188) quotes the case of the machine tool industry where one-half of the employees were classed as skilled craftsmen, having attained this status without any obligation to attend courses of instruction or to pass any practical or theoretical proficiency tests, and whose remuneration was in no way dependent on the attainment of any specific standard of competence, in striking contrast to the practice in Germany. Moreover, as Prais points out, the persistent intractability of the problem of improving the level of skills among British workers was reflected in the fact that even by the late 1970s proposals were still being made on such matters as national tests of proficiency and the linking of pay to achievements in recognised testing of abilities rather than simply to 'serving time'.

In fact by that time the apprenticeship system in its old form was well on the way to disintegration. Apprentices in manufacturing peaked at around 240,000 in the mid 1960s after which they fell steadily to just over 140,000 in 1974 and barely 54,000 in 1989 (*Training Statistics 1990* 27). Several factors precipitated the decline. The system was ripe for change given its inflexibility and increasing irrelevance to modern needs. Secondly, the introduction of new training initiatives from the mid 1960s onwards (see below) made inroads into the established practices. Thirdly, the increasingly difficult economic conditions in the 1970s and early 1980s led to a sharp cutback in industrial training by many firms. Finally, and perhaps of most significance, the high costs of initial training, due to the narrowing of pay differentials between skilled and unskilled workers, affected both the demand for and the supply of training places. The high level of apprenticeship wages relative to adult earnings – around 60 per cent in Britain compared with 17–25 per cent in Switzerland and Germany in 1978 – meant that training costs were two to three times higher in Britain compared with those in other countries. Such high differentials constrained the offer of training places by firms, especially in cases where the resultant skills were highly transferable so that workers could move elsewhere after completing training. On the other side of the equation, the squeezing of pay differentials also reduced the incentive to embark on apprenticehsip courses, though this could have been offset in part by the lessened financial sacrifice from so doing as a result of the relatively high level of apprenticeship remuneration. On balance there was probably a surplus of unsatisfied aspiring trainees which suggests that firms did not offer enough places to satisfy the demand because trainee rates of pay were set above the market clearing level by collective agreement (see Ryan 1980; Jones 1984 1985 1986).

The creation of the industrial training boards

During the later 1950s and early 1960s there was a flurry of interest in education in general and in vocational education and training in particular, the latter prompted by the growing concern about the alleged shortage of trained workers in key skills, and the belief that Britain's poor provision in industrial training was adversely affecting her competitive ability. The Crowther report of 1959 had expressed concern about the inadequate provision for the education and training of school leavers and recommended a major expansion in part-time and full-time facilities for 16–18-year-olds. 'The long-term aim should be to transform what is now a varied collection of plans for vocational training into a coherent national system of practical education' (Peters 1967 111; McCulloch 1984 57).

The upshot of this concern was the passing of the Industrial Training Act in 1964. This gave the Ministry of Labour power to set up Industrial Training Boards (ITBs) in individual industries to be financed by a levy on firms, the proceeds of which were to be distributed to those firms providing adequate training facilities. Eventually, by 1972, twenty-seven boards had been created covering some 15 million workers. The twin aims of the boards were to increase both the quantity and the quality of training (Chapman and Tooze 1987 26). The basis of funding, following employers' criticisms of the original proposals, was modified in 1967 and again in 1973 under the Employment and Training Act of that year. The latter also transferred responsibility for the training boards to the newly created Manpower Services Commission. This body took on wider and more general powers relating to manpower and training and it subsequently ushered in a new phase of policy which will be discussed in due course.

Despite the wide coverage in terms of the number of employees covered by the new scheme, the ITBs did not solve Britain's long-standing training problem. In quantitative terms they failed miserably. From the peak in the mid 1960s the number of apprentices and other trainees in manufacturing fell steadily, being particularly vulnerable to recession. Total numbers declined from just over 389,000 in May 1964 to 296,000 in May 1974, 266,000 in May 1979 and 122,000 in May 1984. As a proportion of the workforce in manufacturing this represented a decline from 4.8 per cent in May 1964 to under 2 per cent by the early 1980s. Engineering and the construction industry were particularly badly hit though the number of apprentices held up rather better outside manufacturing (*Training Statistics 1990* 27).

On the qualitative side the results were somewhat mixed. The work of the boards did introduce a greater degree of professionalism into the management and execution of training which helped to raise overall standards and methods of assessment. This was achieved by raising the number of training officers, by the more systematic organisation of courses and through greater facilities for off-the-job instruction. The Engineering Board in particular achieved notable results in raising the quality of off-the-job training and the certification of proficiency. By 1978–9 around 90 per cent of first-year craft and technician trainees received some off-the-job tuition as against only 52 per cent in 1966–7 (Chapman and Tooze 1987 31; Locke and Pratt 1979 156–7). In-service training within the larger firms is also said to have shown some improvement. Yet old customs died hard. Traditional practices and short-term horizons still dominated employers' attitudes to training. Training among many employers was still associated with apprenticeship, and serving time rather than objective testing of proficiency continued to remain the main route to becoming a skilled worker (Sheldrake and Vickerstaffe 1987 42). The Manpower Services Commission in their review of training published in 1980 concluded that little advance had been made towards a fundamental reform of training practices: 'In general, in the traditional crafts, it is still the passage of time rather than objectively assessed performance standards, which decides whether a trainee is accepted as skilled' (quoted in Jones 1982 68).

Thus not only did the new measures fail to alleviate Britain's skill shortage but the prospects for the majority of school leavers remained as bleak as ever through to the 1970s. On the basis of the General Household Survey for 1973 Prais (1981a 31) showed that 60 per cent of those aged 16–19 were receiving no further education whatsoever, while only 10 per cent were attending part-time vocational classes, 4 per cent were at evening recreational classes and the remaining 26 per cent were in full-time schooling. 'Thus the median English youngster finishing his full-time schooling joins the labour market as an unskilled worker, whereas only a tenth of the corresponding age-group does so in Germany' (Prais 1981a 31). By the end of the decade, despite some further limited improvement including supplementary measures, the education and training of intermediate workers was still woefully inadequate. Not only was the proportion of workers apprenticed very small compared with other countries – for example Germany 5.2 per cent against only 1.9 per cent in Britain – but a very much larger segment of young people was receiving no education or training than in other European country. As can be seen from Table 4.3 over half of 17–18-year-olds fell into this category compared with only 21 per cent in Germany. Perhaps the only consolation is that even this was an improvement on the position in the later 1950s when some 70 per cent of 17-year-olds had no part-time education (Ahier and Flude 1983 60).

Table 4.3 Activities of 16–18-year-olds in 1978 (%)

	Age	Full-time education and training	Part-time education and training	No education and training
UK	16–17	60	7	33
	17–18	32	12	56
West Germany	16–17	50	35	15
	17–18	33	46	21
EEC	16–17	61	15	24
	17–18	41	18	41

Source: Ahier and Flude (1983 145).

If we now turn to examine the stock of certified skills in the total labour force, as opposed to the flow of recruits into training in any one year, the position is even worse since current stock levels reflect the low levels of skill formation in bygone years, including the earlier very low levels of formal qualification. Professor Prais and his colleagues at the National Institute of Economic and Social Research have provided, in a series of detailed studies carried out during the 1980s, a wealth of comparative data on vocational qualifications in different countries. A summary of the vocational qualifications of the labour force in Germany and Britain in the 1970s is presented in Table 4.4. It can be readily seen that the main shortfall in Britain is at the intermediate stage of qualifications rather than at university or equivalent level. In both manufacturing and non-manufacturing only about one-third of the total labour force had any qualifications compared with some two-thirds in Germany; or to put it more starkly, two-thirds of the British labour force lacked any recognised vocational qualifications. Even more disturbing was the fact that of those reporting no qualifications in the British case some four-fifths did not have any educational qualifications either (that is school leaving certificates). In several sectors of activity, for example food, drink and tobacco, textiles, leather, clothing and footwear, bricks, pottery and tiles, mining and quarrying, the distributive trades, transport and communications and agriculture, some three-quarters or more of the labour force lacked formal vocational qualifications. Only one or two sectors, gas, electricity and water, insurance, banking and finance, and professional and scientific services, had anything approaching a

Table 4.4 Vocational qualifications of the labour force in Britain
(1974–8) and West Germany (1978) (persons with stated
qualifications as % of labour force in each group)

	University or equivalent	Intermediate	None
Manufacturing			
Britain	3.3	28.7	68.0
Germany	3.5	60.8	35.7
Non-manufacturing			
Britain	6.5	30.7	62.8
Germany	8.9	59.4	31.6
All activities			
Britain	5.5	30.0	64.4
Germany	7.1	59.9	33.0

Source: Prais (1981b 48).

reasonable stock of skills, that is in the region of 50 per cent. Finally, in every sector the proportions qualified fell considerably short of the German levels (Prais 1981b 48).

At the time there seemed to be little prospect of bridging the skills gap between Britain and her nearest competitors given the still very low level of skill formation taking place in Britain compared with that abroad. Even on the most generous assumptions the proportion of post-compulsory school youngsters taking up full-time vocational education and apprenticeships was only just over a third that in Germany and Switzerland: 24 per cent in Britain, 68 per cent in Germany and 61 per cent in Switzerland (Jones 1982 70; Prais and Wagner 1983 64). Comparative data on the incidence of training among the relevant age cohort reveal a large gap between Britain and other countries. In the mid 1970s, of young persons finishing full-time education at 16 or 17, only about 40 per cent obtained some useful and effective training compared with around 80 per cent in Germany and Sweden and possibly 90 per cent in Japan.

Expenditure data on training, both by the state and from industry sources, confirm the gap in provision. The proportion of public expenditure on education devoted to vocational training was low by international standards: in 1978 it averaged 16 per cent in the European Community as against only 8.1 per cent in Britain, with only Belgium and Italy having lower shares. Since, as we have seen, there is not a great deal of difference in total educational spending per head or as a proportion of national income between Britain and some of her main competitors, one may justifiably question whether too large a share of national resources has not gone into other sectors of education at the expense of shorter intermediate courses with a vocational content, where the social rate of return is estimated to be higher and the subsidy cost less than in, for example, higher education (Landymore 1985 705; NEDC 1983 15).

Low public funding of vocational education and training has not been compensated by private sources of finance. Expenditure by firms on training has generally been considered to be low by international standards. Unfortunately the data on this item are far from reliable partly because of the difficulty of computing accurate figures together with definitional problems as to what should and what should not be included. Many of the outside professional estimates that have been made are hotly disputed by industry sources as being too low so that we need to treat them with some caution. For Germany educational training expenditure by employers has been estimated at £7 billion for 1980 as against £2.5 billion for the UK, with the former being put to more effective use (NEDC 1984 90). Ashton (1986 176) suggested that US employers spent some 3 per cent of annual turnover on manpower training compared with 0.5 per cent in Britain. Porter (1990 498) produces an even less favourable tally. He suggests that investment in training by British industry was only 0.15 per cent of revenues in 1980 compared with 2 per cent in Germany and 3 per cent in Japan. Industry sources however take strong exception to these low estimates and argue that the British level of spending is much closer to that of other countries (Leadbeater 1987; Banham 1989). If this is the case then their figures need to be reconciled with the low level of skill formation in Britain.

New policy initiatives in the 1980s

By the end of the 1970s it was becoming increasingly clear that Britain's training system was far from satisfactory. After two decades of debate and policy action many of the old problems remained unresolved, namely the low levels of qualifications among the workforce, inadequate training facilities for many of the nation's youngsters, continued skill shortages in key sectors and the unresolved uneasy relationship between vocational training and general education. Moreover, by the turn of the decade two other problems were looming to complicate the situation: mass unemployment, especially among young workers, and rapidly changing patterns of skills due to technological obsolescence and renewal, some of which had been caused by the oil crises of the 1970s. These changes called for training and retraining in new skills, together with much greater emphasis on the teaching of transferable skills including of course information technology, as opposed to the traditional specific skills of the typical apprenticeship training. A conceptual shift in the pattern and structure of training from that which had prevailed hitherto was therefore urgently required.

Following the Manpower Services Commission's disparaging remarks on Britain's training facilities in 1980 the government launched a white paper: *A New Training Iniative: A Programme for Action* (Cmnd 8455), at the end of 1981, outlining several new training iniatives. This stressed the need for (1) the provision of a period of planned education, training and work experience for all those under 18 years of age; (2) the more rigorous certification of standards for occupational skills and (3) facilities for adult workers to improve or update their skills or to retrain in new skills. During the next few years there was action on all three fronts.

The first initiative to be implemented was that for the reform of the training of young workers with the launching of the Youth Training Scheme (YTS) in April 1983. Although ostensibly one of the main aims of YTS was training, it should be stressed that an additional motive for its introduction was the very high level of youth unemployment at the time – around one-quarter for 16–17-year-olds not in full-time education. Furthermore, it may be noted that in many respects it was a logical successor to the hotch-potch of youth labour market measures sponsored by the Manpower Services Commission in the 1970s, none of which had achieved very much other than keeping youngsters off the dole. The main element of these earlier schemes was the Youth Opportunities Programme (YOP) which had been introduced in 1978. It was aimed primarily at jobless school leavers and designed to give them work experience through a mixture of tuition and practical work studies. At the peak in 1982–3, prior to the introduction of YTS, there were reported to be around 630,000 young people engaged on the YOP schemes, many of them without either GCE or CSE passes to their credit (Hough 1987 107). From a training point of view it had very little merit. The training period was too short and there was no obligation on the part of employers to offer a structured training programme. It was difficult to find sufficient work experience of a suitable type for such large numbers and many of the trainees ended up in college courses. Employers for the most part regarded it as a cheap form of labour (Hough 1987 107; Jones 1988 54–5).

The YTS was clearly intended to be a more sophisticated replacement for the YOP. Indeed such was the confidence in the new scheme that public support and funding for the Industrial Training Boards system was withdrawn. Most of the boards were wound up and the seven that remained in existence covered some 30 per cent of the workforce. These were transferred to non-statutory industrial bodies whose basic source of income was derived from employers' contributions (Sharples and Carty 1987 67). Thus in contrast to the YOP scheme, the chief objective of the YTS was said to be that of securing a radical improvement in youth training rather than a vehicle for removing youngsters from the unemployment register. It was to provide some form of education and training plus work experience for all those under the age of 18 and also for some adults. The maximum period of training was to be one year compared with six months under the YOP schemes, which was to be on a full-time basis for those unemployed and part-time for those already in jobs. Training facilities and methods of training were to be monitored closely by the Manpower Services Commission to ensure that they met recognised standards, including a specified period of off-the-job tuition, the teaching of transferable skills, and the submission of records of attainment of the candidates. The MSC had power to reject YTS projects which did not meet the specified criteria (Ryan 1984 38).

The numbers involved in the YTS may look impressive, but the intake in the first year (1983–4) of around 370,000 fell short of the original target of half a million. In subsequent years the number of entrants varied very little, though following the introduction of a two-year programme in April 1986 it was hoped to reach the base target by the end of the decade.

How successful was the YTS as a mechanism for improving both the quantity and quality of training? As far as quantity is concerned it did help to raise the proportion of 16–18-year-olds in education and training to around 65 per cent by the middle of the decade. This is certainly an improvement on earlier years though reliable comparative data are lacking. Estimates suggest a proportion of around 40 per

cent in the early 1970s and perhaps 25 per cent in the later 1950s
(Ahier and Flude 1983 60; Sharples and Carty 1987 30). Yet even this
advance fell well short of experience in other countries many of which
were recording participation rates of 75–90 per cent (OECD 1989 37)
as the figures in Table 4.5 indicate.

Table 4.5 Participation in education and training of 16–18-year-
olds (%) in 1986

	Full-time	Part-time	All
Belgium	77	4	81
Canada	75	–	75
Denmark	70	6	77
France	66	8	74
Germany	47	43	90
Japan	77	3	79
Netherlands	77	9	86
Sweden	76	2	78
UK	33	31	64
US	79	1	80

Source: DES (1991 31).

From the point of view of raising the standard of training and
improving the total stock of key skills in the labour force, the YTS
scheme was little short of a disaster. Much of the training was at a low
level and many of the early recruits left the scheme prematurely and
without gaining any qualifications. Less than a quarter of the YTS
trainees under the one-year scheme secured any sort of qualification
and often at a very elementary level (Jones 1988 66). Qualification
rates improved subsequently to around 66 per cent by the end of the
decade but often at low grades in GCE and GCSE examinations
rather than in vocational courses. In many subjects British youngsters
are trained to much lower standards than their continental counterparts in Germany, France, Sweden and Japan even after a two-year
training course. This could largely be due to the fact that many of the
entrants to YTS have not reached a satisfactory standard at school in a
range of core subjects so that the best they can aspire to is a semi-
skilled training below craft level. This again raises the question of
pre-vocational training and education in schools and the need for a
much more comprehensive approach including the expansion of the
TVEI scheme in order to ensure that pupils reach some recognised

standard of competence to enable them to proceed further.

YTS has had very little impact on the stock of key skills in the economy. Much of the programme has been devoted to the more elementary levels of training so that there has been little improvement in the flow of higher qualified youngsters, that is craft and technician levels, equivalent to City and Guilds Part II or NVQ level 3 (see below). As Hilary Steedman (1990 50–6) has shown, the flows of young people obtaining recognised craft qualifications in major occupations in manufacturing barely changed in the twelve years through to 1987, whereas the numbers increased by 50 per cent in France and 30 per cent in Germany. By 1988 some two-thirds of the British labour force was still without vocational qualifications (though at least half of this group had some low level educational qualifications) which was very little different from the position in the 1970s. Only 26 per cent of the labour force (an increase of 3 percentage points since 1979) had intermediate vocational qualifications, mostly at lower levels, compared with 40 per cent in France and 64 per cent in Germany. In fact in some trades the numbers of craftsmen actually declined in the 1980s; in mechanical engineering for example the numbers gaining City and Guilds Part II qualifications fell by more than a half (*Financial Times*, 24 November 1988).

The monitoring of the YTS has left much to be desired. Despite declared intentions it is clear that standards of training have tended to take second place to the goal of reducing unemployment. This was clearly apparent at the end of the decade when cuts in govenment funding for training were announced on the grounds that unemployment was falling (*Financial Times*, 9 May 1990). Emphasis on this aspect has inevitably meant that the MSC (later the Training Commission) has been prepared to waive some of the original criteria for training programmes. The downgrading in the priority given to training and qualifications *per se* has encouraged the proliferation of low quality schemes on which youngsters have learned little and with few opportunities therefore to obtain qualifications. Though a minority of employers, mostly the larger companies who already had good training schemes anyway, no doubt provided worthwhile training for YTS recruits, many have seen the scheme as a source of cheap labour rather than as a way of improving skill levels. In fact only half the organisations providing training schemes initially secured MSC approval (Deakin and Pratten 1987 491–7).

In other words, YTS has been regarded as a second-class option for training purposes, one that drew in the weaker recruits for which firms were obliged to provide additional facilities over and above their normal provision. It has never been seriously regarded as a means for improving the stock of key skills in the economy and many employers have regarded it as a chore to provide training facilities and work experience for youngsters who may never make the grade. Like the former secondary modern school, YTS has no status appeal and so for many participants it has been regarded as second best.

Adult training

In contrast to the move in the direction of making youth training available to all, the opportunities for adult training, retraining and the upgrading of skills have been very limited. Yet in a rapidly changing technological world and for a country with an already low stock of skills, adult refurbishment is just as important as youth training. The 1981 initiative held out promise of much better opportunities for adults to improve their skills. This therefore pre-supposed a reformulation of existing policy based on the Training Opportunities Scheme (TOPs), originally introduced in 1972, which provided short courses of training, mostly for unemployed adults, in skills intended for new jobs. The main drawbacks of this programme were that the courses were too short to be of much practical use and they therefore lacked skill depth. Moreover, increasing unemployment at the turn of the 1970s led to a sharp fall-off in the placement ratio from the peak of 70 per cent recorded in 1979. Funding for the scheme was therefore cut back since it seemed impractical to train people for jobs which were not available (Ryan 1984 41–2).

The new initiative of the early 1980s did bring some reprieve to funding for adult training but no major programme for improving adult skill formation. In fact during the decade there was an unbelievable patchwork of minor measures – nearly forty in all – none of which had much impact. Most of these schemes were of a temporary nature and few had any great merit in terms of offering really worthwhile training. Not surprisingly therefore, recruits became disenchanted and many trainees, as in the case of the New Job Training Scheme of 1987, tended to drop out at an early stage.

This piecemeal policy was eventually replaced by a more coherent programme of Employment Training (ET) which was announced in the summer of 1988. This was designed to provide an average of six months training for some 600,000 unemployed adults a year at an estimated cost of £1.5 billion, employers bearing about 10 per cent of the outlay (Leadbeater 1988b). As with YTS much of the success of the scheme depends on the response of employers and the quality of training they provide. Past experience has shown that too often it has been of a low quality standard.

Standardising qualifications

The third element in the new iniative concerned the attempt to clean up the qualifications jungle. In 1986 the National Council for Vocational Qualifications (NCVQ) was set up, charged with the task of rationalising and evaluating the mass of courses and qualifications which had been proliferated over many decades by a plethora of institutions. It was also to vet new courses in sectors where previously there had been none (Cantor and Roberts 1986 54). Qualifications covering the whole spectrum of occupations were to be graded on the basis of four ascending levels between I and IV, mostly comprising those occupations which required only limited educational qualifications. There were plans to extend the classification to level V and beyond for management and professional activities (Wood 1990b).

While clearly a step in the right direction, the initial work of the Council has been subject to criticism on the grounds that their criteria guidelines fall well short of continental standards. In particular, it has been argued that there is too much reliance placed on practical testing and workplace supervisor assessment rather than independently assessed written and oral work. Secondly, some of the skill requirements laid down are both narrow and very low grade, especially those in level I (Prais 1989b 53–4; Steedman 1990 56). This is in contrast to the broader-based type of vocational courses in Europe which incorporate both trade and core academic subjects, and which provide trainees with a wider range of transferable skills both for immediate work needs and for more advanced training. Prais (1989b 53) reckons that longer-term needs and flexibility in the British system may be sacrificed in the interests of employers' more immediate requirements.

Prospects

The prospects for improvement in training and skill formation still remained very mixed at the turn of the decade. On the one hand, the government accepted the need for further reform by endorsing the creation of a network of eighty-two employer-led Training and Enterprise Councils (TECs). Their main duties are to assess local training needs and to assume responsibility for meeting them under the publicly financed training programmes for young people and unemployed adults respectively. Additionally, they will be responsible for local enterprise programmes as well as for persuading local companies to improve their training provision.

Further reforms followed in 1990–1. Their main obejective was to boost the numbers of 16–18-year-olds in education and training. The YTS, which since its inception in 1983 had provided training for over 2.7 million youngsters, was replaced by a new scheme, Youth Training (YT), in May 1990. The main aims of YT are to increase the volume and quality of vocational training by making it more flexible than the previous system. It offers to all 16- and 17-year-olds who are not in full-time education the opportunity to acquire skills and qualifications, while at the same time ensuring that the needs of the local labour market are met. Compared with YTS, the rules are remarkably flexible. There is no fixed training period, nor any specifically designed framework of training, and there are few detailed rules as to the way training should be conducted. Within this loose framework the training providers are supposed to meet both the future needs of the trainees and to satisfy local labour requirements. The present government obviously regards the new scheme as a key component of its education and training strategy for the future, since in the spring of 1991 it was announced that it would be accompanied by an extension of training credits, allowing young people to purchase approved training from employers, and a streamlining of the system of vocational qualifications (*Financial Times*, 21 May 1991). Furthermore, through proposed changes in further and higher education including the introduction of vocational diplomas the government hopes to establish an integrated system of education and training.

The new structure did not get off to a very promising start. At a time of rising unemployment the government announced sharp cutbacks in funding in an attempt to shift more of the burden on to employers. The budget for youth training for example was to be pruned by 25 per cent over three years, and much higher in real terms, with similar treatment for ET. This implied that the TECs' budgets for 1990–1 would be of the order of £2.5 billion as against an anticipated

£3 billion (Wood 1991a). Negotiations between companies and the Training Councils have not always been easy at a time of rising unemployment when many firms are less willing to offer training places. Some large companies have become disillusioned with the youth training programme and recently several announced withdrawal from it (*Financial Times*, 2 July 1991).

On the other hand, we would question whether the recent changes mark a radical break with past policy. Though the first year of the YT has been hailed as a 'great success in offering well-planned training to young people' (Bridges 1991 398) it appears to offer more of the same. It is still very much a non-compulsory system focused on dealing with unemployment rather than on improving skill levels. Some 90 per cent of the budgets are likely to be targeted on young jobless and adult unemployed. In other words, it gives priority to short-term expediency at the expense of longer-term needs. The bulk of the workforce is neglected and it provides no substitute for the rigorous training programmes in other countries many of which are being upgraded. The YT programme is too loose and unstructured to ensure that trainees match the attainments of their foreign counterparts, and in any case, as under the YTS, there still remains the problem that many are lacking in their basic education to take full advantage of the training offered. Thus, with the best will in the world the current programmes are not going to produce a radical transformation in Britain's stock of skills. Indeed, since new entrants will account at most for only 2 per cent of the labour market, it will be a long time before there is much impact on the total stock of skills. Meanwhile, since other countries are continuing to upgrade their own training programmes this means that Britain will have great difficulty in marking time let alone improving her relative standing, especially since the quality of output is still inferior to that in other countries (Hague 1991 12–14).

Assessment

Vocational education and training in postwar Britain can scarcely claim a record of achievement. As one *Financial Times* leader (9 May 1990) commented:

> The history of British vocational training and education is largely a history of failure. Good intentions have never been translated into effective action. As a result, more than a century after concern was first

voiced, Britain still possesses neither a network of high quality technical schools nor a flourishing training scheme. Companies, schools and governments have all failed to address the needs of the average employee.

Despite many years of intense debate, much expenditure and many changes in policy Britain still does not have a comprehensive and coherent programme of training of good quality in place. Policy has lurched from one scheme to another with the result that there has been a bewildering plethora of conflicting, overlapping and uncoordinated programmes, together with a veritable jungle of qualifications, so confusing as to merit the description 'a non-system' (Cantor and Roberts 1986 63). Keep and Mayhew (1988 xii) summed up the situation as follows:

> To date, attempts to erect a national VET system have been characterised by a series of fragmented and narrowly-focused incremental changes with little or no attempt being made to view the education and training system as a rational entity, or to undertake a complete restructuring from first principles. The result of this ad hoc style of reform has been the promotion of a jumble of uncoordinated, overlapping schemes sponsored by rival bodies. Rather than a single, over-arching focus for policy making, there are instead a multitude of competing agencies and government departments – the Training Commission, NEDO, the DTI, the DES, and, holding the purse strings, the Treasury.

Little wonder therefore that Britain had, and still has, one of the least educated workforces in the western world, which Bryan Nicholson described in uncomplimentary terms as 'a bunch of thickies' when chairman of the MSC in 1986 (Sanderson 1987 127). By international standards the flow and stock of qualified persons at intermediate level has been distinctly inferior. *The World Competitiveness Report for 1989* ranked Britain close to the bottom of twenty-two OECD countries in the training and availability of skilled labour. Even by the end of the 1980s, after years of trial and error, Britain's workforce remained under-educated, under-trained and under-qualified. One-third of school leavers had no useful qualifications to show for eleven years of compulsory education; one-half of those employed had no educational qualifications equivalent to the old GCE 'O' level; and two-thirds of the workforce had no worthwhile vocational qualifications. Furthermore, just over one-half (two-thirds in manufacturing) of the workforce received no systematic training in 1987, fewer than one in three employers had a training plan or training budget, only one in five evaluated the benefits of training in any way, while only one in ten had formal training targets for the whole workforce (CBI 1989 16–17; MSC 1987 6). Many of the very large firms had good training schemes but these still seem to have been the exception rather than the rule.

A combination of circumstances seems to have been responsible for this sad state of affairs. An education system which gave pride of place to academic distinction, and which left little room for anything else, is one possible line of explanation. Hence the divorce of education and vocational training in the schooling system and the failure to develop a tier of technical schools comparable with those found on the continent, regarded by some as the biggest mistake in postwar educational policy (*Financial Times*, 9 May 1990). Secondly, the failure to implement a compulsory programme of education and training for school leavers along the lines of the German model meant that many youngsters received no initial training at all. Of the many programmes that have been launched all have been of a voluntary character, often designed to satisfy immediate requirements, including that of relieving unemployment, rather than the longer-term skill needs of individuals and the economy. Employers too must share the burden of blame. Too few have been prepared to see manpower management and training as a central part of their corporate strategy or to appreciate their relevance to profitability and competitiveness. Thus training and skill formation have been seen more in terms of coping with the immediate or pressing needs of skill shortages in specific sectors rather than as a more crucial element in longer-term business strategy designed to raise the overall level of skills. This complacency no doubt accounts for the fact that as many as half the Non-Statutory Training Organisations (NSTOs), set up by employers following the abolition of most of the statutory ITBs in the early 1980s, were found to be ineffective (*Financial Times*, 10 March 1988). Nor has there been much pressure from workers themselves or their trade unions to improve facilities for training, details of which could have been incorporated into collective bargaining agreements (Coopers and Lybrand Associates 1985 4–5; Leadbeater 1987b). As Ryan (1984 35) observes:

> Vocational education has been squeezed between a school system informed by liberal ideals, geared to academic standards and inadequately funded, on the one side, and an industrial system attuned largely to the immediate needs of employers, on the other.

Britain's poor relative economic performance since the war has certainly not been helped by the low level of skill formation at a time when the skill intensity of international trade has been increasing steadily (Katrak 1982). There are numerous comparative case studies which illustrate the disadvantages of a lagging skill base and some of these are referred to in the penultimate chapter which discusses the economic consequences. For the moment we might spare a thought for the social considerations. The absence of a rigorous system of vocational training and education, as practised in other countries, has deprived many non-academic children of the opportunities for self-advancement and respect. As the *Financial Times* (24 November 1988) commented:

> The continued neglect of rigorous vocational education is denying thousands of non-academic teenagers the status, job satisfaction and pay expectations they could reasonably expect in any other advanced industrial economy.

5
HIGHER EDUCATION

Britain's system of higher education has frequently been criticised for its past deficiences. Before 1939 the universities were said to have produced too few graduates, they produced the wrong type and they did little to foster industrial research through contacts with the business world (see Barnett 1985, 1986; Locke 1984; Ahlstrom 1982; Argles 1964). Thus Locke (1984 52–3 237–8) argues that Britain, and France too, failed to emulate the German model of higher education whose institutions produced a growing élite guard of scientists, engineers and business economists to meet the needs of industry. Between the wars the total output of graduate engineers in Britain was only 9997, whereas in 1923 the German technical institutes had twice as many students as those graduating in engineering from British universities for the whole of the period 1925–39. Indeed, if anything the balance of activity in universities during the interwar years shifted away from science and technology, especially the latter, in favour of the arts, which Barnett (1986 223) sees as 'a clear manifestation of the British scale of academic snobbery'. Not all interpretations of the prewar position are unfavourable, however. While there is probably fairly general agreement that the total output of graduates was small by international standards, Sanderson (1972) infers that engineering graduates were more or less sufficient to meet the needs of employers. Moreover, the links between universities and industry, with respect to both research and the teaching of undergraduates, were perhaps rather more extensive than often assumed (Sanderson 1969, 1972; Divall 1990, 1991).

Expansion in numbers

Whatever the earlier situation, things did not change dramatically in the first decade or so after the war. The numbers graduating with degrees or their near equivalent remained low and only a small proportion found their way into industry. Between the academic years

1950–1 and 1960–1 the number of graduates from British universities increased by only 6000 to a total of 25,699, of which 3273 were in higher degrees (*Annual Abstract of Statistics*). Consequently, graduates in British industry at any level were conspicuous by their absence. As Austen Albu (1963 86) noted, some industries were only just beginning to emerge from the George Stephenson age as far as the recruitment of technical expertise and the training of management were concerned. Even by the late 1950s the machine tool industry had only 1.3 per cent of its employees qualified as scientists and engineers, shipbuilding and marine engineering 0.6 per cent, and textiles even less, while British Railways, with over half a million employees and in the midst of a major modernisation programme, had but 1400 scientifically and technically qualified staff, not all of whom had degrees by any means. Few firms, moreover, had much understanding of, or employed many specialists in, economic forecasting, business management or market analysis.

The poverty of qualified personnel in industry was not solely a function of supply. There was still a deep-rooted prejudice against university graduates on the part of British management, perhaps scarcely surprising in view of the fact that the educational qualifications of most managers and directors were very limited. Only a small proportion of managers, even in large companies, had degrees, many had no technical qualifications, very few had had experience of management education and training, and some lacked any kind of educational or technical qualification. Practical experience and part-time study tended to be the preferred route to advancement, at least at lower managerial levels, while social background was a potent factor for promotion to the top (see Chapter 6). As late as 1950, 90 per cent of those who became mechanical engineers in England were non-university educated, their training mainly consisting of part-time (evening) study for professional examinations (Locke 1984 58).

Subsequent decades saw a massive growth of higher educational provision following the Robbins report of 1963. As Table 5.1 shows, the total number of students in all branches of higher education (universities, polytechnics and other degree-granting institutions) tripled between the early 1960s and the late 1980s, though not all were on full-time degree courses. The number of first degree graduates rose even faster, from 22,000 in 1962, to 75,000 in 1975 and 127,000 in 1987, including the output from polytechnics, the Open University and colleges from 1975. In fact higher education became the fastest

Table 5.1 Number of students in higher education establishments in the UK (000s)

	Universities				Colleges of Ed./teacher training	Public sector higher education			Total all students
	Undergrads	Postgrads	Part-time	Open University		Full-time incl. sandwich	Part-time day	Evenings	
1961–2	97.3	19.6	19.3	–	44.0	37.3	52.4	52.8	328.1(a)
1975–6	218.0	51.0	26.0	56.0	113.0	133.0	96.0	41.0	734.0
1987–8	265.0	56.0	46.0	86.0	38.0	267.0	176.0	58.0	922.0

(a) Includes 5.4 on below degree-standard courses.

Note: Higher education is dispensed by a wide range of institutions, though the universities and polytechnics accounted for over 70 per cent of students in 1983–4 (full and part-time) and an even higher proportion of degrees awarded. In addition, there are a large number of colleges of one sort or another, including the Scottish Central Institutions and direct grant/voluntary colleges which are engaged in higher education in varying degrees.

Source: *Education Statistics for the United Kingdom* (1971; 1989).

growing sector of education and by the mid 1980s it was claiming
some 23 per cent of the total educational budget even though in real
terms spending per student was declining (Fulton 1990 145–6). The
expansion in numbers led to a significant rise in the stock of graduates
in the labour force, from 1.4 per cent in 1951, 1.9 per cent in 1961, to
3.6 per cent in 1971 and 6 per cent in 1980 (Matthews, Feinstein and
Odling-Smee 1982 108; CVCP 1986 2).

Higher education is a costly business: in per caput terms far greater
than that of other forms of education. It not only involves a preparatory period of at least two years to acquire the requisite qualifications for entry to the sector, but then there is an even longer
period of three years or more, depending on subjects studied, at
university or college before graduation is achieved. Most of the cost is
funded by the state. For this reason we need to determine whether the
massive public commitment to higher education has been worthwhile
from a national point of view, as opposed to the private gain to the
individual, and how well it compares with provision elsewhere. This
task can be approached in several different ways. First, we take a look
at the mode of entry to higher education via the 'A' level examination
system. Then we turn to the delivery system itself, that is the universities and other degree-awarding institutions, to see what they have
produced relative to the country's needs in terms of quantity, quality
and product mix. Next we examine the employment patterns of
graduates to see if these shed any light on the utilisation of manpower.
Finally, we conclude with a reference to rates of return analysis for
different levels of education.

The entry route to higher education

For most potential students access to higher education is secured by
the 'A' level examination system: passes in two to three subjects at
varying grades depending on course and institution selected. These
are acquired by students after two or three years' study at a wide range
of institutions on either a full-time or part-time basis. The most
common practice is still full-time study either in schools or at sixth-
form colleges. A small but growing number of candidates now gain
access by other means (Macfarlane Report 1981 8).

The preferred 'A' level route has been criticised on several grounds:
for being too narrow and selective; leading to premature over-
specialisation and lack of flexibility; and for the way it has dominated

the curricula pattern of both schools and pupils. All of these allegations have some truth in them.

The 'A' level syatem, originally designed for a small academic élite en route for the university, has remained remarkably resilient in the face of changes elsewhere in the educational world. Despite a large growth in numbers taking 'A' levels there has been little change in the basic structure of the examination pattern. The majority of students still study no more than two or three subjects in some depth, most of whom hope to acquire sufficiently respectable grades to allow them to gain access to some form of advanced education, preferably of degree level standard. The structure of the examinations and the subject mix has not changed radically over the years. In terms of subjects offered at 'A' level there has been a strong emphais on the traditional academic disciplines, as opposed to more vocationally orientated subjects. One of the few exceptions has been the remarkable growth of economics in which 'A' level entries rocketed from 1181 in 1951 to over 40,000 in the early 1980s (Mallier, Morwood and Old 1990 26). Until very recently there has been strong resistance to the idea of developing a separate technical and vocational 'A' level stream along the lines suggested by Steedman (1987 68) to end the discrimination against less academic students.

The high level of specialisation at the age of 16 plus (though not in Scotland) is almost unique in the western world. Most competitor countries require their 16–18-year-olds to study a range of subjects, at least six to seven, with core subjects such as mathematics, science and languages usually being compulsory. This is possibly another reason, incidentally, why British enrolment rates in higher secondary education, at 40 per cent or less, are so much lower than those in most other countries where they range between 60 and 90 per cent (OECD 1985b 50). Where they are lower, as in the case of Germany, this is backed up by an adequate system of compulsory part-time education and training for those in work under the famous 'dual system'.

Over-specialisation on a narrow band of academic disciplines has had unfortunate consequences for those concerned. It locks students in at an early stage to a specific culture – arts/humanities or science – which effectively limits their future options in terms of study and career choice. For most students it is difficult to change courses in mid-stream, say from arts to engineering or vice versa, because of the extent of specialisation, which means in effect that the demand for places at universities or colleges is very much determined by the pre-selection of courses at the age of 16. Moreover, the narrow curriculum has helped to foster the production of innumerate arts students, and semi-illiterate scientists and technologists

Another disadvantage of the 'A' level system is that it has helped to perpetuate the academically élitist structure which has permeated the whole curricula pattern and examinations system of the schools. In part this has been due to the influential role of the universities – and to a lesser extent the polytechnics and colleges – in the interests of their narrow entry requirements (Burgess 1977 69–70). The university-dominated examining boards and the reluctance of schools to depart from traditional patterns of teaching have also done much to perpetuate the narrow academic orientation of the educational system. The problem may not be unique to Britain as the OECD (1985a 76) explains:

> There are few sectors of the formal system, particularly in European countries, that have such an entrenched power structure and are as resilient as the academic-type secondary schools or lines of study providing the main route to university entry. Moreover, in view of their strategic role in the selection and certification for entry into higher education, these schools exert an influence which clearly extends beyond their own boundaries.

For the individual pupil success depends very much on the choice of school. There is a far better chance of obtaining good grades in the independent schools, in the few remaining grammar schools and at the top comprehensives than there is in the rest of the state sector. This inevitably works in favour of youngsters from good social backgrounds and it is not surprising to find therefore that even by the late 1970s less than 10 per cent of the student population in university and other higher education came from working class backgrounds (Morgan 1990 425–6). Thus the expansion of higher education did little to reduce class inequalities by widening the opportunities for the lower orders (see Le Grand 1982). The independent schools (including direct grant schools) have had far the best record when it comes to 'A' level performance and entry rate to university (Rae 1981 158–9; *Readers Digest* 1987). Moreover, contrary to popular conception, the independent schools have adapted their teaching and curricula structure much more readily than the state sector to the modern world. Classics have almost disappeared, science, mathematics and economics have grown enormously in popularity, while even engineering and technical subjects have made a strong advance. Furthermore, the prejudice against engineering as a career has diminished sharply among pupils in such schools. Of 14,000 boys leaving 160 independent schools in 1976–7, engineering was found to be the most popular career choice; similarly, one-half the boys from public schools entering university in 1980 were bent on studying engineering, science or medicine (Rae 1981 160–61). Clearly a quiet revolution was taking place within the sheltered cloisters of the public schools. The 'A' level system moreover has perpetuated the very thing which comprehensive schools were designed to eliminate, that is social segregation. Early specialisation on a narrow range of academic disciplines to a high standard effectively pre-empts the field of advanced secondary education for a small group – 20–25 per cent – of the age cohort, most of whose members come from socially advantaged backgrounds. They are reared on a diet of book learning and examinations and are expected to achieve high attainment in public examinations before passing into some form of higher education. For the majority of 16-year-olds who cannot, for want of ability, inclination or background, aspire to these goals, or who are more vocationally orientated, there is little on offer for staying on at school after 16. As one observer (Siedentop 1986) noted:

> Having a core of basic subjects which everyone does until a relatively advanced age provides a kind of social melting pot, whereas early specialisation has the effect of humiliating those whose social origins point initially in a vocational direction.

The introduction of the national curriculum and the modernisation of the examinations syllabi for school leavers in the 1980s brought into prominence the shortcomings of the 'A' level system and the need for its overhaul. Various proposals for reform have been put forward, including the widening of the syallabus proposed by the Higginson Committee (1988), the introduction of a new examination between GCSE and 'A' levels, and the Institute of Public Policy Research's suggestion for the equivalent of a British baccalaureate. The latter would replace all existing examinations and would be taken in a balanced range of subjects at the age of 18.

However, none of the proposals so far has been able to bridge the dichotomy between academic and vocational disciplines. Nor is it clear that any of them would satisfy the needs and abilities of a far larger cohort who might be expected to stay on after the age of 16. After all, the raising of the school leaving age to 16 threw up this very problem because of the failure to adapt the curricula to the differing needs of a varied cohort of pupils, and there is no reason to suppose that it will not resurface again if a much larger proportion of youngsters continue beyond compulsory schooling.

The only attempt to address the problem so far has been the introduction of the Advanced Supplementary (AS) examination in 1987. The declared objective was to provide breadth and depth in advanced studies by taking say two 'A' levels and two 'AS' courses. This offers little in the way of a solution. Though the 'AS' level takes only half as long to complete as an 'A' level it is pitched at a similar level of difficulty as 'A' levels and therefore effectively rules out enlarging the catchment of 16–18-year-olds. Secondly, 'AS' courses do not cater for the more vocationally-orientated student since the format of the syllabi and examinations are closely modelled on those of 'A' levels. Finally, there is little prospect of achieving greater breadth with the new examination. Many schools and colleges are not offering the alternative examination, while in cases where it is on offer most pupils tend to be taking complementary rather than contrasting subjects to their 'A' levels, or using 'AS' levels as a stepping stone to 'A' levels.

One of the reasons for the poor response is because the universities have been slow to respond to the need for reform in the advanced examinations system. They have been reluctant to recognise the 'AS' examination for entrance purposes and they have offered little in the way of an alternative. One way out of the impasse would be to scrap the 'A' level system and substitute 'AS' levels in six or seven disciplines, with compulsory core components in mathematics, science/technology and languages. To cater for a larger cohort of pupils it would also be necessary to introduce a proper vocational component or stream and to lower the standard compared with the present 'A' levels. Those intending to proceed to higher education would have to acquire a specified number of 'AS' levels of sufficiently high grades to secure entry. This would have the advantage that pupils could study a broader spread of subjects over a range of disciplines thus bringing this country more in to line with international standards. In fact one institution, the First City Technology College, Kinghurst, has already made a pre-emptive strike in this direction by ditching 'A' levels, and instead has started a BTEC sixth-form with the top stream taking the International Baccalaureat (*Financial Times*,

17 July 1990).

So far the government has signalled its intention to retain the original 'A' level format and to graft on to it cosmetic changes in the form of a system of diplomas awarded to candidates securing passes in two 'A' levels or their vocational equivalents. A similar diploma is proposed for the GCSE examinations. These proposals were announced in the spring of 1991, as part of a package of measures designed to boost participation rates in higher education and improve facilities for the study of vocational subjects. Though the details are still to be clarified, there does not seem much prospect that they will provide any solution to the issue discussed above.

The output of graduates

There are two main questions to be considered with respect to the delivery of graduates: first, whether the quantity supplied has been sufficient to meet national needs, and secondly, whether that output has been of the right balance in terms of subject mix. These questions have been at the forefront of the debate on higher education in more recent years partly because it has been alleged that Britain has lagged behind other countries on both counts (DES 1978; Cmnd 9524 1985). It is a well-known fact that participation rates in post-compulsory education have been low by international standards – less than half those of some countries – and that consequently enrolment rates in higher education (principally degree standard) have also been low. In fact Britain has had one of the lowest enrolment rates among OECD countries, averaging between one-half and two-thirds of member countries during the 1970s (NEDC 1983 15–16; OECD 1981 74–6). However, as we shall see, this does not necessarily mean a comparative shortfall in the final output of graduates.

As to the product mix, there have been frequent criticisms that the British system provides the wrong sort of graduates with the result that we have therefore suffered from a shortage of scientists, engineers and technologists. More specifically, it has been suggested that the specialised academic orientation of the 'A' level examinations system, coupled with the demand-driven approach to university expansion, has produced an unfavourable output balance between subject areas thereby leading to a low level of technological and scientic expertise. Some of these claims can be supported by cross-country comparisons on stock levels and by data on graduate employment destinations. (see below). It is not however axiomatic that the higher education system *per se* is wholly to blame for any deficiences.

Estimating future manpower requirements in a mixed economy, at either the aggregate or sectoral levels, is by no means a simple task. It is difficult to predict exactly the actions of employers and students, while the long lead times involved in training, the variable re-cruitment and retention rates and the unpredictable re-entry rate of women following withdrawal from employment for child-bearing, can render manpower plans hopelessly out of date (Fulton 1990 155). Even in more closely defined professional occupations such as teaching and medicine, attempts to forecast future manpower needs have not met with a great deal of success. As Fulton (1982 122) points out, neither social demand nor manpower forecasts have performed at all well as a basis for determining the provision of higher education. Indeed, manpower forecasts are unlikely to be met if the supply is largely demand-driven, and any resulting imbalance between the two is the inevitable consequence of an imperfect market system. The alternative is to replace the market system by a formal planning mechanism to ensure closer correspondence between demand and supply, but this would lead to rigidity and the curtailment of indivi-dual choice.

In fact, it was largely in deference to the ideal of freedom of choice that the expansion of higher education was based primarily on social demand, though with periodic efforts, most of which were largely ineffective, to influence the balance of take-up between subjects. '. . . from the early 1960s onward both the overall size of the higher education system and the distribution of places across fields within it have been determined primarily in response to student demand' (Fulton 1990 146). The Hudson Institute (1974 86–9) was highly critical of the post-Robbins approach to expansion, regarding it as 'a haphazard response to a bulge in the national population curve'. More specifically, it attacked the lack of strategic purpose of the programme for generating graduates which, because it was based on access and individual choice, precluded a structured approach to meeting the future needs of society and the economy.

As far as the total flow of graduates is concerned, the expansion programme performed far better than its most ardent critics were prepared to admit (Hudson Institute 1974 86). Though enrolment rates in higher education remained well below those of most major countries, the final outturn in terms of degrees awarded was far better.

In a careful analysis of the complex data, Cerych (1983 132–40) has shown that because of higher drop-out rates and longer courses in many other countries, Britain has an above average performance compared with continental countries in terms of the final delivery of graduates. On the basis of the relevant age cohort, only the United States and Japan had a superior record at first degree level, as the figures in Table 5.2 indicate. Moreover, in terms of quality (student/ teacher ratio) and expenditure per student year, the UK also tends to compare favourably with other countries.

Table 5.2 Proportion of age cohort receiving first level degrees and non-university qualifications in 1977 (%)

	University first level degree	Degrees or diplomas of non-univ. type higher education (below degree level)	Total
UK	14.5(a)	3.8	18.3
Germany	9.0	3.1	12.1
Austria	4.9	–	–
Spain	6.9	4.9	11.8
France	7.5	4.4	11.9
Italy	9.4	–	–
Netherlands	4.7	10.0	14.7
Sweden (1976)	12.2	6.2	18.4
US	25.3	–	–
Japan	20.3	9.5	29.8

(a) Degrees awarded by universities, Open University and CNAA.
Source: Cerych (1983 143).

Do these figures imply that Britain was in fact producing too many graduates by comparison with her continental neighbours? Evidence on this point is somewhat conflicting. The stock of graduates in the total labour force, and especially of scientists and engineers, has remained low by international standards partly because of the earlier backlog (see below). Secondly, rates of return analysis suggest that better returns may be found elsewhere in the educational system, a point taken up in the final section of this chapter. Thirdly, broadly speaking the large expansion in graduate numbers since the early 1960s has been absorbed fairly readily. It is true that the demand for graduates, like that of labour generally, tends to wax and wane with the fortunes of the economy. Graduate unemployment was especially high in the recession of the early 1980s, exceding that of the total labour force (Landymore 1985 710), and again in the late 1980s downturn in economic activity, when many firms deferred recruiting. On the other hand, in the mid 1980s (1986–7) there was a growing shortage of graduates despite the fact that student numbers were still rising. On a longer-term view graduate unemployment rates have been better than those with lesser or no qualifications which scarcely merits fear of vast oversupply problems (Fulton 1990 49). Government moves to enlarge the participation rate, after some qualms about oversupply in the early 1980s, would seem to indicate a degree of confidence on this score.

On the other hand, Tarsh (1987 141) sounds a note of caution on this matter. He believes that a case can be made for removing resources from higher education on the grounds of 'the persistent signs of oversupply of graduates, the lack of evidence of shortages except in very specific areas and the increasing movement of graduates into areas of general and lower level employment'. He favours highly specific course shifts rather than broad steers. Some of these points are in fact worth bearing in mind in view of recent proposals to enlarge the participation rate in higher education. There is no clear indication that Britain suffers from a sheer shortage of graduates, except in certain specific areas, which the current expansion plans are not equipped to deal with. What Britain does suffer from is a shortage of intermediary skills and it is far from clear how this can be solved by what is ostensibly going to be more of the same. The universities, while embracing the expansion plans, are uncertain as to what their future role in the education system will be. There is the inherent danger, already apparent in some areas of study, that the quality of output will be sacrificed in the interests of quantity, more specifically by a process of trading down in tuition in an attempt to satisfy educational and training needs that are best provided elsewhere. This is yet another example of muddled educational strategy which has been so endemic in Britain.

The pattern of student recruitment

There has also been concern about the sectoral distribution of the output of graduates. The major complaint is that demand-driven expansion has produced a sub-optimal output mix in terms of subject areas with the result that there have been too many arts graduates and not enough scientists and engineers. Despite the widely held view in the 1960s that British industry and its research dimension were being impaired by a shortage of scientific and technological expertise, there was no concerted effort to repair the lacking. The University Grants Committee (UGC) made no serious attempt to expand provision in science and technology; rather in fact the reverse since it announced, in November 1967, that the main increase in university places would occur in arts subjects rather than in science and technology. One effect of this decision was to limit the expected growth of the Colleges of Advanced Technology (CATs), later incorporated into the university system, which could have acted as the spearhead for the expansion of technological studies (Hudson Institute 1974 88–9).

The decision to favour arts expansion meant that effectively the provision of higher education was determined largely by student choice. Since most of the new recruits came from the secondary schools this choice was constrained by the narrowness and inflexibility of the sixth-form curricula and the accompanying examinations system and by the predilections of sixth-form teachers. Thus in the initial phase of expansion the growth of student places was fuelled by a demand for arts and social science courses and for law and education rather than for engineering and science. Britain's higher education establishments were, it seemed, busily churning out large numbers of arts and social science graduates and, as one cynic remarked, almost as many students of the Welsh language as production engineers (Lockyer 1976 70–1), at a time when industry was said to be desperately in need of more engineers and applied scientists. Thus though the number of students studying science and enginering and technology increased by some 26 per cent in the decade from 1966–7, their shares of the total student population fell quite significantly in the face of an overall increase of 46 per cent in enrolments. The main gains were to be found in arts and social science and education (see Table 5.3). In subsequent years there was some relative improvement in the position of science and technology but by the mid 1980s they still accounted for a smaller share of the total student population than two decades earlier. On the other hand, though the data for earlier years are not directly comparable with later statistics due to differences in the basis of classification, there does seem to have been a quite noticeable shift towards science and technology in the 1950s and early 1960s (*Annual Abstract of Statistics*).

The trend away from science and technology in the big expansion

Table 5.3 Courses taken by full-time students in universities in Britain (excluding Open University)

	1966–7 000s	%	1975–6 000s	%	1984–5 000s	%
Education	6,488	3.5	11,297	4.2	12,267	4.0
Medicine, dentistry, health	19,689	10.7	29,006	10.8	33,325	10.8
Agric. forestry and vet. science	3,785	2.1	5,268	2.0	5,868	1.9
Engineering and technology	30,044	16.3	38,917	13.7	47,723	15.4
Science	48,559	26.3	62,182	23.1	71,887	23.3
Social administration, business studies	37,219	20.2	61,831	23.0	72,321	23.4
Architecture and other professional studies	3,029	1.6	5,636	2.1	6,110	2.0
Language, literature and area studies	26,264	13.2	31,275	11.6	35,004	11.3
Arts other than language, music, drama and visual arts	11,146	6.1	25,593	9.5	24,503	7.9

Source: *Annual Abstract of Statistics*

phase was more serious than the data in Table 5.3 indicate, since the figures do not include non-university degree-awarding institutions, principally the CATs, the polytechnics and a number of miscellaneous colleges. These ideally should have formed the core of a technological university sector modelled along German lines, but in practice they did not fulfil this role. The CATs, as we have seen, were absorbed into the university system and became indistinguishable from the older civic universities. The polytechnics, some thirty of which were set up between 1966 and 1972, soon became subject to what was known as academic drift. In an attempt to enhance their prestige, they sought to ape the universities, which meant a relative shift away from technological and industrial courses, a dilution of vocational and part-time tuition and greater emphais on research activities (Cantor and Roberts 1986 116; Glover and Kelly 1987 102–3). Only the Scottish Central Institutions retained their technological and vocational orientation. Thus was missed an opportunity to meet the nation's manpower gap in technological expertise. However, in all fairness to the polytechnics, their role in the education system was never clearly defined and even today they are in the anomalous position of being expected to provide tuition in courses ranging from BTEC and 'A' level through to postgraduate studies.

When we turn to international comparisons of the distribution of places among broad subject groupings, Britain does not appear to have been badly placed in science and technology. In 1970 Britain had a higher proportion of its students in both subject categories than did most other major countries and correspondingly fewer in the humanities (OECD 1981 51). Sanderson's (1987 134) data for the later 1970s appear to confirm this favourable position.

Stock levels tell a rather different story. These show a continuing lag in the supply of scientists and engineers in the population compared with the position in other countries. In 1977 the United States employed 57.4 scientists and engineers per 10,000 persons in the labour force, Japan 49.9, Germany 40.5 and Britain just over 30 (Collins and Robbins 1990 171). Comparable figures for research scientists alone per 10,000 head of population in 1978 were as follows: the United States 25, Japan 23, Germany 19, France 11 and Britain 8 (*Financial Times*, 24 April 1980). Thus even though the output of graduates in total and the distribution by subject areas was not unfavourable by international standards, Britain clearly had a backlog to make good and should therefore have been directing more students into science and technology.

In some subjects areas, engineering in particular, there was clearly a deficiency in the flow of qualified recruits. Prais (1981 50–2) has shown that in the early 1970s British universities were producing about one-third fewer graduate engineers than Germany (rising to 43 per cent if allowance is made for foreign students in engineering and technology at British universities). The relative gap in the stock of engineers and technologists on a uniform population basis was even greater, 71 per cent for graduates and 36 per cent if those professionally qualified but without degrees are included in the British figures (see also Cassels 1990 43; CBI 1989 18–19).

The employment of graduates

An even more serious matter is the possibility that Britain may not have utilised her graduate population to the best effect. There has been a wastage element in the graduate outflow each year as some graduates do not enter the domestic labour market at all. Industry moreover has tended to take a diminishing share of the total flow, while many scientists and engineers move into defence work or are not employed as scientists and engineers at all but in some quite different capacity. This wastage or drift is one reason, but not the only one, why industry has had difficulty in recruiting graduates in engineering and science.

The figures in Table 5.4 provide a breakdown of the destinations of first degree graduates for selected years. It can be seen that at any one time only one-half or fewer actually enter employment. The rest moved into a variety of activities, including research or academic study, further education, unemployment or overseas work. Not all of these were lost to productive activity of course since some, after further study for example, no doubt entered the labour market. Nevertheless, it is clear that a very significant proportion of graduates do not initially join the workforce.

Of those who do take up employment directly on graduation, many go into activities other than manufacturing. The big growth areas of student recruitment have been the public services and the financial sector, including accounting (Table 5.5). By the later 1980s the intake of new graduates into public services was almost as large as that of manufacturing, while financial services had become by far the largest

Table 5.4 First destinations of first degree graduates in the UK (000s)
(Universities only up to 1975–6; plus polytechnics, Scottish colleges 1980–1, colleges in England and Wales 1986–7)

	Research or academic study	Further education or training	Entering employment	Unemployment/short-term unemployment	Overseas graduates returning home	Other known destinations	Unknown	Total
1965–6	6.4	7.0	12.9	1.7	1.0	1.7	1.5	32.2
1975–6	7.8	12.4	23.1	7.9	1.9	3.0	7.6	63.7
1987–8	9.4	12.1	61.7	11.0	4.8	6.3	14.6	120.0

Source: *Training Statistics 1990* 102–3.

Table 5.5 Employment categories of first degree graduates by subject known to have entered employment in the UK (000s)
(Universities only up to 1975–6; plus polytechnics, Scottish colleges 1980–1, colleges in England and Wales 1986–7)

	Public services	Schools	Other education	Agric. and forestry	Manufacturing	Building and public utilities	Accounting, banking, insurance	All others	Total entering employment
1965–6	1.9	1.3	0.7	0.1	5.4	1.5	1.1	0.9	12.9
1975–6	6.9	0.6	0.7	0.2	5.7	1.9	4.8	2.2	23.1
1987–8	11.9	5.3	1.6	0.3	12.3	5.7	18.3	6.1	61.7

Source: *Training Statistics 1990* 102–3.

source of recruitment. The numbers going into manufacturing scarcely changed in the decade through to the mid 1970s, though there was some recovery in subsequent years despite the decline in the sector's overall employment base. Nevertheless, over the whole period manufacturing's share of graduate recruitment declined from 41.8 to 19.9 per cent. This trend deterioration partly reflects the relative decline of manufacturing during this period, but it also suggests an inability or reluctance to recruit qualified expertise. The proportion of postgraduates going into industry was even less; in 1980 only 15 per cent of postgraduates with engineering or technological qualifications did so (*Investors' Chronicle*, 21 November 1981 548).

What is perhaps even more remarkable is that many qualified scientists and engineers (QSEs) do not actually work as such. Lindley (1981 23) notes that some 60 per cent of QSEs did not work in their chosen fields, against which the annual increase in the stock of about 5 per cent a year looks quite small. Not only that, but 45 per cent of those working in the category designated as scientists and engineers were not actually qualified in that capacity, having neither graduate nor equivalent professional qualifications. Thus, in so far as some sectors, for example manufacturing, appear to have suffered from a shortage of high level expertise, there would seem to be an obvious solution to the problem.

A further factor to take into account is the drain of resources to the defence sector to which the Finniston Committee (1980 27) drew particular attention. Apart from the United States, Britain has one of the largest defence sectors in the western world, accounting for some 5 per cent of gross domestic product and about 4 per cent of the workforce including the armed forces (Johnson 1990). In addition, 25 per cent of all R & D spending (49 per cent of that funded from public sources) is directed towards defence work, much of it going into aerospace, electronics, nuclear power and military equipment. The sector has attracted the cream of the country's supply of high level skills partly because it offers work in exciting and prestigious fields apart from the attractions of the remuneration. It has been estimated that over 30 per cent of all highly qualified scientists and engineers are engaged in defence activity. Unlike its American counterpart, the British defence sector has not been a very fruitful source for the development of civilian spin-off projects partly because of its low critical mass and the method used for awarding contracts to firms. But what it has done is to reduce the skilled expertise available to civilian industry with detrimental consequences for its advancement. The authors of one recent survey (Kaldor, Sharp and Walker 1986 39 45–6), argue forcibly that it has drained civilian industry of valuable manpower: in effect the military sector has crowded out civilian employment and the diffusion of new technologies at a time when creative skills are at a premium in the exploitation of new technologies. In short, they conclude, 'the drain on skilled manpower, particularly in electronics, has been a major factor inhibiting the expansion of high technology industries and, equally important, the take-up of new technologies in older industries'.

The Finniston inquiry also laid great stress on the shortage of engineers in manufacturing and the way that this adversely affected the capability of many firms, especially in export markets. It also noted however that industry often found difficulty in recruiting high quality expertise. This came as no great surprise since it was by no means the first to draw attention to this problem. It was a well-known fact that manufacturing had not been the most popular choice of occupations among graduates. A survey of over a thousand graduates reported in the *Financial Times* (14 July 1989) showed that only 7 per cent had seriously considered a career in industry, though engineering itself fared somewhat better at 15 per cent, most of whom were males. The most popular choices were the media and communications, education, banking and finance, computing and information technology and tourism and leisure.

If industry has a poor image overall when it comes to attracting skilled manpower, it is in an even worse position with regard to the recruitment of engineering expertise. It is not only that there has been a shortage of engineers in some sectors of business such as production management and at the boardroom level for example, but also that industry has been unable to attract the best talent since the most able candidates tend to go elsewhere. Industry itself is largely to blame for this predicament. It has not done a great deal to promote the image of an engineering career in industry, especially in the less glamorous branches. Pay, conditions of work and career prospects have been poor and engineers have often been accorded a low status profile. Initial training has been limited and many graduates have been thrown in at the deep end, into technical and applied jobs for which their academic training has not prepared them. Not that industry is alone in the latter respect. Stories of dissatisfied graduates are not uncommon and these are frequently the result of unsuitable positioning or lack of training. Most graduates, whatever profession they enter, appear to receive very limited training from their employers. A survey of 9000 graduates and higher diplomates ('A' level plus two years' advanced training) qualifying in 1980, found that one-half the sample received no formal training from their employers, while less than one-third experienced on-the-job training. Formal training was most common in utilities (gas and electricity), the armed forces, the police, prison and fire services (thankfully), and in computing and financial work (Clarke and Rees 1989 491–500).

More generally, engineering, so crucial to many industrial operations, has found great difficulty in shaking off the traditional 'boiler-suit and spanners' image of the profession, one reason no doubt why so few women have chosen it as a career (Finniston 1980 71). Quite unjustly, the press, the media, the teaching profession and the public at large continue to depict a misleading stereotype of engineering as a dirty, greasy occupation, to do with mending cars and machinery and carried out by men in all-in-one suits well-covered in oil. As David Thomas, a correspondent to the *Financial Times* (7 March 1989) put it:

> An engineer is someone who dresses in a boiler suit, covers himself in oil, loves nuts and bolts and, at a pinch, will help you wash your car. This misleading view of engineers is formed early on by primary school children and goes a long way to explain Britain's failure to recruit enough professional engineers.

This initial conception of engineering is perpetuated throughout school life, and is re-enforced by the intellectual snobbery and anti-technology bias of many teachers trained in the humanities and in what are regarded as the more prestigious 'clean' sciences. Technological issues are relegated to a peripheral role and few school children receive careers advice on engineering (Glover and Kelly 1987 110). It is these social values which explain why engineering has been accorded such a low status in Britain compared with its prestigious role in most other countries. They are very much a reflection of Britain's inglorious cultural heritage which has clung tenaciously to a two culture dimension – arts/humanities and pure/natural sciences – with engineering being assigned to a subordinate status as an applied science, rather than as a third culture, *Technik*, embracing knowledge and skills relevant to the making of artefacts, as in Germany for instance. In that country engineering and technology have a status on par with, if not superior to, other disciplines and engineering graduates rise high in the managerial hierarchy. It is obviously going to be difficult to break down the intellectual blockage in Britain. Perhaps the first point of attack should be in the schools where the initial damage is done (Finniston 1980 79–80; Hutton and Lawrence 1981). Better careers advice and practical instruction about the world of work and industry together with stress on the important role of the engineering dimension in industry would certainly help for a start. At the same time industry and the engineering profession need to improve their public profile in order to remove misleading conceptions as to what the world of work is all about.

Rates of return analysis

Should Britain have produced more graduates? This is a key question but not an easy one to answer since not all indicators tell the same story. By the 1970s aggregate graduate flows appear to have been quite respectable by European standards, but not by the American and Japanese ones. It is possible of course that the latter countries were producing too many graduates. Stock levels however were still inferior, especially in science and technology, reflecting the slow accumulation in earlier periods when graduate flows were very low. In some sectors, notably engineering, the graduate flow still left room for improvement, though industry's inability to attract the most able graduates may have been more a function of conditions of employment than one of supply. There are question marks over the utilisation of graduate manpower, especially the large proportion of scientists and engineers engaged in defence work.

As to the distribution of resources between different sectors of education, rates of return analysis may offer some general guidance. Many of these show very low rates of social return on postgraduate education, moderate rates at first degree level and very high rates of return on intermediate training up to HNC (see Morris 1973; Morris and Ziderman 1971; Psacharopoulos 1985). Differentials between arts and science at first degree level tend to be small, with the balance running in favour of the former. This has raised some doubts as to the alleged shortage of scientists and engineers at graduate level (Layard 1971 20–1).

There are many imponderables in this type of exercise, not least the earnings-based derivatives used for calculating rates of return, to caution drawing firm conclusions from it. None-the-less, in broad terms most of the studies do seem to indicate that a resource switch from expensive higher education to less expensive intermediate education and training would not have come amiss. This would be in accord with more circumstantial evidence on the state of the graduate labour market as outlined by Tarsh (1987 141). It also fits in with Hollenstein's (1982 78) doubts as to whether industry would have been better placed had it had a larger input of top level expertise, on the grounds that skill deficiences lower down the line, that is at the intermediate level, were still so large as to cause a mis-utilisation of graduate manpower through trading down, thereby lowering the workforce's capacity to absorb innovations.

Final assessment

For the whole of higher education there is not a single unequivocal conclusion that emerges from our survey. At the pre-entry stage to higher education we would question the wisdom of specialisation on a narrrow band of subjects usually in related disciplines. This has perpetuated the traditional cultural divide between humanities and science and has left no room for the emergence of a third culture, *Technik*, with parity of esteem. Moreover, it has seriously curtailed student choice and flexibility since subsequent study patterns are virtually frozen at 16 when the 'A' level selection is made. It is perhaps not surprising therefore that we tend to produce more semi-illiterate engineers and innumerate arts graduates than is the case in other countries where premature specialisation does not occur. A further disadvantage of the system is that it discourages the less academically-gifted from staying on at school.

   Low participation rates at the post-compulsory school stage, in contrast to the high levels in many other countries, are echoed later in the enrolment rates for higher education. However, the effects are considerably muted at the final output stage because of the higher retention rate of students in this country due to better screening on entry. Thus, following the big expansion in higher education from the 1960s, the system delivered an annual flow of graduates which compared favourably with those of other European countries. But because of earlier deficiences stock levels remained low, especially in key subject areas, which suggests that more effort should have been made to monitor entry rates within the broad subject groupings. This would not of course have been compatible with the declared policy of freedom of student choice, though no doubt it could have been engineered surreptitiously had there been a will to do so.

As for the deployment of graduates, there is cause for concern. The initial wastage rate was quite high, while occupational dispersion data suggest a mis-utilisation of manpower resources, especially among QSEs. Poor training and positioning of graduates also had a similar effect, which partly explains why industry failed to attract the best recruits. This however is fully consistent with the low priority given to manpower strategy as a whole. Rates of return analysis would seem to indicate that resources might profitably have been switched from higher education into intermediate training and this is supported by more indirect evidence. Clearly an *a fortiori* case for first things first.

6
THE EDUCATION AND
TRAINING OF MANAGEMENT

The education and training of managers is just as important as that of scientists, technologists, technicians, craftsmen and other productive workers in society. Each level of expertise is complementary and interacting and a deficiency in one sector will tend to have important repercussions elsewhere. Thus a shortage of craftsmen and technicians relative to scientists and technologists will result in the latter 'trading down' or 'filling in' for the lacunae lower down the ability range. Similiarly, a shortage of good managerial talent in any organisation will lead to substitution effects, for example technicians doing the work of general middle management, administrators taking on the role of enterprise initiators, or more seriously at higher managerial levels, the neglect of new investment opportunities through sheer shoratge of top quality management. Thus there would be little point in spending large sums on training scientists and technologists to develop advanced technology if there is an absence of equivalent effort in developing managerial expertise which can exploit the new opportunities. The Finniston Committee (1980 36–7) reporting in 1980 on the engineering professions drew particular attention to the way in which the lack of technological understanding among top management affected the capability of many companies both to devise and to implement new technology. In turn of course, an under-trained managerial cadre may fail to perceive the need to employ many personnel with advanced expertise and in time this could well damage a company's competitive strength.

Business and society

Many writers have in fact stressed the important role of management in the economy and the need to devote adequate resources to training (Kempner 1983–4). Political and Economic Planning in their illuminating study of postwar managerial experience and behaviour (PEP 1966 15) argued that in the last analysis the growth of the economy as a whole depends on the efficiency and growth of the individual firms within it and these in turn are determined largely by the men who run them. A similar sentiment was expressed by the National Economic Development Council in their report on the conditions for faster growth published in 1963 (NEDC 1963 220).

Conversely, other observers have sought to lay much of the blame for Britain's poor economic performance on the weak response on the part of management. After all, Freeman argues (1980 132), the policy mistakes of past governments and other failings of the economic system might not have been so serious if 'British industrial management had been as strong and efficient as German industrial management in coping with the problem of international competition and the associated technical change. But this is manifestly not the case. In sector after sector long-term weaknesses have become apparent which require concerted long-term strategies to rectify.'

Blanket generalisations about management can of course be highly misleading. There have been several well-known success stories, especially in the more sheltered sectors of activity such as services and retailing. But whether the managerial talent in these sectors can be said to be any better than that in the industrial sector is an open question, given the fact that many service trades are sheltered from the invigorating winds of foreign competition. However, even within the manufacturing sector there have been significant differences in performance between firms. No one would dispute the fine records of firms such as Glaxo, BTR, Hanson and Unilever. Yet in the big league there are many more companies with an indifferent or patchy record than there are clear winners. Moreover, it should not be forgotten that small and medium sized companies still account for a considerable share of ouput and their performance overall can scarcely be regarded as exemplary.

A second point to bear in mind is that the performance, attitudes and characteristics of managers are inevitably affected by the social milieu in which they work. Despite their key role in the economic system, business leaders, no less than trade unionists, have long since been the target for denigration by the British public. In fact from the dawn of modern industrial society they have received a bad press and they have been awarded few of the accolades accorded their counterparts in other countries, especially the United States and Germany. During the nineteenth century they were seen as the harsh exploiters of labour and their general status in society left much to be desired.

Many of the classic novels of the period bear witness to the lowly esteem in which trade and industrial pursuits were held by the established pillars of society. A self-made businessman with little education found it an uphill struggle to raise his social standing against the established bastions of landed gentry, the church, the army and the civil service, together with a growing band of professional élites. This no doubt explains why many sought to ape the life-styles of their 'betters' and sent their sons to be educated for similar positions (see Wiener 1981; Ward 1967).

In the twentieth century the position of businessmen in society improved somewhat compared with the previous century, but they have never attained the elevated status of their counterparts in other countries. They have frequently been the convenient scapegoats for attack when things went wrong, or branded as the wicked capitalists when success was rewarded by high profits. The British have never respected their businessmen and managers in the way the Germans, the Americans, the Japanese or the French do theirs, nor has Britain got folk-hero business leaders of the type revered in the United States or Germany. It is the professional classes – the bankers, the financiers, the lawyers, doctors, accountants and civil servants, the armed forces, even the teachers and the clergy, but not unfortunately the engineers – who draw rank on the captains of industry. It is to these occupations that the best graduates – unlike their continental counterparts – gravitate, rather than to industrial management.

The educational background of top management

Whether the legacy of the educational system has been responsible for society's attitude to industry and management is a moot point. Certainly there has been much debate about the way in which the historical structure of the educational system – with its preference for humanistic and pure science studies as opposed to engineering and technology – produced the educated amateur or gentleman at the helm of British industry (Wiener 1981). Coleman (1973 108) has drawn attention to the linkage between class, education and business leadership among the larger companies between the 1860s and 1940s where the top posts, as in the civil service, the church, the government, the armed forces and finance, tended to be filled by members of an élite group with a common educational background, namely public school, Oxford, Cambridge, humanistic. Drawing on the example of

Courtaulds, he finds a typical example in John Coldbrook Hanbury-Williams who became chairman of the company in 1946. In contrast to his predecessor Samuel Courtauld, Hanbury-Williams 'was a snob, liked titles, married a Byzantine Princess, and relished Court appointments. (He) knew little or nothing about production technology, despised technical men, remained ignorant of science, and wholly indifferent to industrial relations' (Coleman 1980 23–5). Who better than to run one of Britain's major companies in the postwar period!?

In fact the choice of Hanbury-Williams as leader was wholly consistent with the traditional pattern of recruitment to the top posts, an approach which above all else emphasised continuity and the belief in the concept of the gentleman: 'that gentlemen are likely to be better leaders. And that is precisely what this particular choice failed to demonstrate.' It epitomised the composition of the Courtaulds' board, the majority of whom were ex-public school pupils, while one-third had attended Oxford or Cambridge (Coleman 1980 23–5).

This was by no means an atypical example. Many other large companies had similar structures and patterns of recruitment to top posts at this time. Copeman (1955 149) in his sample of 1243 directors of large public companies in 1951 found that 58 per cent had attended public schools, though only one-third subsequently went on to university. Most surveys of business leadership of the period also tend to show that it was one's social background and where one was educated that mattered most, rather than the educational expertise most relevant to industry. Thus an analysis conducted by the Acton Society Trust (1956) in the mid 1950s found that the most advantageous background for promotion at all managerial levels ran in the following (descending) order of importance:

(1) Arts degree from Oxford or Cambridge
(2) Major public school education
(3) Non-technical qualifications
(4) Arts degree from other university
(5) Science degree
(6) Lesser public school education
(7) Grammar school
(8) Technical qualification
(9) First job technical or senior clerical

Note the low standing of technical subjects as a route to higher management and the absence of formal management training (Lewis and Stewart 1958 66; Stewart and Duncan-Jones 1956 66–7).

Too much should not be read into the apparent élitist domination of top managerial posts. It would be dangerous, as Coleman (1973 110) points out, to link it directly with enterprise failure since in banking and finance, where it was even more prominent, it appears to have succeeded. Moreover, the popular sociological conception that top management is riddled with élite groups sharing an exclusive educational background (Fidler 1981; Stanworth and Giddens 1974), needs to be put in a comparative international context. Britain in fact is by no means unique in terms of the make-up of her top management cadre. In the United States, Europe and Japan an even larger proportion of top executives are graduates of the élite educational institutions: for example the French grande écoles, the American Ivy League universities, the German technological universities, and the prestigious top ten Japanese universities. They also tend to share a common cultural and social background. The social origins of British top executives are very similar to those in Europe in that the majority (two-thirds) come from well-to-do families with only a sprinkling from the lower classes. In this respect it is Europe, including Britain, which differs from the United States where a higher proportion of managers spring from the lower orders (De Bettignies and Evans 1977 280).

One of the big differences however is that business executives have been less qualified than their counterparts abroad. This is as true today as in the past. In the mid 1950s only about one-third of top managers and directors had university degrees, while an even smaller proportion had any engineering or scientific experience. Even in the engineering industry itself only just over one-fifth were found to be technically qualified, and of these only a small number had been to university. At the general managerial level, an Institute of Directors' study in 1959 found that some 50 per cent of general managers had no qualifications whatever, while over half the directors in charge of production were without engineering or scientific qualifications (Copeman 1955 149; Granick 1962 246–7; Koestler 1963 87 89; Bartlett 1977 171; Lewis and Stewart 1958 66). As for management training, this was still very much in its infancy and few executives had had any formal training in this field. The comments of Urwick and Brech (1953 218) make this clear:

British industry . . . has not been concerned with management, has found difficulty in understanding that it exists as a subject, and has certainly never felt that it needed any special skill other than that assumed to be inherent in the acquisition of a share in ownership or a seat on a board of directors.

The situation did not change radically over the next two decades. A sample survey in the early 1960s found that the majority of managers, irrespective of the size of the company and the level of management, were not qualified in technical or science subjects (Nichols 1969 82). By contrast some 60 per cent of the board members of major German companies had an engineering background. According to Hutton and Lawrence (1981 45,100,111), the Germans are said to find the idea of a history graduate becoming a management trainee quaintly amusing. By the early 1970s only about one-half of top executives in large British firms were university graduates as against 80–90 per cent in France, Germany, Sweden, Belgium, France and the United States (Fores and Clark 1975 69; Leggatt 1978 811, 818; Glover 1978a 158). Formal management training was still the exception rather than the rule, while the majority of managers received little in the way of regular in-house training or performance monitoring (Channon 1973 213, 226–7).

The second major difference compared with other countries is that British top management tends to be very deficient in technical expertise and production skills to the detriment of the primary function of manufacturing. The German concept of *Technik*, the making of industrial artefacts, as a specific and identifiable culture, is almost unknown in Britain. The mechanics of the production process tend to be regarded as little more than a necessary evil and graduates tend to fight shy of going into production work, or if they do they try to escape from it as quickly as possible. This of course reflects the low status accorded to the engineering dimension and the limited opportunities for promotion from those within its ranks (Fores, Lawrence and Sorge 1978 168). One of the main conclusions to emerge from the Sussex Research Unit's study on technical innovation was the marked lack of professionalism among British managers:

> While much of British industry has been run by managers possessing few, if any, formal technical or managerial skills, our major competitors' industries have been controlled more often by trained managers possessing a range of such skills. It might be that, as in English cricket, in British industry the days of the amateur are numbered (Rothwell in Pavitt 1980 306).

Elaborating on the same theme, Nuala Swords-Isherwood (Pavitt 1980 93–5) raised some of the wider educational and social issues relevant to management generally:

The major and significant differences between British managers and their rivals in most other countries are in their professionalism, in the number of engineers among them, and in their social class. The educational system in Britain is such that the most favoured subjects of study are not those most directly relevant to industry. It has been geared to non-industrial pursuits, and the pinnacle of achievement has been as far removed as possible from production. Signs can still be seen in the unpopularity of industrial careers, with consequences for the quality of industrial entrants, for their competence and for their status. The vicious circle once established is difficult to change, although there is some suggestion that such changes are occurring.

Though industry has frequently been criticised for not recruiting sufficient numbers of men qualified in enginering or in some branch of science, one of the problems has been that of finding enough applicants with such qualifications who were likely to be suitable material for managerial posts. But whether science or engineering graduates necessarily make better top managers than those trained in arts, law or accounting is a debatable point which we shall take up later. Nevertheless, the scarcity of the former did raise problems for middle management recruitment and particularly for the production side of industry. Arts graduates did not prove entirely satisfactory substitutes since it was often said that they took years getting over being at the university and that they were even proud of their complete ignorance of the sciences (Aldcroft 1982 57).

The position in smaller companies

Most of the comments so far have been related to the experience of larger companies, which accounted for some 40–50 per cent of manufacturing output and the bulk of innovations in the postwar period (Utton 1982 50–1; Tisdell 1981 83). As far as smaller and medium-sized companies are concerned, the situation with respect to managerial education and expertise was far worse. Many smaller firms had originated in the days of the practical man and hence they had inherited the characteristics of that time. Managers or owner-managers tended to be born rather than made and problem – solving was done on a pragmatic, rule-of-thumb basis with little support from education and training (Warner 1987 92–3; Locke 1989 97). Many entrepreneurs saw their businesses in personal rather than organisational terms, as family estates to provide a steady stream of cash for the owners and a source of family employment and succession, rather than as corporate entities with long-term asset growth the main goal as in the United States (Chandler 1990 286 390). Some of these attributes, especially the long-retention of family control and inheritance, apply equally to many larger companies, well into the twentieth century. The consequence has been that British firms, with a few notable exceptions such as ICI, BP and Unilever, were slow to develop clearly defined managerial hierarchies of the modern corporate structure and this meant that there was relatively little call for formal management training and technical expertise. In fact many smaller companies continued to extol the virtues of the practical man and in some cases, as in branches of engineering, there were far too many 'Dickensian firms, controlled by autocratic and often highly conservative managing directors' (Rothwell in Pavitt 1980 139). Newly-established small firms proved little better. Their founders, as Bannock (1981 37–8) explains, were often from socially disadvantaged backgrounds – immigrants, broken homes, interrupted education or ex-employees – rather than members of the articulate and educated élite who tended to gravitate to the professions. In such firms education and training were accorded very low priority.

The management problem in smaller companies has been examined at some length by Boswell (1973 180–3). In part it stems from the institutional rigidities of the family-dominated firm with little or no infusion of external talent. Not only does this sometimes present a succession problem, but more important it tends to deprive such undertakings of much-needed expertise for general mangement purposes. This leads to below average performance as increasing obsolescence sets in and family domination and inheritance preclude the recruitment of more dynamic expertise at the management level. This means that they tie up valuable resources in terms of land, capital and labour which could be used more effectively elsewhere

Several studies have drawn attention to the dearth of ability in the smaller enterprise. Deeks (1972) in an analysis of the furniture trade found but one graduate among 229 managers in small firms, and it is not without significance that this industry has had one of the worst records when it to comes skill formation (Steedman and Wagner 1987). This was by no means untypical, however. The Bolton Committee (1971) found that few chief executives of smaller firms had degrees or any higher educational qualifications. Emphasis instead was on trade-based skills and learning on the job which meant that the scope for career opportunities based on educational merit was very limited. This would explain why many small firms are not very well adapted to cope with growth and change since they lack the human resources which would enable this to take place. For some owner-dominated small enterprises there is often little way out since the owners' concept of business is influenced by a craft mentality which spurns the need for the infusion of expertise of a type which would effectively destroy the original character of the business (Scase and Goffee 1982 101–10 157).

A broader inquiry based on information contained in the National Training Survey 1975–6, and covering a cross-section of managers at all levels in both large and small firms, found that managers in general were only marginally more qualified than the population as a whole. Over half of the managers in the survey had no qualifications at all, while the proportion of managers with university education was a mere 3 per cent, and no more than 11 per cent among general managers. Since many of the degree holders were employed in large firms, the incidence of degree holders in small firms was bound to be very low.

The most disturbing feature of the survey was the very large number of managers without any formal qualifications, with 20 per cent having had no formal schooling beyond the elementary stage. Many moreover had little prospect of acquiring relevant qualifications or training for the tasks in hand. They worked their way up from lower levels in the enterprise, either from craft-based occupations or from clerical activities, picking up experience as they went along. Few received any worthwhile training and one quarter of all managers in the survey had not had as much as one day's vocational training for any job since leaving school. As the authors (Crockett and Elias 1984 42) commented: 'We found that the majority of firms do not train their managers for the jobs they hold other than the usual "Cooke's [sic] Tour" of the establishment.' Except for general mangers and office managers, most of the recruits to management left school at an early age and worked their way up from the shop floor. For the individuals concerned there was no great incentive to acquire qualifications and undergo training since neither had a significant bearing on earning power and promotion. Earning potential and access to the higher echelons of management were determined primarily by the level reached in the hierarchy of control.

Education and management recruitment

Crockett and Elias (1984 42) hint that the problem of management recruitment may lie in the class structure of the British educational system with its negative attitude to industry and management as a career because of its lack of prestige compared with other occupations. In this approach it is the educational system which is at fault since it does not produce the products suitable for managerial careers. Britain has never developed the type of prestigious technical institutions of the continental model, nor the American management schools, which provided a steady flow of very able and technically trained personnel who took up managerial careers (Hutton and Lawrence 1981a). Instead it produced specialists in academic subjects who, sometimes with additional professional training, filled middle management staff posts, and generalists who made good administrators for the civil service, the army and the Empire, but who were ill-suited to the needs of industry because of their lack of technical training.

Sorge and Warner (1986 199–201) maintain that the generalist management concept emerged as a result of the historical development of functionally differentiated professions. Management became the specialism of the generalists who could not easily slot into the professional groups, which have little counterpart abroad, because of the non-technical tradition of managerial activities. 'The classification of the hierarchy as management could only emerge to the extent that managerial functions were not inherent to specialist careers and forms of vocational education training.' In Germany, on the other hand, where education was less divorced from vocational practice, management retained strong links with functionally constituted tasks relevant to the production process.

This pattern of development has had serious consequences for management recruitment in British industry. Because of a shortage of top technical talent and the reluctance on the part of the most able graduates to take up an industrial career, companies have been forced to rely on the traditional sources of recruitment to top posts, that is from arts graduates, pure science graduates, those with a prestigious social background, and latterly members of the legal and accountancy professions. For the most part they were generalist administrators or amateurs when it came to production since few of them had much knowledge of or contact with the making of artefacts. They were good at organising and administering things and often very competent in matters of high finance but, as Ian Macgregor (1987 68) has pointed out, the British predilection for administrative excellence may well have swamped out the ability to manage. 'Administration', he argues,

> is the perpetuation of existing systems and the status quo. It is the essence of management to change and improve things; management has to seek efficiency, identify the need for change and have the will to effect it. Administrators, by their nature, do not make changes; they set up a committee to consider them. Perhaps the greatest postwar manifestation of the growth of administrators was in the field of personnel and industrial relations.

Approaches to management development

There is of course no common route to management status. Natural, cultural and historical forces have produced a variety of different models or approaches to the rearing of managers, each one of which is to some extent unique to its specific cultural context and cannot readily be transplanted *en bloc* elsewhere (Warner 1987 91). Thus the French approach is very much an élitist one routed through the grandes écoles with very strong emphasis on mathematics and engineering studies. On the other hand, the German one is less élitist: the accent is on technically specific subject areas such as engineering and business economics studied in the technological universities. The latter do not however train students to be *berufsfertig* (or ready for the job) which is left to the firms that employ them to carry out (Locke 1988 92). The Germans, and other continental countries for that matter, have spurned the American generalist approach to management training: there are relatively few specialised MBA (Master of Business Administration) programmes of the American type, and management issues and problems tend to be incorporated within the individual subject specialities (Locke 1985a, 1985b). The American and Japanese systems are different again. Both are more broadly based than their continental counterparts. The former is strongly orientated towards the business schools and the MBA programmes which produce the generalist scientific management expertise on which American industry has placed so much reliance. By contrast, the

Japanese focus on rigorous in-house training following high level general academic education at one of the top educational institutions. The British system does not fit into any of these categories and it might be more aptly described as a 'non-system'. 'If there is a UK culture of management, organisations and their mutual development, it would seem to embrace qualities of parochialism, insularity and "muddling through" ' (Constable and McCormick 1987 47). It has in fact been suggested that the lack of a generally accepted route into the managerial class is possibly one reason why so many accountants become managers in this country (*Financial Times*, 29 April 1987).

If anything Britain has gravitated, albeit slowly, towards the American pattern, a move more in keeping with her generalist philosophy towards management development. Whether this is the most suitable approach is another matter. Sorge (1978 103) questions the value of general management training in the absence of significant specialist knowledge in the art of manufacture, especially in engineering. Continental countries have for the most part eschewed the practice of management science as a distinct discipline divorced from specialist instruction in specific skills and techniques. Not that Britain has made a great deal of headway in this direction anyway. British efforts in management training pall in comparison with those of America (Collins and Robbins 1990 164–5). By 1970 there were nearly as many business schools in the US as there were university schools of education, and by the mid 1980s some 320,000 students graduated annually with either a bachelor's or master's degree in management, almost as many as the number of new entrants to management each year (Constable and McCormick 1987 16).

Developments in Britain were painfully slow. Despite the emergence of what might be called a management movement in the interwar years, which preached a gospel of management education based on scientific principles, rather than management as an art, the response from business, government and the universities was indifferent and at times even hostile to the new ideas that were being propagated. Employers for the most part rejected the notion that management practice and techniques could be taught by formal education, apart from which they 'were suspicious of university graduates, and tended to believe that the proper mode of access to managerial positions was either by inheritance or through the grisly process of working one's way up from the bottom' (Whitley, Thomas and Marceau 1981 35). Such negative attitudes therefore provided little incentive for educational institutions to make a move in this direction by mounting courses of instruction, irrespective of the fact that management education would scarcely have passed muster as a respectable discipline within the groves of academe. Thus except for a few business and commercial courses, and the odd postgraduate management course, notably that offered by the Manchester College of Science and Technology from 1926, there was very little in the way of formal management instruction in educational institutions before the second world war.

Partly as a result of wartime experience which revealed how far British management practice was slipping behind that of the United States, somewhat greater interest was shown in the subject in the immediate postwar years. In 1947 the British Institute of Management (BIM) was set up. This body not only acted as a centre for information on management methods, but it also helped to sponsor a national management training scheme following an initiative by the Ministry of Education at the end of the war. The courses under this scheme were to be run by technical and commercial colleges and were to be taken on a part-time basis over a period of several years. The initial response to the scheme when it was first launched in 1949 was quite good but enrolments steadily declined in subsequent years, partly because of doubts about the quality of the tuition offered by the colleges, and partly because of the generally unenthusiastic response of employers who were reluctant to sponsor candidates or to recognise the qualifications of what were regarded as downmarket institutions.

The universities for their part made only a very modest contribution to management education in this period. Apart from traditional courses in business and commercial studies, notably at Birmingham and Manchester, only a handful of universities established either full-time or part-time (post-experience) courses in management or business administration. For the most part they were not well supported by industry not least because of the strong academic orientation of the curricula on offer. Thus what little training there was in management techniques and practice tended to be based on in-house programmes run by some of the larger companies, supplemented in some cases by short external courses at one of the private colleges or residential centres which had sprung up since the war. By 1965 there were reckoned to be over sixty of these in existence, the most famous of which was the Administrative Staff College at Henley, founded in 1947 (Whitley, Thomas and Marceau 1981 34–42). Private sector provision was far better suited to the perceived needs of the business world than that of the state institutions since courses were run on more informal lines in congenial surroundings, they were tailored to employers' requirements, they were normally of short duration, and their main aim was to broaden and develop the minds and capacities of existing businessmen, rather than rearing new managers from scratch.

Despite these various developments management training still remained very limited in practice. In the early 1960s Political and Economic Planning (1965 234) estimated that less than 1 per cent of managers in industry received any form of external management training. Fortunately, growing concern about the quantity and quality of management education and training came at a time when educational expansion and human capital needs were much in vogue. Thus following the reports of the Robbins Committee on higher education (1963) and that of Lord Franks on business schools (1963), both of which strongly supported expansion of facilities in management education, two postgraduate business schools, financed jointly by the state and private enterprise, and modelled along Harvard lines, were set up in London and Manchester. It was a very modest beginning since they produced only a handful of graduates in the first few years and even by the mid 1980s, with the addition of programmes in other universities, the total output of MBAs was probably no more than about 1200 a year (Wagner 1987 94). By that time however a large number of other institutions had jumped on to the business bandwagon, offering a variety of courses of varying degrees of quality in management and business studies. Altogether there were over a hundred universities, polytechnics and colleges offering undergraduate, postgraduate and diploma courses in management or business studies. One estimate suggests that in 1984–5 about 12,300 people were receiving instruction in management at levels ranging from Higher National Diploma to postgraduate degrees (Constable and McCormick 1987 16). This was about double the number a decade earlier.

While certainly an improvement on what went before, the annual flow was very small beer when compared with the number of new entrants to management each year, and even more so in relation to the total stock of managers. Assuming a thirty-year managerial life-span and a total stock of managers of some 2.75 million (including junior and first-line managers), then the combined output of graduates and diplomates was equivalent to about one-seventh of the total national required intake of new managers annually (circa 90,000). If we add in the numbers on post-experience external training courses (part-time) of around 45,000, then no more than about 2 per cent of all managers were effectively getting some kind of external training in management practice. This is not a very large improvement on the position in the 1960s though the sample count for that estimate was somewhat smaller (Constable and McCormick 1987 16; Warner 1987 94; PEP 1965 234).

Though by this time there was greater recognition in the business world of the need for more and better management training, there remained the unresolved issue as to who should provide it. Most employers were probably still very ambivalent about the utility of academically-based provision since it was deemed to be somewhat out of touch with the more practical needs of industry. Their indifferent response to the graduates of the MBA programmes, the uneasy partnership in the business school ventures, and the criticisms levelled at many of the university and polytechnic courses, all point to a disenchantment on the way academia has responded to the needs of the business community. There is still a gulf between the academic and business worlds which neither side has been willing to bridge. As a consequence, the business community has preferred to rely more on its own in-house training programmes and the private sector staff colleges and centres for external instruction to enhance its existing managerial talent, though, as we shall see below, the extent of the provision has fallen far short of what is deemed by outside observers to be adequate.

The situation in the 1980s

Despite the progress made in the previous two decades, the education and training of management still fell a very long way short of that of Britain's competitors by the later 1980s. The level of formal educational qualifications among managers was very low, the scale of management training was totally inadequate, and there was still no 'widely used, clearly understood method for educating and training ... managers' (Constable and McCormick 1987 21). In a scathing report prepared for government sources by Professor Charles Handy (1987), the British were denounced as amateurs trying to compete in a world of professionals.

The conclusion that many British managers are uneducated in business and management terms is inescapable. It must also be true that management training in Britain is too little, too late, for too few. It is finally probably true that most management development is left to chance in a Darwinian belief that the fittest will survive. They probably will but it is a wasteful process' (Handy 1987 11).

While recognising that there was no one route to the top, it was nevertheless apparent that Britain fell a long way short of other countries in the depth and breadth of training its managers. Three 'A' levels and a degree in the humanities was no substitute for a baccalaureate followed by a course at a grande école in business and engineering with work assignement, or for the rigorous in-house training following graduation from one of Japan's top universities. But for the majority of British managers qualifications fell a long way short of this anyway. Using the analysis of the Labour Force Survey for 1985, which covers some 3.3 million self-defined managers of all types, the breakdown of qualifications is shown in Table 6.1. Only just over 12 per cent had degrees, though this figure would be closer to 50 per cent for top managers in larger companies. If qualifications down to HND are included, the proportion still only rises to around one fifth. At the other end of the scale, there was almost an equal proportion with no qualifications at all. Most of the remainder, apart

Table 6.1 Educational qualifications of British managers 1985 (%)

	Men	Women
First or higher degree	12.1	12.8
Professional qualification	6.2	2.5
HNC/HND	5.6	1.4
Nursing or teaching qualification	1.6	13.4
Apprenticeship (completed)	9.6	3.0
ONC/OND, City and Guilds, 'A' levels	24.2	15.2
'O' levels or equivalent	15.0	18.9
CSE below grade 1	1.5	2.2
Other	3.3	4.6
No qualifications	19.1	24.7
Don't know/no reply	1.7	1.2
Total numbers	2,541,000	729,000

Source: Handy (1987 11).

from those with teaching or nursing qualifications, ranged between 'A' and CSE level qualifications.

On management training the report made equally depressing reading. Though most of the large companies (80 per cent) did provide some management training, fewer than half their managers took part in it. Over half of all companies carried out no management training whatsoever, while in those that did only about one-third of the managers actually participated. On average the UK manager received about one day's training a year, which effectively meant that many probably never received any training since starting work. External instruction was conspicuous by its absence. Moreover, one interesting point, and one that crops up at the vocational stage as we have seen, is that education and training at management level often involved repairing deficiences earlier down the line. 'Much of executive education is the teaching of sixth-form subjects to middle-aged executives; it is remedial education instead of executive education' (Handy 1987 11; Mangham and Silver 1986 1).

No other country has neglected its managerial stock to the extent that Britain has done. Nor for that matter have few other professions, except university teaching until quite recently, received so little in the way of professional training. As Handy continues:

> For no other important role in life, other than parenting, is there no proficiency test, no preparatory education or early apprenticeship. Managers in Britain have, for the most part, been exempted from such requirements because many used to believe that managing was like parenting – something which you picked up as you went along. The other countries do not believe that so important a task can be left to that sort of accidental process.

A combination of circumstances has been responsible for the underlying weakness in management education and training. For one thing corporate executives have shown great reluctance to give manpower issues the priority they deserve. This applies at all levels including the professionalisation of management. The days of the practical man and the gentlemanly amatuer lingered long in the boardrooms of British companies. As Hussey (1988 58) reflects:

> The story of management training in British industry can be summarised as inadequate resources ineffectively managed, and with most effort being devoted to the wrong things. The fault is rarely that of those who perform the training function in industry: it is with the

senior and top management who give little or no attention to the activity. If there is one area where amateurism prevails more than in any other it is in the management of training.

Mangham and Silver (1986 20–3 34) came to a similar conclusion in their survey of management training in Britain. While they were unable to demonstrate a well-defined link between company performance and management training, partly because their study only took account of the incidence of training rather than its extent and quality, they stressed the need to ensure that appropriate mechanisms were available in companies so that effective training could be undertaken. In particular, they urged a greater involvement of boards of directors in the training process and the need to clarify the language of competence.

What is clear is that there is no widely shared set of specific qualities, skills and attributes that will enable anyone to rate jobs or people, let alone create training programmes. The statements which find ready acceptance – communication, leadership, motivation – are too global to be of much use in selection or development.

Higher educational institutions must also share part of the blame. It is true that industry may not have articulated its requirements in terms of skilled personnel very explicitly, but the universities and other higher educational establishments have been slow to respond to the needs of industry unless forced to do so (Divall 1991). Until fairly recently the universities have maintained an arms' length approach in their dealings with industry in the belief that they should not contaminate academic studies with vocational matters. Alford (1988 104) blames the prevailing social values in Britain which, he maintains, 'conditioned the educational system to inculcate the belief that manufacturing is an inferior form of economic activity'. Thus enginering and technology courses bore little relevance to the world of work and production, while engineers and scientists, many of whom might expect to become managers, had little chance of gaining experience in business subjects during their degree courses. It is scarcely surprising therefore that some of the more ambitious technically qualified recruits have been frustrated in their career prospects since their narrow educational background means that they are often not considered suitable management material. This is one reason why many have sought to escape from the rigid confines of functional activities in research and production where the career prospects are bleak, by retooling themselves with an MBA or some other management qualification in the hope that they may gain entry to the fast track. This problem does not arise to anywhere near the same extent in continental countries since scientists and engineers are valued much more highly as potential management material, while their broader educational background places them in a favourable position from the start. Graduates in European countries emerge from higher education with qualifications which equip them to become both generalist managers and technical experts (Department of Industry 1977).

Similarly, the response of the universities and polytechnics in providing courses in business studies and management science has been derisory in terms of the total output of graduates, quite apart from the fact that some of the courses have been criticised for their over-academic content and divorce from the practicalities of the real world. Nor is there reason to suppose that lack of demand has been a constraint on provision in this area: in 1986–7 only 27 per cent of those applying to universities for business management degrees were accepted (Shapinker 1987).

Another factor, mentioned by Kempner (1983–4), is the extraordinary lack of mobility among the educated élites between different sectors of activity. The products of the grandes écoles, and for that matter those of the German technische hochschulen, are much more mobile between the different sectors of government, civil service, business and academia, whereas once British élites are on the occupational ladder 'little further movement across the divides of business, government and civil service is likely'. This not only reduces the prospects for the cross-fertilisation of ideas, practice and needs, but the greater emphasis abroad on applied science, mathematics, enginering and business studies is more likely to produce a greater awareness of the needs of industry than the arts background which is still so typical of many of Britain's élite groups in government, the civil service, finance and industry (see Fores and Glover 1978; Granick 1972; Fores and Pratt 1980).

The management and control of production

Whatever the causes for the lag in management education and training there is fairly general agreement that the quality of management in this country has had an adverse influence on the economy.

Several writers (Fores and Glover 1978; Davies and Caves 1987) have stressed the inherent weakness of management as a factor in the underperformance of the economy. They point to the lower educational qualifications of British managers and their relative lack of technical training compared with their European counterparts which means that British management is less qualified for the tasks in hand.

> In particular, engineering posts which are considered in most countries to be the key to in-service training for top management are seen to be less prestigious in Britain. The role and importance of management, and in particular the role and importance of technical functions concerned with production, are estimated too lowly in Britain. We believe this to be a major cause of the country's poor use of resources and hence, also, for a poor rate of economic growth. (Fores and Clark 1975 69)

This is substantiated by Horovitz's detailed comparative study (1980) of top management control and corporate strategy in France, Germany and Britain. The most illuminating contrast is that between Germany and Britain and their different approaches to organisation, planning and control practice. British company structures were found to be loose and rather flexible, orientated towards autonomous product markets with a high degree of decentralisation in decision-making. There was a lean central staff which concentrated on long-range planning. By contrast Germany company structure was more formal and rigid; it was functionally and divisionally based and there was a large central staff who were responsible for many decisions. Planning was geared to operational efficiency through tight project programming. As far as control procedures were concerned, the British top control was less frequent and detailed than the German and it tended to concentrate on financial matters where it was most effective. Production control, on the other hand, was less emphasised and less successful, and it relied heavily on line management self-control. Production control in the German case was both more frequent and more detailed, it was directed specifically at operational efficiency of the production process where it was very effective, and it entailed strong central control rather than autonomy at the production level.

Horovitz (1980 148–53, 185–7) attributes these differences in control procedures to the disinclination of British managers to focus on technical and production matters, because their cultural traits and educational backgrounds in finance, marketing and personnel render them ill-equipped to deal with technology-loaded subjects such as production, design and research and development. While he admits that German control mechanisms may be somewhat overcentralised and formalistic, he believes that British managers may have something to learn from German practice as far as production control is concerned, 'not only in terms of its utility in focussing on key efficiency objectives and key tasks in the production process which would help to close the gap between actual performance and strict financial flows, but also for purposes of evaluating long-term planning strategy'.

Production management has long been a weak spot in British companies and production managers and production engineers have been regarded as the Cinderallas of the profession, whereas continental and Japanese engineers are highly valued for their technical production skills. One of the main problems in Britain has been the quality of the recruits into this field: 'There is a small group of people who are able and well-motivated but . . . a long tail of people who are not' (Department of Industry 1977 31). This again partly reflected the inadequacies of the education system which failed to produce the right quality of people. The Economist (1981) reckoned that Britain's problem was not so much one of too few engineers, but too many of the wrong quality emerging from second-rate engineering colleges. Yet in some areas there were shortages too, production engineers being the most prominent. At one point in the 1970s the universities were producing almost as many graduates of the Welsh language as they were production engineers, while polytechnics such as Lanchester, Birmingham and Hatfield had only a handful of students studying production management. There was in fact no first degree available in production management, the nearest equivalent being production engineering (Lockyer 1976 70–1). Equally of course the poor demand for places may well reflect the lowly esteem with which top mangement regarded such expertise. Pay, prospects and conditions were poor and the more able graduates steered clear of going into production management (Hutton and Lawrence 1980 9, 16).

Any shortfall in management skills and education at the top level is more than likely to be reflected lower down the managerial hierachy at the middle and junior levels. Davies and Caves, (1987 44, 80, 93, 95) in their study on productivity for the period 1968–77, infer a deficiency of managerial intensity at the plant floor level, especially in large plant industries, and that this, in conjunction with other labour factors, acted as a productivity depressant. And as they stress, the solution was not to be found in adding yet more managers to the total stock, but in improving the quality of the existing managerial complement through improved education and training (see Mangham and Silver 1986 23).

Unfortunately, the arms' length style of generalist top management to the crucial areas of technology and production processes has had serious implications for a wide range of issues including industrial relations, workforce supervision, R & D and product development. Some of these matters are developed more fully in the next chapter and so we can simply make a few illustrations here. In worker relations, for example, top management has maintained a strong personality cult and a view of consultation as a one-way process in which lip service is paid to workers' interests. According to Jean Millar (1979 65), a large group of managers in Britain still cling to the old style of leadership and of rights, which only serves to reinforce the 'them and us' attitude at the shop floor level. In the case of R & D and product development, these are not seen by top managment as being strategic issues in corporate strategy. More often than not they are delegated down the line so that effective control is lost, with the result that R & D and marketing departments can sometimes end up with conflicting goals (Goldsmith and Clutterbuck 1985 120). Consequently, innovation and product development are slowed down and distorted and eventually competitiveness suffers. Again this problem arises from a lack of technical knowledge and interest at the board level because:

> Top managers with little technical experience, and who have been educated to focus their attention on short-term issues, see technology as complex, long-term, narrow (just research and development) and highly uncertain. They are not only "technology-averse" . . . but they often find it downright intimidating.
> Whether or not they also make this mistake of underspending on technology, they therefore delegate the management of it, either well down the line, or to a senior executive. To do the latter might be all well and good, except that they don't then pay much attention to what he tells them.' (Goldsmith and Clutterbuck 1985 120, quoting Christopher Lorenz).

Finally, we might refer to the subject of workshop supervision. It is a well-known fact that many British companies have paid too little attention to many aspects of the production process. Nowhere is this more apparent than in the supervision and control of workshop practice – the province of front-line management comprising supervisors and foremen. Mant (1977 1978) among others has drawn attention to the differential commitment and attention to detail between British and German companies with respect to the more mundane aspects of production. This arises largely through the divorce of career managers from the technicalities of the production process which he believes to be an important contributory factor in Britain's poor productivity record. One obvious consequence has been the failure of management to give clear guidance as to the role of supervisors and foremen, whose status and prestige have been slipping steadily in the postwar period due to full employment, a limitation of their disciplinary powers and the usurping of their technical functions, often by non-technical specialists (Carter and Williams 1957 67–8). Not only has the erosion of their position generated resistance to change and increased the unionisation of supervisory staff, but it has also helped to diminish the efficiency with which shopfloor operations are carried out. Child (Child and Partridge 1982 9–12, 191–2, 210–16) believes that supervision is widely regarded as a problem area in British industry and that low productivity is a question not simply of investment, but of its utilisation at the point of production, which is unlikely to be improved unless management takes a firm line on the critical role of supervisory grades.

There is abundant evidence, especially in the engineering industry, of lax management practices in terms of organising and maintaining production flows efficiently (Lewchuck 1987; Beckerman 1979; Lawrence 1980; Dudley 1977; Lockyer 1976). In some branches of engineering, especially mechanical, not only have operational practices often been chaotic, but the whole structure and organisation of production was so antiquated that it required complete scrapping and redesigning to bring it up to modern standards. A not untypical picture of the day-to-day operations in one engineering factory was described by a leading consulting engineer (Bruce 1983) as follows:

> Fork trucks hauling material everywhere, damaging and losing parts; progress chasers and half the supervisory staff trying to find parts for their next operation; operators going for tools while their machines sit idle; aisles full of people dodging fork trucks; complex production control systems trying to keep track of thousands of transactions each day; inspectors trying to separate bad parts from good throughout the process; late deliveries; delivery lead time measured in months for products with a routed manufacturing time measured in a few hours.

That British operating practices at the plant level show up poorly compared with those in other countries, Germany especially, can partly be explained by the failure of management to support and reinforce the front-line staff. The contrast with Germany is instructive for there the foreman, or *Meister*, has retained much of his status and prestige and he plays a much more substantial and effective role in supervisory and technical matters. Nor has the German *Meister* lost out to non-technical staff specialists to the same extent as in Britain: one reason which may explain why the proportion of staff personnel is lower in German firms (Fores, Lawrence and Sorge 1978 87–9, 188). In fact the chairman of the British Institute of Management Council, in a report published in the mid 1970s (BIM 1976 18–19), admitted that it had been a stagnant sector of management in terms of age, education and training for many years. Very few foremen, most of whom had left school before they were 16, had any significant educational or technical qualifications, and the training received prior to, or in, work, was little short of derisory compared with that of his German counterpart (Prais and Wagner 1988). Yet given his crucial role at the interface between the shopfloor and higher management for ensuring the smooth and efficient functioning of the production process, the neglect of this area of control is all the more reprehensible.

Drawing on his industrial experience, especially at British Leyland, Michael Edwardes (1983 163 281), argued that British management's authority had been challenged and eroded in the postwar period and that it had therefore lost the will to manage. The reason we suggest for this outcome was that management was increasingly less able to manage because of its poor education and training which fell far short of that required to meet the challenging climate of later years. Whether management was a prisoner of the society within which it operated is a question that has been much debated. It has frequently been argued that British business behaviour was conditioned by the attitudes and cultural values of a society which had traditionally put a low premium on education for business. Tylecote (1981 27–32, 1977 22) refers to the lack of *unternehmerfreundlich* values in schools, in universities and in the mass media, in contrast to their dissemination in Germany. Turner (1971 473–6) has commented on the unhealthy attitude to monetary rewards in Britain compared with the American, the low social status of business in Britain, and the attempt by businessmen to improve their standing through leisure and land. The latter, Alford (1988 105) speculates, may have prompted businessmen to favour short-term horizons in their decision-making. Safety and security have been more important to the British executive compared with his American counterpart, which could explain his predilection for defensive mergers and acquisitions rather than organic development (Channon 1973 45–6, 206, 210–11; Hussey 12). Granick (1972 364, 370) believes that the low prestige of industrial careers attracts the less able and less dynamic recruits into business. British managers play a modest and low profile role in society and they compensate for their low status and low pay by taking considerable leisure on the job. 'The demand for results that American managers expect would be resented by British managers just as bitterly as the imposition of an American work pace on the factory floor would be resented by blue collar workers. British managers share in the national value system of placing great importance on preserving the workplace from speedup' (Granick 1972 370). Perhaps, at the end of the day, the shop floor and management are not always poles apart as is often suggested.

7
ECONOMIC CONSEQUENCES

Though the volume of public resources devoted to education and training has been quite respectable in relative terms compared with some of Britain's major competitors, the same cannot be said for the levels of educational attainment and skill formation. By international standards these have been distincly poor: one need only recall the low level of achievement in mathematics and languages among school leavers or the low levels of accredited skill formation among the workforce to confirm this conclusion. Thus there is certainly more than a grain of truth in the disparaging remarks of Barnett and Bryan Nicholson to the effect that Britain has spawned or reared a 'nation of coolies' or a 'bunch of thickies' (Barnett 1986, 203; Sanderson 1987, 127).

The shortfall does however have both quantitative and qualitative aspects, though the extent of the incidence of each varies between sectors. In resource terms compulsory schooling has been more than sufficient, especially following the raising of the school leaving age to 16 in the early 1970s. But in qualitative terms there was much room for improvement. Here the delivery system preformed badly given the level of resource provision, with the result that many youngsters emerged from school with inadequate literacy and numeracy skills. This is borne out by the large number of YTS trainees who require remedial tuition in these subjects before they can cope with a vocational training programme. Such deficiencies moreover, are by no means confined to those who leave school at the age of 16. Many university students, after a much longer period in education, have been found wanting in both language and mathematical skills.

By far the largest quantitative deficiency has been at the intermediate-vocational training level where Britain has underperformed badly by international standards. This has not simply been a question of the low participation rate in advanced secondary education, though this is one aspect of the problem, but a much wider issue involving the training of the bulk of the nation's youth for the world of work. Until recently only a relatively small proportion of the workforce received any worthwhile training for employment. Moreover, even the many policy measures relating to vocational training of the past decade have not brought industrial training to anywhere near the levels obtaining in other European countries, especially when qualitative aspects are taken into account.

At higher levels of education – university or near equivalent – the volume gap between Britain and other countries had narrowed some-what by the 1970s, especially when allowance is made for differences in rates of completion and drop-out – but the product mix of the output was inconsistent with the needs of a dynamic industrial economy. The main thrust of university expansion was centred on satisfying the demand for arts and social science courses to the detri-ment of technological and vocationally-orientated subjects, though here one has to be careful in distinguishing between a pure supply problem as opposed to market incentives which have affected the final destination of many graduates. At the managerial level, both educa-tion and training have been very limited except among top firms, and even today the majority of managers compare unfavourably in both respects compared with their counterparts abroad.

What is most noticeable throughout the education and training system is the anti-technology, anti-vocational and anti-industry bias on the part of those providing the teaching and training services, coupled with the cult of amateurism and the practical man among industrialists. As a result education has never, by any stretch of the imagination, been geared to the world of work and industry in the way it has been in other countries (Carter and Pinder 1982 105). This has bred a nation almost proud of its vocational ignorance. Quite why Britain should have remained so out of step with other countries as far as educating and training its people for the world of work is something of a puzzle, the subject of which we take up in the final chapter. The main focus of attention in this section is to explore some of the economic implications of the educational deficiency.

Skills and competitiveness

A question in a recent JMB 'A' level examination paper (June 1990) offered candidates the following statement: 'Modern economies require an educated workforce', and asked them how far the British government had met that need during the first half of the twentieth century. The implicit assumption herein is that the statement is by definition true, but we should ask ourselves why this should be so.

For most advanced countries in the postwar years the level of skill formation has become increasingly critical as a factor in international trade competitiveness. This is largely because the main growth area in the trade of these countries has been the exchange of more sophisticated, technological and skill-intensive products, rather than capital intensive ones. Success in the exchange of such products among high income countries depends very much on comparative levels of productivity and also increasingly on non-price factors, which in turn are partly determined by the level of skill formation (Stout 177; Wragg and Robertson 1978). Furthermore, high income countries cannot compete with lesser developed or newly industrialising countries on the latters' labour cost terms for obvious reasons, so that it behoves them to move upstream to high unit value products which of necessity embody substantial inputs of human capital formation. Innovation, and with it R & D, lie at the heart of this process since it is one of the few comparative advantages left to developed nations (Schott 1981, 65).

Stoneman (1984 56, 61, 69) has warned of the perils which lie in store for an economy (or for that matter a sector or firm) which persistently lags in innovation: resources will tend to shift into the sheltered non-tradable sectors of activity and eventually the country will become a low wage, non-trading economy. There is no alternative escape route. Devaluation and wage reductions may ease the situation for a time but in the long run no amount of tinkering along these lines can compensate for technical backwardness. There is no way that such solutions can rejuvenate a traded goods sector which is continually under threat from superior foreign product innovation for, as he points out, cutting the price of an obsolete product cannot restore a market that is lost for good. Notable examples in this context might include mechanical calculators versus electronic ones; mechanical versus quartz watches; or in telecommunications equipment, mechanical switchgear as against electronic switchgear. A significant micro-example is provided by Courtaulds' experience at one of their spinning mills in Oldham where it was found that wage reductions could not possibly provide a substitute for investing in new and much more efficient capital intensive technology to supply the needs of the market and thereby remain internationally competitive (Prowse 1986). Stoneman believes that Britain's poor technological record, particularly the failure to turn technology rapidly into commercial products, is at the root of the country's industrial malaise, though he admits that its contribution is difficult to assess precisely because of intermittent compensations through wage and exchange rate changes.

Britain's relative economic decline since the early 1950s has been well documented. It shows up most noticeably in the marked loss of trade shares, the weak trade elasticities, the low unit values of exports, and the poor trade performance in high technology and skill intensive products (Aldcroft 1991 116–18). It is also reflected in the low levels of productivity by international standards and the declining significance of the manufacturing sector. Thus by the early 1980s Britain's share of the value of world exports in manufactured goods had fallen to less than 10 per cent, compared with nearly one-quarter in 1950, while productivity in manufacturing, once the highest in Europe, had sunk to less than 60 per cent of the average for western Europe (Williams, Williams and Thomas 1983, 116; Rowthorn and Wells, 1987, 1). It is perhaps not surprising therefore that Britain's former surplus in trade in manufactured goods had moved into deficit by the early 1980s.

It would be churlish, and of course incorrect, to argue that Britain's relative economic decline can be attributed solely to educational and training deficiences. Indeed, a wide range of economic and behavioural factors have been adduced to explain the slippage (see Caves 1980; Jones 1976; Pratten 1976; Smith, Hitchens and Davies 1982; Davies and Caves 1987). Nevertheless, it is significant that skill factors do feature quite prominently as an explanatory variable in analyses of postwar decline. Gertrude Williams (1963 177) was one of the first to stress the fact that 'the shortage of skilled labour is already recognised as one of the greatest handicaps in our efforts to increase productivity and raise standards of living'. Since then most commentators on the British economy have listed skill shortages as a causal factor, but with varying degrees of emphasis. Davies and Caves (1987 94–5), for example, in their study on the productivity gap infer a strong impact from the low level of technical skills. Productivity, they argue, has suffered from a pervasive under-investment in human skills, in everything from simple technical skills to business administration. 'The substantial effect of differential human capital found in our results, the seriously limited labour mobility, Britain's slippage in comparative advantage for 'quality' products (reported in other studies) imply either that the nation under-invests in training or that its populace is uneducable.'

The evidence certainly suggests that skill shortages have been an endemic feature of postwar Britain. Every upturn in the business cycle has been accompanied by complaints of shortages of skilled labour, especially in the engineering industry, while even in recessionary periods some growth industries such as electronics have encountered difficulties in recruiting qualified labour (Smith 1983). It can be seen from Fig. 7.1 that in the boom periods the problem has been quite acute. In the early 1970s the percentage of manufacturing firms affected by skill shortages rose to over 50 per cent, while in the later 1980s some 47 per cent of respondents to a CBI skills survey reported that they were unable to meet their skill needs (CBI 1989 16). These figures moreover probably understate the true position since they refer mainly to intermediate level skills, while they tell us little about the actual quality of the existing skilled labour force.

Fig. 7.1 Percentage of manufacturing firms expecting skill shortages to limit output, January 1972–October 1989

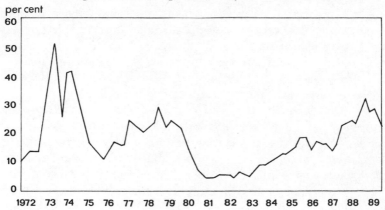

Reproduced from Department of Employment Training Agency, *Labour Market Quarterly Report*, GB, November 1989, p. 5.
Source: CBI, *Quarterly Industrial Trends Survey*, October 1989.

The link between skill shortages and declining competitiveness may be a direct one in so far as output growth is checked, especially in boom periods, by resource constraints with consequent adverse effects on exports and imports. There is certainly evidence that during cyclical upswings exports are squeezed and imports, especially of finished goods, rise sharply to satisfy the demands of the home market with the result that the balance of payments deteriorates. But perhaps even more serious for trade competitiveness are the indirect and longer-term consequences of continued skill deficiencies. What is most significant taking the long view is not that Britain has had the wrong product structure, nor that costs have run amok compared with those of her main competitors, but that Britain's trade pattern has been moving steadily downstream, that is into lower quality, lower unit value goods, less technologically sophisticated and less skill intensive products than those of competitors (Aldcroft 1991 116–18). This has been caused by several factors including too little investment in research and innovation and under-investment in human skills at all levels. Moreover, as time wears on the deficiency in human skills becomes almost an insuperable handicap since, unlike capital shortages which can be remedied comparatively quickly even if this means importing equipment for a time, a shortfall in workforce skills takes a very long time to repair (Coyle 1991 14–15).

The down-market trend in Britain's trade has been a notable feature of the postwar period. Several studies (Stout 1977; Connell 1979) have shown that British producers have found increasing difficulty in competing on non-price terms, that is in design, quality, technical sophistication, reliability, delivery schedules and the like. Hence their products do not attain a premium rating in world markets; instead, because of poor quality characteristics, they move to the bottom end of the market and receive a low unit value. To take one specific example of mechanical engineering exports which account for some twenty per cent of British exports; in 1975 one tonne of German mechanical engineering exports fetched 60 per cent more than a similar equivalent of British exports, a differential that had been increasing steadily for the past 20 years (Williams, Williams and Thomas 1983 14).

Further confirmation of the competitive deterioration can be seen from the international trade data. For the decade 1968–78 Katrak (1982) found that the skill and R & D intensity of British imports increased relative to those of exports, while trade capital intensities showed the reverse trend. These adverse movements he attributed to Britain's relative lag in technological development and in its supply of skills. Similarly, the technological-intensiveness of British exports has been steadily declining in the postwar period. By 1984 the share of world exports in this category (defined in terms of R & D intensity greater than 2.36 per cent of value added) was very much lower than those of the United States, Japan and West Germany: respectively the shares were 8.5, 25.2, 20.2 and 14.5 per cent (de Jonquieres 1987).

The way in which skill deficiencies at different levels can affect trade performance may be readily demonstrated. For example, poor mathematical attainment in the lower ability ranges may be the cause of delivery delays, poor stock control and slipshod quality approval. Alternatively, inadequate vocational training may impair the ability to deliver quality products, limit the utilisation of sophisticated equipment and discourage the proper servicing and repair of equipment. Shortages of higher level expertise may in turn impair the ability to innovate, as we shall see below.

A detailed illustration of the handicap presented by skill deficiencies may be taken from one of the National Institute's many studies on skills and training (see below), that on kitchen furniture (Steedman and Wagner 1987). This involved a comparison of matched plants in Britain and Germany which showed a substantial productivity gap of the order of 50–60 per cent in favour of German firms. Germany produced high quality products using advanced methods and machinery and about one-third of the kitchens produced were exported. British firms, on the other hand, tended to concentrate on the middle and lower quality ranges, they had less sophisticated machinery and poor organisation and production control, and sold only about 4 per cent of their output overseas. Imports accounted for nearly one-third of domestic sales in 1986, two-thirds of which came from Germany. But the really big difference between the two countries was in the level of skill formation. Nine-tenths of German employees had undergone a three-year vocational training course after having completed a school leaving certificate with the equivalent of at least four 'O' levels. By contrast, barely one-tenth of British employees had any equivalent vocational qualifications and few had any worthwhile school credentials, so that it is not surprising that the firms experienced constant skill problems. Nor was there all that much hope for the future. The low level of attainment of school leavers coupled with the inadequate training facilities either in-house or under government-funded schemes (for example YTS) held out little prospect of ever raising the workforce capabilities to anywhere near the German level.

The low level of skill formation in kitchen furniture production had several implications as far as performance and opportunity are concerned. In the first place it led to poor quality products and low levels of productivity. Secondly, the organisaton of production was often chaotic because of the limited training of supervisory staff. Thirdly, British firms were unable to take full advantage of advanced machinery, for example computer numerically-controlled machinery, because of a lack of in-house expertise in such equipment. Finally, it was difficult to introduce new methods and production processes based on computer programming at the plant level when 'computer printouts are not in shopfloor language'. With these sort of handicaps it is scarcely surprising that British firms performed so poorly in international trade compared with their German counterparts.

Innovation and R & D

The last point well illustrates the difficulties of introducing innovation at the shop floor level when the workforce is poorly trained and educated. Not only do workers lack the capability to digest and implement new and advanced methods, but their very ignorance may well render them unreceptive to change. Ignorance tends to breed suspicion, contempt and sometimes open hostility to new ideas and different ways of doing things, one reason no doubt why workers in Britain have been less willing than their counterparts abroad to aid and abet technological progress. However, as Rothwell (1977 201) has argued, the initiative for innovation, whether it be new technology, new methods of working or improved marketing systems, must come in the first instance from the top. 'Top management should be open-minded and progressive; indeed, unless top management has the will to innovate, there is little that other members of the company can do to generate and expedite an effective innovation policy.' But it is in this very capacity that British management has failed to deliver, partly because of a lack of training and expertise on the part of management itself.

We have already stressed the importance of innovation as a factor determining competitive strength. This point was brought home forcibly by the empirical studies carried out by the Science Policy Research Unit at Sussex University (Pavitt 1980). Innovative activity and export shares were found to be closely associated in chemicals, durable consumer goods and capital goods, especially the latter where quality rather than price was often the over-riding factor in sales performance. Yet for a developed country whose main comparative advantage must inevitably depend upon her innovatory prowess, Britain has had precious few success stories. In fact outside the government-backed glamour sectors such as aerospace, defence equipment and nuclear power, and one or two others, notably pharmaceuticals, Britain has not distinguished herself in the exploitation of new technologies. In machinery, vehicles, metals and metal products, which accounted for about one-half of world exports of manufactured goods in the 1950s and 1960s, Britain's technical effort was decidedly poor (Freeman 1979 70). If anything innovatory effort in these sectors tended to deteriorate over time.

Britain, it is often said, has been good at inventing things but weak when it comes to exploiting them commercially. One could quote a string of success stories in invention which failed to hit the commercial market in Britain. Moreover, aggregate figures for research and development spending (R & D) as a proportion of GDP have generally compared favourably with those of other countries. However, one should be wary of using R & D effort as a proxy for commercial innovatory performance. There is not necessarily a close association between research effort and innovation since much depends upon the structure of research spending and the subsequent exploitation of its fruits (see Stoneman 1984; Rothwell 1977). Nevertheless, there is some association at the sectoral level between R & D and growth and it is significant that Britain's export weaknesses have been especially pronounced in machinery, vehicles and metal products in which research intensity has been low by international standards and getting worse over time. Secondly, Britain's relatively favourable R & D ranking at the aggregate level owes much to the high proportion of government-sponsored research on a few chosen fields such as aerospace, defence and nuclear power. This has entailed a concentration of research and development effort and resources, especially skilled manpower, on areas with small markets (nuclear power), limited civilian spin-offs (defence) and product groups facing formidable international competition (aerospace). As we saw in Chapter 5, the government-backed research sector has claimed a high proportion of the nation's most qualified scientific manpower and indirectly aborted developments in the civilian field.

At the same time, both government and industry have neglected some major growth areas in electronics and electrical products, in capital equipment, specialist chemicals and in the older machinery sectors such as machine tools and textile machinery (Smith 1986 92–3). Even more disturbing was the fact that from the mid 1960s industry-financed research activity actually declined quite significantly. Through the period 1967–75 Britain was the only major OECD country in which industry-financed R & D activities declined in absolute terms. The decline was fairly widespread, with the exceptions of chemicals and pharmaceuticals, though by far the worst performance was recorded in mechanical engineering where R & D manpower was halved and R & D expenditure as a percentage of net output fell from 2.7 to 1.9 per cent. It is perhaps not surprising to find therefore that mechanical enginering was one of the weakest performers in international markets during the 1970s.

No doubt the recession and crises of the first half of the 1970s could partly account for the cutbacks, reflecting the belief that innovation was a luxury only to be indulged in during good times (Twiss 1974 xviii). But the long-term record suggests that in trade sensitive sectors British industry has had a persistently poor record in research and development and innovation by international standards. Surveys indicate that the major British firms spend considerably less on research and development than their counterparts in Germany, the United States and Japan (*The Independent*, 10 June 1991). Yet experience does seem to indicate that, in general, firms which have committed themselves to research and to exploiting new technologies have been successful, while those that do not tend to lose market share and decline. The exception proves the rule even in the British case. The pharmaceutical industry is one of the few sectors which has managed to hold its own in international trade largely because of a heavy commitment to research and the commercial development of new products. Glaxo in particular, now one of the world's top drug companies and also one of the most profitable, has had an exemplary record in organic growth and product development through intensive research during the last two decades.

Such success stories are few and far between. The far more common experience has been a persistent loss of market share due to declining competitiveness, brought about by a failure to innovate and adapt to changing market circumstances. Shipbuilding, vehicles, engineering, steel and consumer products are some of the most notable examples, but the list could be extended to include some of the more modern growth industries such as electronics. Two examples taken from engineering – textile machinery and machine tools – may serve to illustrate the above points in greater depth.

In the case of textile machinery Britain once reigned supreme in world markets, and even as late as 1954 her share of world trade in textile machinery was as high as 30 per cent. The subsequent history of the industry makes dismal reading. By 1975 Britain's share of the world market had dropped to a mere 11 per cent, yet that of West Germany had risen from 18 to 35 per cent over the intervening period, and even Switzerland's share had increased to 15 per cent. Employment meanwhile more than halved between 1951 and 1973, from 75,000 to 35,000. By the latter date many British textile producers were in fact buying foreign machinery, not because it was necessarily cheaper, but because of its technical superiority. The plain fact was that the majority of machinery makers failed to respond to the technical transformation in textile machinery which meant that international competitiveness was increasingly determined by the technical sophistication of the product. Neglect of research and development and the limited recruitment of technical expertise, in contrast to the experience in Germany, go far to explain the collapse of the industry in Britain. The failure of the machinery makers to adapt or improve their products to meet changing markets demands, or to produce an entirely new generation of machinery, is exemplified by the disastrous record of British Northrop which originally pioneered the automatic loom (Rothwell and Zegveld 1979 79–83). Rothwell (1980 307) draws attention to the paucity of engineering expertise and the growing number of accountants at top level decision-making which in some cases led to a neglect of investment in new technical developments.

Much the same fate befell the machine tool industry and for very similar reasons, though in this case the skills deficiency was even more pronounced. Once a pioneer and world leader in machine tools, Britain now no longer ranks as a significant force in the industry. By the early 1980s Britain accounted for a mere 2.8 per cent of world production as against nearly 20 per cent twenty years earlier, then ranking fourth as a producer after the United States, the USSR and West Germany. Employment in the industry has more than halved since the late 1960s, as has the trade share down from 13 to less than 6 per cent, whereas Germany's remained stable and Japan's rose sharply. At the same time import penetration of the home market increased steadily (Daly 1981 60–4). As with textile machinery, technical inefficiency was a major factor in the machine tool industry's loss of competitiveness. The industry failed to capitalise on its initial advantages in numerically-controlled machine tools, and it performed badly in terms of both the design and the production of new tools (Rothwell 1980 302–3). Technical inferiority can be attributed to low investment in new machinery, skill shortages and a lack of a long-term commitment to R & D. The latter, having risen significantly in the decade or so from the later 1950s, subsequently collapsed from a peak of £5.4 million in 1967–8 to a mere £1.6 million by 1972–3; by which time it accounted for less than 1 per cent of total sales as against more than 3 per cent at its peak (Daly and Jones 1980). This, moreover, in an industry which received considerable public support from the 1960s onwards.

Given the machine tool industry's appalling record with respect to investment in human capital it is scarcely surprising that it was unable to exploit new opportunities. For an industry which ostensibly relies heavily on skilled expertise at all levels, it has probably had one of the least trained workforces with the result that it has suffered from a permanent shortage of skilled labour. At the higher level for example, design and production engineers have been conspicuous by their absence. A sample survey in 1958 revealed that there were only twenty-five graduate engineers working in the ninety largest concerns which employed a total of 30,000 workers. The position had improved somewhat by the later 1970s when some 277 scientists and technologists were recorded as being employed, though the number subsequently fell to under 200 by the early 1980s. As a proportion of the total workforce this was still well under 1 per cent, compared with about 4 per cent for the engineering industry as a whole. Moreover, the quality of British engineers and technologists was said to be inferior to those employed in German firms, while a large proportion were engaged on product design and development to the detriment of marketing and manufacturing production. Production engineers, as in the engineering industry generally, were very thin on the ground (Aldcroft 1987 33–4).

At the operative or intermediate level the position was even worse. The machine tool industry depends on craft skills to a greater extent than many other branches of engineering, with around one-half of its employees being classed as skilled craftsmen. Yet compared with Germany, Switzerland, Sweden or Japan, the training received by many of these so-called craftsmen has been little short of derisory. The traditional apprenticeship system provided little in the way of formal or structured training. Apprentices were required neither to attend courses of instruction, nor to pass any externally assessed examinations and so most of them ended their indenture with no formal vocational qualifications. For the majority of trainees the craftsman's badge was secured simply by 'serving time'.

Thus in terms of both quantity and quality the machine tool industry has suffered from a serious shortage of skills. Low pay and the low status accorded to professional engineers have been partly to blame at the higher levels, a narrowing of craft pay differentials and the inadequacy of facilities for proper vocational training are relevant factors at the intermediate level. Whatever the causes however, the implications of the under-investment in skills have been serious. The industry has never had sufficient top level expertise to enable it to maintain a presence at the frontiers of technical development. At the same time, the shortage of intermediate skills coupled with the inadequate training given to craftsmen and technicians have meant that highly trained personnel have had to spend too much of their time doing what should have been done by those with lesser or intermediate skills. Consequently, the former had less time to spend on advanced development work with the result that 'As one generation of employees succeeds another . . . products with a low skill-content are increasingly produced, and products with a high skill-content need increasingly to be imported' (Prais 1981a 185). Hence the unfavourable export–import unit values in British trade.

Ultimately this problem stems from the poor calibre of management, as Rothwell (1980 306) has stressed. It is not so much a question of the want of professionalism in terms of training in managerial techniques, but a lack of managerial personnel with appropriate technical qualifications so that a proper appraisal of technical matters and skill formation can be carried out. The cult of the technically ignorant manager, in sharp contrast to the situation in Germany with its third culture *Technik* enjoying parity of esteem with the other two, has been a favourite topic of derision both in this country and abroad. As the *Investors' Chronicle* commented in 1979:

> The situation to which this system of management has led is this: the worker on the bench or line knows what he is doing and his chargehand has a pretty fair idea. The foreman knows enough to stay in his office. The factory manager knows very little and the chairman and the board are in total ignorance, in ideal cases not even knowing where the factory is or what it makes! (quoted in Prais 1981a)

The Germans, it is said, not only find it quaint that historians and arts graduates can aspire to managerial responsibility especially in technically-based industries, but they are frankly amazed that Britain manages to cope at all with such low levels of skill formation. German firms too suffer from skill shortages but they are much less severe than those in Britain, and their response in terms of training is much more constructive than that of most British companies (Leadbeater 1991). The Finniston Inquiry (1980 36–8,112–13) deliberated at some length on the consequences of the shortage of technical expertise in British industry, especially at the top, and the implications this had for research and development, innovation, productivity and competitiveness. They were of course particularly concerned with the neglect of the engineering dimension in industry and the paucity of engineering expertise among industrial leaders and managers. The lack of technical understanding among top management set limits, they felt, to the ability of firms to devise and implement technology-based responses to market changes or new competitive environments. Additionally, it might also forestall improvement in production methods and reorganisation of plant layout etc., because of a lack of understanding of, and even an absence of interest in, such matters. Quoting a study by the Engineering Industry Board on innovation and enginering, it was observed that:

> The impression was frequently given that new techniques were unused, not because they were inapplicable to the firm concerned, but because senior staff in the firm lacked the necessary knowledge to implement the innovations. The converse was also true. In many cases (in both large and small firms) almost the only factor that distinguished firms using a new technique from those not doing so was the existence in the 'innovative' firm of one or two key individuals who had the necessary expertise.

If the level of R & D and the rate of innovation are important determinants of economic success then it is important to stress, as Pavitt (1980) does, that they do not necessarily take place automatically in response to economic growth or a high level of investment. Favourable economic conditions will no doubt induce greater innovative effort, while many innovations will involve substantial additional investment. Similarly, research spending, at least in Britain, appears to be more buoyant when the economic climate is good. Furthermore, a rapid rate of investment will itself give rise to new developments and improvements in products and processes, though the line of causation may well be reversed where the rate of product innovation is autonomously rapid and/or randomly determined, as in the case of electronics and pharmaceuticals for instance. In the latter case therefore, investment opportunities and the level of investment will be determined primarily by the speed with which new technologies are exploited. However, whatever the line of causation, it is ultimately the choice of techniques which is crucial, and the correct choice will depend not only on a firm's in-house development capability, but also on the general level of managerial competence. In other words, Britain's poor track record in innovation and research cannot be explained away simply or solely by perverse market signals or the general economic background. 'It is the consequence of an accumulation of discretionary decisions reflecting the conservative characteristics and lack of professional competence of British managers, engineers and workers; relatively little research (i.e. innovative) activity, bad choices, and slow adaptation and learning' (Pavitt 1980 9).

Resource utilisation and manpower management

The problem is more than simply one of sluggish innovation and low spending on research, however. The poor record in technological innovation has been matched by an equal deficiency in the utilisation of resources. It is no doubt true that industry's weak productivity record compared with that of its major competitors reflects the slow pace of innovation and in some cases the low capital stock per worker. Nevertheless, numerous industry surveys have also stressed the inadequate utilisation of existing resources, with the result that the productivity of factor inputs is low in comparison with the returns from identical or similar inputs in other countries. Thus many manufacturing activities have not been making the most of their potential, that is there has been considerable scope for improving the productivity of existing resources by better industrial housekeeping. The shift of labour out of manufacturing over the past decades is in part a reflection of the serious overmanning in British industry in the past, to which American commentators have frequently drawn attention (Caves 1968). Some estimates for the 1960s suggested that British industry had excess labour to the tune of several million.

Motor manufacturing provides a classic case of overmanning and poor resource utilisation, among several other defects it might be added. The efficiency and competitiveness of this industry has deteriorated steadily over time partly because of the very low priority accorded to the actual process of production. Yet in 1955 Britain still had the highest labour producivity in Europe and was a leading exporter of both cars and commercial vehicles. Two decades later output per head was not only below that of 1965, but it was around one-third lower than in Germany, France and Italy. In some cases differences of up to 80 per cent were found in the number of man-hours required to assemble similar cars, while Ford's Halewood plant had an efficiency of about half its counterpart site at Saarlouis in Germany. As the Central Policy Review Staff noted in their report of 1975, there were many things wrong with the industry, including insufficient R & D, poor production methods, badly designed vehicles, inadequate technical facilities, excessive overmanning and generally bad labour management, testimony to which is all too evident in the atrocious industrial relations record. As a consequence, though nominal labour costs per hour tended to be lower in Britain than elsewhere, the unit costs per car assembled were higher because of lower factor productivity (Cairncross, Kay and Silberston 1977 10; Dunnett 1980).

The scope for improvement at the factory floor level was amply demonstrated by the findings of a research team from the University of Birmingham's Department of Engineering. They carried out a study of the distribution of time spent by operatives and machines during a working day in forty engineering and metal working firms in the period 1968–72, with a series of follow-up studies of forty-five firms between 1970 and 1974. It was found that on average operatives spent only 48 per cent of their working time actually engaged in productive activity, while no less than 16 per cent was taken up with just 'waiting'; the machines were idle for about half the time. With only relatively small-scale adjustments in work organisation and technical improvements labour productivity could have been improved almost instantly by more than a third, and capital productivity by no less than 100 per cent (Beckerman 1979 176; Lawrence 1980 129; Dudley 1977 127).

This and many other studies point to a serious failure in the production side of industry to which Anne Mueller (1977 261–6) drew particular attention in her instructive paper. She emphasised the widespread inefficiency of resource use, especially in engineering, rather than a low level of investment *per se*, as a cause of poor industrial performance. In turn this could be attributed in large part to lax managerial practices in terms of organising and monitoring production processes, that is such things as methods of working, workflow practices, maintenance of equipment, technical improvements and factory layout. Similarly, factors which determine non-price competitiveness, such as product design, quality control, technical specifications and delivery schedules, all the province of management, left room for improvement.

The basic problem in all this is the traditional one of the low priority accorded to the actual process of production in Britain, which contrasts sharply with the keen attention the Germans devote to this side of the business. To a large extent it stems from inadequate skills and expertise at all levels of industrial operations. But probably the major shortcoming has been the deficiency of managerial intensity both at the top and among middle management, with the technical and engineering expertise and knowledge about production to ensure that things are run efficiently. Ford UK, for example, has for many years found great difficulty in recruiting adequate middle managers and line workers capable of keeping assembly plants running efficiently (Griffiths 1989). But as Mant (1978 71) has pointed out, this may have much to do with the divorce of career managers from the technicalities of the production process since, as noted previously, the latter has been seen as a dead end as far as mobility up the managerial hierarchy is concerned.

But the problem runs deeper than this since the lack of technical competence at the managerial level affects skill formation and attitudes lower down the line. It results in a failure to recognise and a consequent neglect of the importance of skills at both the operational and supervisory grade levels and this in turn has adverse repercussions on the production process. As Ron Mellor, Secretary of the Institution of Mechanical Engineers, enjoined: 'Education standards are so low in some parts of the country that production workers simply don't have the awareness and alertness of line workers in other countries' (Griffiths 1989). Furthermore, poor education and indifferent job training, together with the consequent limited career prospects, lead to low motivation, absenteeism, pilfering, and more generally to a lack of pride in one's job, all of which impinge adversely on productive efficiency. Similarly, the status and training of supervisory grades, especially foremen, falls well short of the German equivalents, and helps to explain why British industry has such a poor record in resource utilisation (see Prais and Wagner 1988).

An additional difficulty at the intermediate level has been the excessive job demarcation rules among craft unions which has tended to perpetuate a narrow range of skill abilities among workers and thereby limited the scope for flexibility in the use of manpower. This in turn inhibits the adoption of more efficient working practices and leads to overstaffing. It has also given rise to frequent demarcation disputes both within and between unions, with the result that valuable managerial time has often been devoted to 'fire-fighting' or the resolution of industrial disputes rather than to achieving macro-economic efficiency (Gordon 1982 34).

In the case of the motor industry, a classic example of this kind of dispute, Lewchuk (1987) has sought to explain the problem in terms of institutional constraints which, he argues, impeded the full adoption of American production techniques in Britain. The managerial dimension, through lack of training and technical expertise, never fully developed to a point where it could establish direct control over effort norms through close supervision of machine pacing at the factory floor level. Thus though British producers moved to mass production techniques these had to be adapted to the peculiarities of the British institutional structure in order to accommodate a more recalcitrant and conservative workforce steeped in the craft traditions of the previous century. Management lacked the ability or will to remove them and this resulted in weak managerial control over the use of manpower. Effort norms could not therefore be maximised and this in turn discouraged the adoption of high capital intensity and more productive technologies. The final outcome was low efficiency and overmanning. Thus both management and labour became locked into a low growth strategy from which it was difficult to disengage given the institutional constraints which helped to perpetuate the system.

One further consequence of skill shortages has probably been an inflation of wage costs. Wages in Britain tend to be less sensitive to recession and unemployment than elsewhere and this may be explained partly by the low level of skill formation. Because of skill shortages employers are fearful of losing trained workers even when demand is slack, while the latter retain a strong bargaining position since unemployment tends to be concentrated among the unskilled. Hence there is little incentive for skilled workers to moderate their pay claims in times of recession, and the prevalence of local plant bargaining, as opposed to industry-wide negotiations, tends to exacerbate inter-regional competition for skilled workers. This has the effect of driving up wages above the warranted rate, that is above the rate of productivity growth which is itself constrained by the low level of skill formation, not only of skilled workers which are in short supply, but also of the less skilled and unskilled workers as a result of the inevitable 'knock-on' effects through union bargaining and the erosion of pay differentials between skilled and unskilled workers.

The OECD in one of its recent reports was of the firm belief that chronic skill shortages and inadequate training of the workforce were so acute in Britain that they undermined the normal operation of the labour market and thereby resulted in low productivity, excessive wage inflation and a high internal rate of unemployment. An upgrading of vocational and general training levels was deemed to be critical for enhancing labour mobility, labour market flexibility and productivity (*Financial Times*, 4 July 1991).

Industry studies

The results of the comparative productivity exercise by Davies and Caves (1987) show particularly clearly the impact of low levels of technical skill in the workforce at large, a feature which arose as much from the qualitative characteristics of vocational training as from the volume of resources devoted to training. Further confirmation at the micro level of the adverse effect of low skill formation is contained in the series of detailed comparative investigations carried out by Professor Prais and his colleagues at the National Instiutute of Economic and Social Research during the 1980s. Most of these studies are devoted to schooling standards and vocational training and include several comparative sector analyses of matched plants in Britain, France and Germany. They seek to outline the differences in schooling, training and general skill formation between Britain and other advanced countries and to assess the consequences of these differences for Britain.

The general conclusions which emerge from these investigations are as follows. First, Britain has had a very low level of vocational training and skill formation in most trades compared with those of other countries. Secondly, the intensity and quality of training has generally been inferior to those elsewhere. Thirdly, pre-vocational educational standards were often found to be very poor. Fourthly, the general inference drawn was that skill formation mattered in explaining productivity and quality differentials. And finally, the reforms of the 1980s do not appear to have made much difference to repairing skill deficiences in Britain largely because of the continued poor quality of the training on offer.

The productivity gap was most noticeable in the comparisons with Germany. In the case of the construction industry for example, there was a productivity differential of 100 per cent in favour of German firms, which the authors attributed largely to the highly qualified nature of the German workforce compared with the British, in an industry in which much of the work is individual and needs to be carried out correctly and efficiently without detailed and costly supervision. In the early 1980s Germany was producing three and a half times as many building craftsmen as a proportion of the labour force as Britain. The majority of those employed in the German construction industry were qualified craftsmen whereas in the British case the reverse was true (Prais and Wagner 1983; Prais and Steedman 1986).

In a similar study of forty-five matched plants in the metal working trades in Britain and Germany there were found to be differences in labour productivity of between 10 and 130 per cent with a mean of 63 per cent, and again 'the centrality of skills at all levels seemed apparent' in explaining the wide gap (Daly, Hitchens and Wagner 1985 49–51, 60). Metal manufacturing in this country has been notorious for its poor record in skill formation with the majority of the labour force having no proper vocational qualifications. In another study, this time on women's outerwear clothing (Steedman and Wagner 1989), skill differences were again highlighted as a reason for Germany's superior performance. Not only did Germany produce about ten times as many skilled clothing workers as did Britain, but it was also found that the majority of supervisors, plant managers and owners in Britain had no vocational or technical qualifications relevant to the industry. By contrast, all the German supervisors in the sample had completed a three-year apprenticeship together with additional course work study.

Similar conclusions can be drawn from most of the other studies in this series including those on hotels (Prais, Jarvis and Wagner 1989), kitchen furniture (Steedman and Wagner 1987), office work (Steedman 1987), retailing (Jarvis and Prais 1989) and engineering (Steedman 1988; Prais 1989a; Steedman and Wagner 1987). What is especially important is the way in which skill deficiencies in Britain affected the quality of production, an important consideration given the increasing importance of non-price factors in international trade competitiveness.

Even more disturbing was the fact that the quality and intensity of training in Britain, limited though it was, did not match those elsewhere. German trainees, in whatever field, generally met higher standards of attainment than their British counterparts, and YTS and other reforms of the recent past have done little to alter the discrepancy between the two countries. In their study of clothing Steedman and Wagner (1989 48) commented as follows:

> It is remarkable testimony to the modesty of Britain's ambitions to improve training that around two thirds of the practical skills that YTS trainees are expected to take *two years* to master, must be mastered by the German trainees within the first *two months* of their training course; the remaining third of the skills required for the 'Clothing Skills Awards' would be acquired by the German trainees by the end of their first six months of training. It is only of limited comfort to learn that the very simple operations which are required for the Clothing Skills Awards constitute a range of competence far wider than that which would normally be acquired by a British Machinist in the course of (non-YTS) training.

In the case of retailing, where YTS did have a sizeable impact, at least in terms of the numbers taking up training, the final outturn in quality was not very encouraging. Only about one-quarter of the entrants gained recognised qualifications under the new NCVQ standards which were generally at a fairly low level of attainment compared with equivalents in France and Germany. Moreover, the standards required were highly job-specific and they excluded externally assessed testing. This inevitably reduced the scope for flexibility and the acquisition of transferable skills with adverse consequences for economic effciency (Jarvis and Prais 1989 61, 68). Similarly, standards of training and qualification in hotel management rarely matched the German levels since 'The current system of training subsidies seems to focus in an undifferentiated way too much on certificating elementary skills rather than promoting higher levels of vocational qualification which would increase flexibility and adaptability' (Prais, Jarvis and Wagner 1989 68).

Schooling standards were frequently referred to in the reports as an impediment to the progress of greater skill formation at the intermediate level. The main stumbling block time and again was the deficiency in core subjects, especially mathematics even at a most elementary level, though literary skills and languages also posed a problem. 'Until schooling standards in Britain are similarly raised (to German levels) for the broad cross-section of school-leavers, the task of raising workforce skills to German levels is bound to remain difficult in Britain' (Prais, Jarvis and Wagner 1989 60; Prais and Wagner 1983). Mathematical attainments among secondary school leavers have been unbelievably low, so much so that vocational trainees often find great difficulty in coping with courses that require a rudiment of numerical skills. To illustrate the point Hilary Steedman (1988 63) quotes the case of a class of 19-year-old car mechanics in their final year before qualification being faced with solving the following simple arithmetic question in the course of their work: 600/0.2. Not one of the class could answer it correctly, yet a group of 15–16-year-old French students all got the answer right in less than one minute. This elementary question in fact featured as part of a question set in a Part II level examination of the City and Guilds Institute. It may speak volumes for the modest standards expected, but which many, judging from this example, cannot achieve.

The problem is not confined to mathematical abilities, though the lacking in this department is probably the more serious for many vocational trainees than deficiencies in other subjects. But foreign language skills among the majority of school leavers are almost conspicuous by their absence. Apart from native language attainments, and the less said about those the better, only a very small proportion of school leavers can be said to have any worthwhile knowledge of a foreign language. In France some 75 per cent of all secondary school pupils take at least one foreign language during their secondary school career compared with only 35 per cent in Britain; at least one-half of all French youngsters continue with one foreign language for a further two to three years after the age of 16, whereas only 3 per cent take a foreign language at 'A' level. Furthermore, the majority taking vocational courses in France also study a foreign language. This again points to the disadvantage of the single subject examination system in Britain and the lack of a designated core curriculum, at least until quite recently. And as Steedman (1987 61–2) points out, why has French dominated the language curriculum in preference to German given that Germany is Britain's most important EC customer?

Differences in skill formation between Britain and other countries are not confined to the intermediate craft skills and below. They are also evident in the limited qualifications among higher grades of workers including foremen, technicians, supervisors, production engineers and plant managers. Prais and Wagner (1988) have drawn attention to the enormous differences between Britain and Germany in the training of foremen and we have already had occasion to refer to the meagre qualifications of supervisors in the clothing industry. More widely, MacGregor (1987 377) refers to the economic illiteracy of large sections of the population which limits the ability to comprehend what is going on in the economic world.

Such widespread under-investment in skills in a skill-intensive world can have quite serious implications for a major trading country since it ultimately has a detrimental effect on efficiency and hence competitiveness. Daly (1984 42) in a comparison between British and American manufacturing industry reckoned that a 1 per cent shift in labour force composition from unskilled to skilled could produce a productivity gain of the order of 2 per cent. If this magnitude is correct then Britain should stand to gain considerably if it can get its act together on the training front. As we have seen, there are many subtle ways in which low skill formation can impede innovation and efficiency: for example the inability to utilise or repair properly sophisticated equipment, lack of attention to quality control, difficulty in meeting customer specifications, and many other non-price factors which help to determine competitiveness. Inadequate shop floor skills may also reduce the flexibility in production methods and give rise to more overhead labour in the form of quality controllers.

Low skill formation may also discourage or retard innovation and the introduction of improved working methods through the prevalence of conservative attitudes. Ignorance breeds contempt for change and adaptation and leads to inflexible production strategies which cannot readily respond to new requirements or changed conditions. Workers who are undertrained in both practical and theoretical knowledge cannot understand properly what they are doing, why they are doing it, or how they might adapt to a new technological environment. Hence their attitude to new technology and new work methods will tend to be defensive if not outright obstructive. This in turn sours labour relations and leads to bad investment decisions. Workers therefore need to have an adequate comprehension of technological matters, among other things, in order to overcome their inability to understand or to master new ideas and processes (Daly, Hitchens and

Wagner 1985 58–61).

Sadly, the educational and training reforms of the 1980s, together with the more recent ones introduced or foreshadowed at the turn of the decade, do not offer much hope of Britain catching up with her competitors. In general terms they are too shallow for this purpose. The standards set in the core curriculum subjects and under the NCVQ levels are not on par with those in other major countries (Prais 1989b). The new vocational training system (YT) is still very weak by international standards and it lacks any compulsory element. After almost a decade of reform Steedman (1988, 1990) found very little improvement in the stock of craft qualifications in major occupations during the 1980s whereas, by contrast, Germany and France recorded significant gains. Their plans for the future acquisition of skills, moreover, suggest that Britain will be hard pressed to prevent the gap from widening further.

8
WHY DIDN'T WE DO BETTER?

It is a curious fact that the British are often complaining about their educational and training facilities and yet they seem unable or unwilling to set about improving them in any substantive way. For a century or more there have been endless official and unofficial reports, learned statements and debates, not to mention the stream of derogatory press comments about the shortcomings in this field. There have also been legislative and policy changes galore and yet we still lag badly behind our competitors in skill formation and coherent strategies for educational provision. Commenting on the latest batch of proposals to reform the educational system Correlli Barnett (1991) writes: 'It has taken about 120 years for the penny to drop with a British government that a coherent national education and training strategy with a logical structure of institutions and qualifications is vital to Britain's ability to survive and prosper.'

Why has this been so? In this chapter we attempt to draw together some of the more important factors which we feel have been responsible for blocking radical reform.

The nature of the problem

In Chapter 2 it was argued that a sheer lack of resources was not a major restricting force in the postwar period. It may well have been the case prior to the 1950s and it could present a problem in the future given the current backlog now to be made up. But for most of the postwar period aggregate spending in relative terms has been fairly satisfactory by international standards. If so, it suggests that we have either misallocated those resources, or else they have been utilised badly. In practice it was probably a combination of the two. Too large an input, for example, into compulsory education combined with inadequate control of the delivery system; too little into vocational education and training; and an incoherent strategy with respect to higher education. At the same time industry itself has spent too little on training, including managerial development. As Lynn (1988) notes, fundamental problems are not necessarily solved by throwing more cash at them if the existing strategies and procedures are in question. That this point is worth bearing in mind is borne out by the fact that examination performance between different local authorities varies considerably even after allowing for differences in social composition and levels of spending, implying that it is important to identify good practice in the educational system before allocating resources (Levitt and Joyce 1987 121).

In this volume the main focus of attention has been on the way in which the education and training system has provided people with the knowledge and skills required for a lifetime's work. We recognise of course that education has purposes and functions other than that of promoting the work ethic, but since a considerable part of life on earth is consumed in working and earning one's living, it would seem legitimate that the educational system, which we all pay for at a later stage of life, should equip us with the tools of trade so that we can make the best of our abilities. This goal the system has signally failed to achieve, at least as far as the majority of the population is concerned.

Before looking at some of the reasons for the failure to develop a coherent and viable education service it may be helpful to recapitulate some of the major shortcomings that have persisted for much of the period covered in this study.

As far as formal schooling is concerned the 1944 Education Act was not in principle the unmitigated disaster that some have alleged it to be. After all the Germans have maintained a workable and successful tripartite system to this day. The fault lay in the way it was implemented, or in some cases the way it was not. The technical schools, for example, never really got off the ground and so there could be little parity of esteem within the tripartite system, as originally envisaged by the Norwood Committee in 1943 (Norwood Report 1943 14). Nor did the proposal for compulsory part-time attendance at continuation colleges following formal schooling see the light of day. Thus there was no basis for a second track or vocational educational route and the academic stream gained all the accolades. The examinations system tended to bolster the latter's prestige. It favoured the academically gifted and this remained true even after the CSE examination was introduced because of its acknowledged inferior status. The bias was maintained and even strengthened at the advanced stage of secondary education, for the 'A' level examination structure catered primarily for the academic élite, and comprehensive schooling did little to change this pattern. As Hilary Steedman (1987 68) quite rightly asks, why was there not a technical and vocational 'A' level at 18 plus to end the examination apartheid 'which has traditionally consigned technical and vocational qualifications to vague limbo with only tenuous links to the mainstream education system'?

At the compulsory schooling stage there were even more serious defects, however. Many pupils at 15 or later left school without acquiring the basic skills of literacy or numeracy, let alone competence in foreign languages or science and technology. The competence of the teaching service comes into question here, but even more important we feel has been the absence of a core curriculum, rigorously devised and tested at different age levels. If this would seem to some a reactionary note against the liberal and progressive educational principles of recent decades, one might spare a thought and a measure of sympathy for many of the pupils who have failed to acquire core skills and have therefore found difficulty in proceeding further with their education and training. It is all very well exposing pupils to cultural and creative activities at school but at the same time they also need to acquire proficiency in basic skills to succeed in the world of work.

Not only did many pupils leave school without worthwhile qualifications but the opportunities for further education and training were far from good. Vocational training for early school leavers was not made compulsory as in Germany and for much of the postwar period the provision of vocational training was limited and often of poor quality. The lack of standardisation of courses and qualifications did little to enhance the prestige of the system. There were many changes in policy especially later in the period, but for the most part they consisted of *ad hoc* bolt-ons to an already precarious system. If anything the quality of the delivery system deteriorated as it expanded. There was still no logical progression from school to vocational education and training as there was for the academic stream.

The system was somewhat kinder to the élite group of academic scholars who went on to higher education. There was a logical progression of examinations and an entry system in to higher education that worked reasonably smoothly. The main problem was that it was unduly narrow and inflexible and therefore offered little to the academically less able. The provision of higher education was largely demand-driven and it tended to favour theory as opposed to the practical. This provided a precept for educational institutions of all types to gravitate towards the style and patterns set by the apex of the system, namely the universities. This had the effect of downgrading the practical and the technological and is most clearly evidenced in the life of the polytechnics, which though initially 'so eager to demonstrate the superiority of public purpose over elitism, soon acquired characteristics remarkably similar to those of the universities' (Kogan 1975 216). Such academic bias seems to spring eternal in educational institutions in Britain since similar patterns can be discerned in schools and colleges (Selby-Smith 1970 150, 159, 173).

There are many factors, some of them interrelated, which have played a part in shaping Britain's educational system. One of the most important, as far as schooling is concerned, has been the devolution of control, and this provides a convenient starting point.

The politics of control

Kogan (1978) has enumerated a wide range of individuals, pressure groups, organisations and other interested parties – politicians, civil servants, local government, parents, teachers, the unions, students, pupils and educational reformers – who have sought to influence or control the pattern of educational progress in Britain. In fact nearly everyone, it seems, would appear to have a view on education, and for this reason, unlike many other issues of national importance which are too esoteric or too complex to be understood by the layman, education has been subject to many diverse pressures at both national and local level. Conceivably this is also true in other countries though probably not to the same extent as in Britain. For, as Levitt and Joyce (1987 121) point out, 'education in the United Kingdom is bedevilled by a remarkable degree of difference of opinion (not found among our competitors) as to what education is for and, in consequence of this, as to the value of cognitive tests and examination results as measures of performance'.

To a large extent this problem has arisen because of the devolution of responsibility in education and the limited degree of control by central government. While major legislative initiatives rest with the central govenment, a large part of the educational service has been effectively controlled by the Local Education Authorities (LEAs).

This has had several consequences. It has led to a wide variation in the provision of school services across the country and thus made it difficult to impose any uniform standard of practice. It has also meant that education has been exposed to a diversity of opinion and interest group pressure at the local level. Education moreover became increasingly politically dominated as the influence of the central government waned until the 1980s (Jennings 1977 9, 27).

Both Kogan (1975 101, 107) and Jennings (1977 88) question the wisdom of allowing the LEAs so much latitude in the execution of education services. Kogan argues that the LEAs tended to be reactive rather than innovative, more interested in the status of local government than anything else, and cites their reluctance to initiate work experience in schools. Their failure to develop the technical schools as a third force in the tripartite system may also be quoted in confirmation of this point. Jennings, moreover, doubts the ability of many councillors to cope with the complex tasks of planning, programming and evaluating the large expenditures involved in administering education at the local level.

Even more disturbing was the latitude the LEAs allowed schools as regards what was taught and how it was taught. Even some head teachers had little idea as to what was being taught by the teachers in their classrooms. This not only led to an enormous diversity of provision between regions and even within the confines of one local area, but it also meant that there was no guarantee that pupils would emerge proficient in core subjects, even less that they would receive any instruction in technical or vocational subjects. In many schools they were allowed to drop subjects at will before the examination stage and in extreme cases they might end up doing their own thing depending on the whim of the teachers concerned: for example the 'flower-power' studies in Brent, or the complete anarchy at the William Tyndale Junior School in Islington, which became a *cause célèbre* in the 1970s following a full-scale investigation into the activities of the school (Kogan 1978 73, 88–9). All great fun no doubt for those involved at the time, but hardly fair on the pupils who eventually had to make their way in the world.

This problem was perhaps most acute at the compulsory school stage and especially for the less able pupils, since at the higher level of secondary education a smaller and more committed group of pupils had prescribed goals to aim for, that is 'A' levels, and had already acquired some proficiency in a range of subjects. Lynn (1988 132–44) argues that the failure of the schools to discharge their responsibilities satisfactorily and the complexities of the objectives of education call into serious question whether teachers should be allowed to determine the format of the curriculum and the way it is taught. He contrasts the British situation with that of Japan (and France in some respects) where there are three powerful incentives making for teacher efficiency: (1) detailed specification of the curriculum by the Ministry of Education; (2) strong competition between schools for examination successes; and (3) large numbers of private schools subject to the discipline of the market place.

The teaching profession has of course jealously guarded what Sir David Eccles (Minister of Education in the later 1950s) referred to as 'the secret garden of the curriculum'. Successive Ministers of Education expressed their belief in the freedom of schools and teachers to devise their own methods of teaching since this they felt was more likely to lead to creativity and individual response in pupils and to satisfy their differing needs. As a consequence, curriculum control by the centre was much less evident than in most other European countries (Kogan 1978 63). In this respect the 1944 Act was found wanting since it laid down few guidelines as to curriculum and its content except for 'religious education' and 'act of worship', which for some curious reason were made compulsory. As Kogan (1978 19) wryly remarks: 'When they were written into the 1944 Education Act their authors must have had the same intentions as the Soviet educational planners who insist on the teaching of compulsory Marxism. That, too, we understand from Nigel Grant's authoritative *Soviet Education*, is a ritual "like compulsory chapel", boring and unreal to most.'

Yet the government was far from powerless under the 1944 legislation which had in fact provided the central authority with considerable leverage to intervene in education matters at the local level should it so wish. But entering the 'secret garden' was not that easy when confronted by the powerful opposition of the teachers and the LEAs who were determined at all costs to preserve their independence from central control. Thus the DES, in the mid 1960s, was thwarted in its attempt to look into school curriculum matters by their combined opposition, perhaps not surprisingly since the proposed Curriculum Study Group was dubbed by Sir David Eccles as 'a commando type unit', which was scarcely likely to endear either the teachers or the LEAs (Shipman 1984 186, 194; Kogan 1978 63). The intentions may have been innocuous since there is no evidence of any deep-laid plot to grab control of the curriculum from the teachers, but the damage had been done. Subsequently, the DES, in conjunction with the teachers and the LEAs, established the Schools Council for the Curriculum and Examinations, staffed largely by teachers and therefore likely to be more sympathetic to their cause.

This probably represented the high water mark of the 'secret garden'. During the 1970s there were to be increasing attacks on the ineffectiveness of the Schools Council, with rising concern over declining standards which were associated with liberal and progressive education. A series of Black Papers, written by academics, teachers and others concerned about declining standards in education, castigated the liberal mode of thought and called for a return to more traditional methods of instruction. Even Prime Minister James Callaghan entered the Great Debate and pontificated about declining standards in the schools. He instituted, through the DES, confidential inquiries into educational standards and curriculum matters, with the intention of promoting improvements in literacy and numeracy in schools through an agreed core curriculum (Morgan 1990 399). By the early 1980s the DES was therefore pressing hard for curriculum reform and rigorous assesment of performance which eventually bore fruit in the Baker reforms later in the decade.

Whether the new core curriculum and testing provisions will prove successful in raising standards in key subjects remains to be seen. The obvious defects of the new system are the wide spread of subjects which will be beyond the capabilities of many less bright pupils, the limited time allotted for core subjects and the specifications of the contents of the subjects. The GCSE mathematics syllabus, for example, falls short of the former 'O' level standard, and yet there is no real alternative for weaker candidates.

Be that as it may, we have discussed the issue of devolved control at some length to illustrate how the interplay of weak central control and powerful grass roots interests have been able to delay a long overdue reform. Critics will no doubt counter that centralised control is inimical to free expression and the independence of the teaching profession, but when the delivery system, as it has operated since the war, fails to provide an equality of opportunity for pupils to achieve core skills because of local idiosyncrasies, then there is a strong case for such action.

Central government policy can be criticised in other areas of education and in these cases there was less excuse for inaction on the grounds of local opposition. We have already referred to the harmful effects of the exclusive dominance of the academic 'A' level syllabus and the failure to introduce an equivalent for vocational studies. Without a reformed curriculum at the post-compulsory stage there was little point in many less academically inclined pupils staying on at school. As Shipman (1984 202) notes, teachers were already finding it difficult catering for many existing 16-year-olds under the traditional subject rubric. Similarly, the anomalous position of the polytechnics, neither fish nor fowl, teaching a whole range of courses from BTEC to degree level and without a clear brief as to their precise role in the educational system. Ideally they should have been removed from local control and designated as technological universities in the German fashion, with a clear mandate of objectives, instead of which they gravitated towards traditional academia, shedding on the way some of their rag-bag of courses, many of which were in any case more suited to the colleges of further education. Ironically, the universities are now in danger of losing their way as a consequence of conflicting government directives. Having resisted reform for so long and having failed to take the initiative in the educational debates, they found themselves powerless to prevent the encroachment of central control in the 1980s. Some of the reforms may have been long overdue – for example more vocationally-orientated courses and stronger links with the business world – but the extent and speed of the changes have been so great that the universities have been unable to respond in a coherent way. In the process of change they may sacrifice much of what is best in university work and end up in the anomalous position of the polytechnics. Unfortunately, until there are clearly specified guidelines as to the roles and objectives of the different branches of higher and further education the present pattern of drift will continue.

It was in the field associated with the vocational education and training of 16–19-year-olds who were not destined for higher education that the greatest lacuna in policy has been perceived. There has never been a coherent and comprehensive strategy to cater for this group of people. Developments have been haphazard and *ad hoc*, often in response to specific problems rather than as part of a rational structure. The result has been a great variety of provision in a multitude of different institutions comprising a myriad of courses and a bewildering range of qualifications which have been aptly described as a 'jungle' (Locke and Bloomfield 1982 43). According to Cantor and

Roberts (1986 37), the absence of a coherent structure has left the 16–19-year-old group without proper educational opportunity, it has created an artificial distinction between non-advanced and advanced further education and it has retarded the proper integration of education and training.

Further education, that is outside the university sector, has been one of the most rapidly expanding sectors of education since the war. Apart from vocational instruction, much of the growth consisted of part-time and recreational courses which were provided for general public consumption. However, the growth in facilities was extremely haphazard and by the 1970s it was badly in need of rationalisation. There was a considerable degree of overlap, wastage and conflict among competing institutions. As one observer (Selby-Smith 1970 173) of the scene noted: 'It lacks a clear rationale and is not designed to efficiently allocate scarce resources. The ultimate effects of changes are perceived only dimly. There is a bias in favour of more expensive and advanced courses, and a clear need for a revised structure of control and larger authorities.' During the course of the 1970s there was a considerable reduction in the number of colleges through closure and merger, but the jungle of courses and qualifications was not tackled until the following decade when, as we have seen, a whole series of new training initiatives was launched.

In this instance the fault can be squarely laid at the door of the central government. Though locally administered, further education and training were the ultimate province of national government. A coherent programme of education and training demanded a lead from the centre, in consultation of course with the colleges and employers. But for much of the time the government worked on the basic premiss that training as such was industry's responsibility and it was therefore reluctant to devise measures which would usurp what were regarded as the traditional functions of industry. This is one reason why so many policy measures in this field have been *ad hoc* or piecemeal and/or supportive, rather than radical programmes designed to overhaul the training system. It may also partly explain the reluctance of past governments to institute compulsory training and education for 16–19-year-olds. Few other countries have had to rely on such an informal and haphazard system of public provision in this sector and it is scarcely surprising therefore that Britain has remained so low in the training league table.

Although government policy has been anything but conducive to the creation of a rational and efficient education and training structure to meet the needs of economy and society, one should also recognise that policy formation in this area was very much influenced by the pressures and interests in society at large. For the most part these were inimical to reform. Employers, trade unions, the academic establishment, teachers, educationists and the public at large have been slow to respond to the need to adapt the education and training system to the requirements of a modern society.

The response of employers and trade unions

As already noted, for many years the government's approach to training was based on the assumption that it was primarily the duty of industry to take care of skill formation. Unfortunately British employers were not prepared to respond to the challenge. Despite repeated complaints about lack of skills and the low attainments of school leavers, employers, especially in manufacturing, were reluctant to do much to rectify the situation. As Ethel Venables (1974 150) observed as late as 1974: 'The message from industry is that "unqualified" school leavers are employable after a minimal initiation on the job. They may complain of the failure of the schools to educate them properly but they see no *economic* necessity to educate them further.' Even today many employers still do not regard training and skill formation as an essential component of corporate strategy or directly related to corporate performance (Leadbeater 1987a 1987b). They have therefore adopted a complacent attitude, preferring to minimise training expenditure by taking a short-term horizon approach and training for the most immediate and pressing needs, while buying in skills where possible to meet longer-term requirements. Moreover, it is not only at the intermediate skill level that industry has been complacent. It has also been slow to articulate its needs in terms of the type of graduate recruits required, while it has done very little to raise the status of engineering expertise in industry. The disposition and training of graduate recruits has often been poor, while management training has been conspicuous by its absence.

It is difficult to explain why such attitudes prevailed in view of the differing experience in other countries. The cultural ethos has frequently been invoked to account for the situation: that is the gentleman player and practical man heritage and society's traditional disdain for industry, commerce and trade. These cultural aspects are dealt with more fully below. Alternatively, it may be that in the two decades or so after the war industry was under little pressure to changes its ways. David Lodge's fictional MD of Pringle's, Victor Wilcox, in *Nice Work* (Lodge 1988 196) summed up the situation thus: 'We were too greedy and too lazy. In the fifties and sixties, when you could sell anything, we went on using obsolete machines and paid the unions whatever they asked for, while the krauts were investing in new technology and hammering out sensible labour agreements. When times got harder, it paid off.' There is more than a grain of truth in this observation as a glance at PEP's report (1965) on management behaviour will show.

Nor has there been much pressure from the workers and trade unions to improve skill formation. The nineteenth-century mechanics' institutes notwithstanding, there has never been a very strong tradition of workers self-financing their own training and further education as in the United States or Japan for instance. And even less so today partly because many school leavers are ill-prepared for the world of work and further study. The schools have not by and large infused youngsters with an irresistible desire to improve themselves by further study, the majority being only too eager to abandon their studies for good once released from compulsory education. This contrasts sharply with the more constructive attitude towards self-improvement in Germany and Japan for example (Lynn 1988).

Nor have the trade unions, which represent the workers' interests, done a great deal to advance their members' cause in this respect. It is true that many national trade union leaders do now believe that training provision should be incorporated into collective agreements but this has not always been the case. However, such views are not necessarily shared by the rank and file, especially the shop stewards, who wield the power at the local level bargaining table and are usually more interested in short-term material benefits for the workers they represent. In any case, trade union leaders, at both the national and local level, have rarely had much education and training themselves, either for their original jobs or for their trade union activities. Much of what they do in their union capacity has been picked up on the job which certainly does not equip them properly to cope with the complex problems of a modern economy. Taylor (1980 91–3) reckons that by the standards of most western nations, Britain has one of the worst educational services of any trade union movement. This may partly explain the limited horizons and lack of effective power of the leaders and officials at the national level, and also what Dore (1973 420) terms the 'antique inflexibility' of Britain's trade union institutions. The restrictive conditions of the traditional apprenticeship system, for example, effectively divided the workforce into skilled and unskilled, often on spurious grounds, and supported by trade unions anxious to preserve craft status and traditions, helped to perpetuate the institutional constraints to change. It also helped to intensify class differences and antagonisms between management and workers.

The educational system itself has contributed to these class differences. Jean Millar (1979 52) makes the interesting observation that there is a world of difference in dress, appearance and lack of differentiation in class accents between workers and management in Germany compared with those in Britain. When British workers and employers appear on television one can immediately tell the difference, whereas this is not the case with their German counterparts. She attributes this to the more egalitarian aspects of German society and education and the virtual absence of private fee-paying schools in Germany. Barnett (1977 240) goes further, maintaining that the cloth-cap working-class culture is almost unique in Europe and that it has been fostered by various factors including distinctions in workplace conditions and status and by the provision of council housing. Few other countries in fact have practised social and economic apartheid against their working members on such a grand scale.

The educational establishment

What is even more remarkable is how little pressure for reform came from the educational establishment, that is the teachers, the higher educational institutions, the colleges or the educational writers and scholars. It is not that they failed to espouse causes, but the ones they backed were rarely designed to widen the window of opportunity for the bulk of the nation's youth. Even the support for comprehensive schools did little to alter the traditional pattern of provision.

Though teachers became more militant as the years went by, they have never, by and large, been a very progressive force in education. They backed comprehensive schooling and the raising of the school leaving age – the latter no doubt much regretted later – but when it came to more crucial issues such as vocational training, work experience or curriculum reform, they showed indifference or even outright hostility. Many teachers, it has been argued, took a perverse delight in explicitly discouraging subjects with a technical and commercial flavour, even typewriting (Worswick 1985 5, 45–6, 50). The teachers have also resisted intrusion into curriculum matters and teaching methods for many years, and the eventual implementation of a core curriculum and other reforms at the end of the 1980s led to heated opposition despite the evidence that Britain was lagging behind other countries in teaching basic subjects.

The reasons for the teachers' obstructive stance are complex. One factor is professional pride. Teachers have always been conscious of their rather tenuous professional status and therefore opposed changes which were likely to demean it. Hence their opposition to vocational studies and their fear of intruders into the 'secret garden'. Secondly, the vicissitudes of their employment conditions as public servants in response to variations in the economic climate have made them more concerned with pay and service conditions than with educational policy matters. As Kogan (1975 230) observes: 'Teachers' associations have become more militant but on salaries and conditions of service rather than on the main educational policies; on the latter they . . . have been reactive rather than creative.'

Two other factors coloured teachers' views. One was the educational debate of the 1960s and 1970s in which the egalitarians, especially the educational philosophers and the sociologists, made the running. They espoused the comprehensive schools and the raising of the school leaving age, but resisted the infiltration of vocational studies into the school curriculum as recommended in the Newsom report (1963). Brennan (1977 99–100) argues that their intellectual endeavour had a considerable impact on the teachers' stance, not because it held out the prospects of greater opportunity for those concerned, which patently it did not in the absence of changes in the curriculum and the examinations system, but because it appeared to safeguard the erosion of teachers' prerogatives with respect to curriculum and associated matters.

It was the examination system however that proved to be the main stumbling block. Despite the introduction of the new CSE examination in 1965, the public examination system continued to be dominated by the GCE 'O' and 'A' levels whose prestige has been out of all proportion to their utility. We are not of course disparaging academic excellence; every country has its élite academic streams and these are no less important to society than any others. What we would decry is the way in which they have tended to dominate the work of the schools at the expense of courses and examinations with more vocational relevance for those not destined for 'academic' careers. These examinations, moreover, continued to be controlled and administered not by employers, but by boards dominated by academia. This meant that the structure and content of the examinations were determined to a large extent by the requirements and priorities set by the higher education authorities. Thus the curriculum pattern met the needs not of the vast majority of pupils who dropped out of the system, but those of the small minority who aspired to a place in higher education. The control exercised by the educational establishment over the examination system ensured that there would be little infiltration of 'base' subjects. To quote Dale (1985 15), 'The status of subjects tends to be measured by the extent to which they have moved away from utilitarian or pedagogic traditions and have become academic.'

In other words, the higher educational establishments set the pattern for the schools, catering for at best the top 20–25 per cent of the ability range. In so doing they helped to perpetuate the existing academic bias of the entire nation's teaching force. Neither the universities, the polytechnics nor the colleges did anything to dislodge this academic stranglehold. The universities resisted any change in the curriculum and the examinations system, while the polytechnics and colleges were more concerned with moving upstream to more prestigious and expensive courses in an attempt to improve their academic respectibility, to give much thought to such matters. At this juncture it is worth recalling the views of the Taunton Commission (1868 88) which, though reporting well over a century ago, argued that the organisation of education in the schools could never be complete unless the universities co-operated to make it so by giving encouragement to every kind of study which the country needs:

> If any studies get no recognition at the Universities, or if no room is made for them, it is impossible for those studies to flourish in the schools. If science has an unpractical character at the Universities, it will be very difficult for the schools to give it a practical turn. If the Universities cut themselves off from the needs of the country, they make it much more difficult for the schools to supply those needs. We cannot but consider it the duty of the Universities, placed as they are at the head of English education, to study carefully the requirements of the country, and to take their part in supplying them.

All sound advice but sadly it went unheeded.

Public opinion

It is difficult to test the strength of public opinion on any particular issue since so much of it tends to get submerged or mis-represented by the noise emitted by specific pressure group interests. Those most able to articulate their ideas and opinions are therefore likely to dominate the expression of views on any specific subject. In educational matters we have already had occasion to refer to the difficulty of achieving national consensus because of the diversity of opinion emanating from various pressure groups. However, the fact that the articulate middle class tends to make the running in the expression of views does not necessarily mean that there is widespread concern on the part of the public at large on such issues. Indeed, Jennings (1977 41) argued that the interest of the general public is not particularly strong and that their knowledge of the educational services on offer is rather poor. Interestingly enough the Taunton Commission (1868 15) was saying much the same thing in the nineteenth century when it critcised the apathy of parents:

> Too often the parents seem hardly to care for education at all. Too often they give inordinate value to mere show. Too often they think no education worth having that cannot be speedily turned into money. In fact, many parents need education themselves in order to appreciate education for their children, and their present opinion cannot be considered final or supreme.

Perhaps then things have not changed that radically today. If one compares attitudes in Britain with those say in Japan, France or Germany, there does seem to be a rather different conception of the value of education and training. The British, Stephen Lewis (1991 20) argues, tend to have a far more negative attitude to education and training than most Europeans and North Americans. They appear to regard education more as a consumption than an investment good, boring and useless, to be dispensed with as rapidly as possible, whereas in many other countries it is highly valued as a long-term asset of benefit to both the individual and society. In some countries youngsters are encouraged – sometimes over-pressurised perhaps – to do well at school and to continue their education and training as long as possible. In Japan and France for example, considerable extra tuition is 'bought-in' by parents to supplement public provision (Lynn 1988). In Britain, on the other hand, while social surveys suggest that most parents deem it important that their children should be reasonably proficient in the traditional three 'Rs' and that they should be taught a certain amount of discipline, beyond that many are fairly indifferent or even opposed to wider and deeper education following compulsory schooling (Jowell, Witherspoon and Brook 1986 199, 223).

There are of course exceptions. The upper middle class who send their children to private or public schools and then on to the universities have had no difficulty in articulating their requirements. The same is true of a segment of the middle class whose goals have been grammar or good comprehensive, university or polytechnic and then into the professions. These groups tend to dominate the system so reinforcing the academic slant of much of Britain's educational system.

This has therefore left little room for the majority of the population to influence or manipulate the educational system and hence in an important sense it has lessened the pressure for reform. Throughout the period a large part of the population was effectively 'shut out' from the system. After all, what was the point? The examination system was dominated by an academic ethos and catered for a minority of the pupils. Even when a new examination was introduced (CSE) it was regarded as second best by all concerned, and most pupils continued to be subjected to the traditional academic diet which held out prizes only for the few (Dale 1985 12). Thus for the majority of pupils who were not academically motivated there was not much incentive to work hard for there would be little to show for it at the end of the day. Moreover, since until recently the practical and vocational content of school courses was so restricted and the opportunities for post-school training were both limited and poor, the prospects for many appeared rather bleak. It is scarcely surprising therefore that many teachers found difficulty in coping with an extra year's schooling when the age limit was raised to 16, or that most pupils and parents should welcome the day of release from compulsory education.

Thus for many parents there has not been a great deal of opportunity to influence the decision-making process in education. Much of the pressure for change has arisen within the education service itself, or has been initiated or prompted by the educational intelligentsia, the press and the local political parties (Kogan 1978 150). These interest groups have been dominated by the articulate middle class, as have the political alignments within the LEAs. The same people also monopolised the school governing boards, the parents' evening meetings, the extra-curricular activities in schools, and much else besides. Effectively they have stifled the views of a wider public and ensured that their own requirements were satisfied. This is one reason why the pressure for better vocational education and training has been so muted.

The cultural heritage

Most commentators when writing about the British economy or the educational system refer to the cultural handicap (Wiener 1981; Lewis 1991; Barnett 1977; 1991; Alford 1988). Some in fact regard it as a crucial impediment to Britain's economic revival and the reform of the educational system, arguing that nothing short of a funda-mental shift in cultural attitudes will solve her long-standing prob-lems (Lewis 1991; Lorenz 1982; Barnett 1977; 1991). However, critics would counter that because it is difficult to put a quantitative value on such factors they must perforce be regarded as of limited significance.

Yet the cultural issue is too pervasive to be ignored altogether given its long lineage and persistance. The basic manifestations are said to be a general disdain for industry as opposed to non-industrial pursuits, an emphasis on intellectual and academic achievement rather than on the practical or productive, and a class system which is unique in the western world. The origins of the problem can be located in the nineteenth century when social values and attitudes were moulded by the writings of the social novelists such as Dickens, Gaskell, Brontë and the Kingsleys, and by the peculiarities of the English educational system. The novelists, while purporting to espouse the social cruelties of the time, became in essence a potent source of antipathy towards industrialists and business. Similarly, the education system, especially the public schools and the ancient universities, transmitted the social and cultural values of the landed and gentry classes to the industrial middle classes, values 'which virtually ignored the economic life of the country' (Ward 1967 52) and which bred an antipathy towards indus-trial pursuits and practical learning. As Barnett (1977 244) observes: 'The outlook of the Victorian public school and university has per-meated into our state education, so that the national outlook is hardly more sympathetic towards achieving industrial success than it was fifty years ago. University students evade scientific courses; they look for careers outside industry.'

The cultural dichotomy has many different facets which can be illustrated by a few simple examples. For example, German hosts when entertaining foreign visitors will more than likely proudly show them some vast industrial complex. Can one imagine the British doing this? They, by contrast, will treat their guests to a tour of some medieval church, baronial estate or museum. An industrial estate or works' tour would be the last thing on the list, if at all, and then it would be denigrated as an aesthetic monstrosity or environmental hazard (Aldcroft 1982 61). On a differnt tack, Christopher Lorenz (1982) contrasts the popularity of a rural soap opera such as *The Archers* compared with the failure of *On the Line*, a sort of industrial *Archers* with lots of technical detail, noisy machinery and other details of the everyday life of a business community. Regardless of the technical merits of the respective programmes, Lorenz believes that their different success rating reflects something more fundamental, namely 'the deep-rooted attraction to rural values, and antipathy towards industrial ones, which has been bred into most middle-class English men and women for over a century by the educational system and by the very structure of society'. In similar vein one might mention the virtual absence in quiz programmes of questions on industry and the economy; or the hostility engendered whenever planning permission is sought for a new factory or industrial estate; or again, the squalls of protest that occur when a firm announces large profits.

Lorenz believes this anti-industrial culture, together with the very closely associated barriers of the class system, to be one of the main reasons for Britain's poor economic performance during the past century. This may be pitching it a bit strongly though there seems little reason to doubt that it has been an important contributing factor in her relative economic decline. The intellectual and social climate in Britain can scarcely be said to be sympathetic to business success or to the idea that management in industry is a worthwhile career for the talented graduate. The intellectual élite tend to seek openings in the professions, in teaching, research and the public service rather than in the making of artefacts, and there is very little transmutation of talent between different occupations as there is in France and Germany (NEDC 1970 2). Fidler (1981 44, 155, 209) notes how top management tends to distance itself from the production process and contact with the workers, thus perpetuating the gap between workers and management to an extent almost unparalleled in the western world

(Tylecote 1977 26–32; Dore 1973 251). This could reflect a genuine dislike or ignorance of the 'dark industrial areas', or it may signify a more deep-seated aversion to being in business and making things.

Bayer and Lawrence (1977 226–7) sought to contrast the different attitudes towards education and industry in Britain and Germany. In Germany vocational subjects enjoy parity of esteem with academic ones and there is no inherent incompatibility between vocational preparation and education. By contrast, in Britain the prestigious subjects are the academic and theoretical ones, and most vocationally-orientated subjects, apart from medicine and law, are deemed to be of lower status and by definition more suitable for less able students. This ranking reflects the low status accorded to industry and engineering, occupations once regarded as not fit for gentlemen, and now it seems not suitable for the intellectual. Such prejudices are almost unknown in Germany where, if anything, vocational and practical occupations are prized more highly than others. As Bayer and Lawrence (1977 226) record:

> There is no stigma attached to making money in Germany and perhaps more important, no stigma attached to making three dimensional artefacts. And to be 'in industry' in Germany is to bask in the sunny legacy of the *Wirtschaftswunder*, whereas the connotation in Britain is one of lame dogs and Government rescues. The point becomes very clear if one notes the only two vocational subjects in Britain which do attract a high proportion of good 'A' level students, notably Law and Medicine. Firstly they are old, established and traditional professions. Secondly, they lead to employment either as a free professional or in the public sector. And thirdly, and this is the key point, they have nothing to do with industry.

The educational system in Britain may not be solely responsible for the persistance of the two-dimensional cultural syndrome in Britain but it does have a lot to answer for. Evans and Summerfield (1990 17), in their overview of a series of informative papers on technical education since 1850, come to the conclusion that institutional values averse to practical training in the educational structure, alongside tensions between local and central control and the absence of a powerful employers' lobby in support of technical education, have been the key factors in retarding the development of technical education. Clearly then the erosion of those values and the breakdown of the cultural barrier, to allow the entry of the third culture, *Technik*, to take its rightful place alongside the other two, will have to occur through the educational system since this is where much of the problem originates. From primary school to university the intellectual climate is still very much geared to preserving the traditional cultural heritage and blocking the emergence of vocational talent on which Britain's economic future depends.

REFERENCES

ABBOT, A. (1933). *Education for Industry and Commerce in England*. London, Oxford University Press.

ACTON SOCIETY TRUST (1956). *Management Succession*. London, Acton Society Trust.

ADONIS, A. (1991). 'Bottom of the Class', *Financial Times*, 21 May 1991.

AHIER, J. and FLUDE, M. (1983). *Contemporary Education Policy*. Beckenham, Croom Helm.

AHLSTROM, G. (1982). *Engineers and Industrial Growth*. London, Croom Helm.

ALBU, A. (1980). 'British Attitudes to Engineering Education: A Historical Perspective', in K.Pavitt, ed. *Technical Innovation and British Economic Performance*. London, Macmillan.

ALDCROFT, D.H. (1982). 'Britain's Economic Decline, 1870–1980', in G.Roderick and M.Stephens, eds. *The British Malaise: Industrial Performance, Education and Training in Britain Today*. Sussex, The Falmer Press.

ALDCROFT, D.H. (1987). 'The Machine-Tool Industry', *The Economic Review*, 4.

ALDCROFT, D.H. (1990). 'Education and Britain's Growth Failure 1950–1980', in G.Tortella, ed. *Education and Economic Development since the Industrial Revolution*. Valencia, Generalitat Valenciana.

ALDCROFT, D.H. (1991). 'Technical and Structural Factors in British Industrial Decline 1870 to the Present', in P. Mathias and J.A.Davis, eds. *Innovation and Technology in Europe: From the Eighteenth Century to the Present Day*. Oxford, Blackwell.

ALFORD, B.W.E. (1988). *British Economic Performance 1945–1975*. London, Macmillan.

ALTERS, P. (1987). *The Reluctant Patron: Science and the State in Britain, 1850–1920*. Oxford, Berg.

ANDERSON C.A. and BOWMAN M.J. (1976). 'Education and Economic Modernisation in Historical Perspective', in L.S.Stone, ed. *Schooling and Society*. Baltimore, Johns Hopkins University Press.

ANDERSON, D. (1957). 'Education and Training for the Engineering Industry', *The Engineer*, cciv.

ANDERSON, M. and FAIRLEY, J. (1983). 'The Politics of Industrial Training in the United Kingdom', *Journal of Public Policy*, 3.

ANGLO-AMERICAN COUNCIL ON PRODUCTIVITY (1951). *Education for Management: Report of a Visit to the US in 1951 of a Specialist Team Concerned with Education for Management.* London.

ARGYLES, M. (1964). *South Kensington to Robbins: An Account of English Technical and Scientific Education since 1951.* London, Longman.

ARROW, K. (1973). 'Education as a Filter', *Journal of Political Economy*, 81.

ASCHER, K. (1983). *Management Training in Large UK Business Organisations: A Survey.* London, Harbridge House Europe.

ASHTON, D.N. (1986). *Unemployment under Capitalism: The Sociology of British and American Labour Markets.* Brighton, Wheatsheaf Books.

BAIROCH, P. (1975). *The Economic Development of the Third World since 1900.* Methuen, London.

BANHAM J. (1989). 'Vocational Training in British Business', *National Westminster Bank Quarterly Review*, February.

BANNOCK, G. (1971). *The Juggernauts: The Age of the Big Corporation.* London, Weidenfeld and Nicolson.

BANNOCK, G. (1981). *The Economics of Small Firms.* Oxford, Blackwell.

BARLOW Report (1946). *Scientific Manpower.* Cmd 6824. London, HMSO.

BARNETT, C. (1977). 'The Hundred Year Sickness', *Industrial and Commercial Training*, June.

BARNETT, C. (1979). 'Technology, Education and Industrial Economic Strength', *Journal of the Royal Society of Arts*, 127.

BARNETT, C. (1985). 'Long-term Industrial Performance in the UK: the Role of Education and Research 1850–1939', in D.J.Morris, ed. *The Economic System in the UK.* Oxford, Oxford University Press.

BARNETT, C. (1986). *The Audit of War.* London, Macmillan.

BARNETT, C. (1991). 'The Educational Battle Begins, 120 Years Too Late', *The Sunday Times*, 26 May.

BARTLETT, C.J. (1977). *A History of Postwar Britain 1945–1974.* London, Longman.

BATES, I. (1984). *Schooling for the Dole? The New Vocationalism.* London, Macmillan.

BAVRITT, D. (1956–7). 'The Stated Qualifications of Directors of Larger Public Companies', *Journal of Industrial Economics*, 5.

BAXTER, J.L. and McCORMICK, B.J. (1984). 'Seventy Per Cent of Our Future. The Education, Training and Employment of Young People', *National Westminster Bank Quarterly Review*, August.

BAYER, H. and LAWRENCE, P. (1977). 'Engineering Education and the State of Industry', *European Journal of Engineering Education*, 2.

BECKER, G.S. (1964). *Human Capital.* Princeton, N.J. Princeton University Press.

BECKER, G.S. (1975). *Human Capital.* New York, Columbia University Press.

References

BECKERMAN, W. ed. (1979). *Slow Growth in Britain*. Oxford, Clarendon Press.

BEECHAM, B.J. (1982). 'The Universities and Technical Education in England and Wales', *Journal of Higher and Further Education*, 6

BELOE REPORT (1960). *Secondary School Examinations Other Than G.C.E.*, London, HMSO.

BERG, I. (1973). *Education and Jobs: The Great Training Robbery*. Harmondsworth, Penguin Education.

BETTS, R. (1967). 'Characteristics of British Company Directors', *Journal of Management Studies*, 4.

BLAUG, M. (1970). *An Introduction to the Economics of Education*. London, Allen Lane, The Penguin Press.

BLAUG, M. (1976). 'The Empirical Status of Human Capital Theory: A Slightly Jaundiced Survey', *Journal of Economic Literature*, 14.

BLAUG, M. (1985). 'Where Are We Now in the Economics of Education?' *Economics of Education Review*, 4.

BLAUG, M. PESTON, M. and RIDERMAN, A. (1967). *The Utilisation of Manpower in Industry: A Preliminary Report*. Edinburgh, Oliver and Boyd.

BOLTON COMMITTEE (1971). *Report of the Committee of Inquiry into Small Firms*. Cmnd. 4811. London, HMSO.

BOSWELL, J. (1973). *The Rise and Decline of Small Firms*. London, Allen & Unwin.

BOSWELL, J.S. (1976). *Social and Business Enterprise: An Introduction to Organisational Economics*. London, Allen & Unwin.

BOSWORTH, D. and WILSON, R. (1980). 'The Labour Market for Scientists and Technologists', in R.M.Lindley, ed. *Economic Change and Employment Policy*. London, Macmillan.

BOSWORTH REPORT (1966). *Report on Education and Training Requirements for the Electrical and Mechanical Manufacturing Industries*. London, HMSO.

BOYSON, R. (1975). *The Crisis in Education*. London, The Woburn Press.

BRANSON, N. and HEINEMANN, M. (1971). *Britain in the Nineteen Thirties*. London, Weidenfeld and Nicolson.

BRAUN, F. (1987). 'Vocational Training as a Link between Schools and the Labour Market: The Dual System in the Federal Republic of Germany', *Comparative Education*, 23.

BRENNAN, E.J.T. (1977). 'The Great Debate: Some Personal Reflections', *The Vocational Aspects of Education*, 29.

BRIDGES, J. (1991). 'Youth Training – Now We Are One', *Department of Employment Gazette*, July.

BRITISH INSTITUTE OF MANAGEMENT (1976). *Front-line Management: Report of the British Institute of Management Working Party*. London, The British Institute of Management.

BRUCE, P. (1983). 'Five Point Revival Plan for Enginering Industry', *The*

Financial Times, 28 April.

BURGESS, T. (1977). *Education after School.* London, Gollancz.

BURGESS, T. and PRATT, J. (1970). *Policy and Practice: The Colleges of Advanced Technology.* Harmondsworth, Allen Lane.

BURGESS, T. and PRATT, J. (1971). *Innovation in Higher Education: Technical Education in the United Kingdom.* Paris, OECD.

BRYCE REPORT (1895). *Report of the Royal Commission on Secondary Education.* C. 7862. London, HMSO.

CAIRNCROSS, A.K., KAY, J.A. and SILBERSTON, A. (1977). 'The Regeneration of Manufacturing Industry', *Midland Bank Review*, autumn.

CANTOR, L. (1985). 'Vocational Education and Training: The Japanese Approach', *Comparative Education*, 21.

CANTOR, L.M. and ROBERTS, I.F. (1986). *Further Education Today: A Critical Approach.* London, Routledge & Kegan Paul.

CARR REPORT (1958). *Training for Skill: Recruitment and Training of Young Workers in Industry.* London, HMSO.

CARTER C., ed. (1981). *Industrial Policy and Innovation.* London, Heinemann Educational.

CARTER, C. and PINDER, J. (1982). *Policies for a Constrained Economy* London, Heinemann Educational.

CARTER C.F. and WILLIAMS, B.R. (1957). *Industry and Technical Progress.* Oxford, Oxford University Press.

CARTER, M. (1966). *Into Work.* Harmondsworth, Penguin Books.

CASSELS, J. (1990). *Britain's Real Skill Shortage and What To Do About It.* London, Policy Studies Institute.

CAVES, R.E. ed. (1968). *Britain's Economic Prospects.* London, Allen & Unwin.

CAVES, R.E. (1980). 'Productivity Differences Among Industrial Countries', in R.E.Caves and L.B.Krause, eds. *Britain's Economic Performance.* Washington D.C., Brookings Institution.

CENTRAL POLICY REVIEW STAFF (1975). *The Future of the British Car Industry.* London, HMSO.

CENTRAL POLICY REVIEW STAFF (1980). *Education, Training and Industrial Performance.* London, HMSO.

CENTRAL STATISTICAL OFFICE (annual). *Annual Abstract of Statistics.* London, HMSO.

CERYCH, L. (1983). 'International Comparisons', in G. Williams and T. Blackstone, eds. *Response to Adversity: Higher Education in a Harsh Climate.* Guildford, Surrey, Society for Research into Higher Education.

CHANDLER, A.D. (1976). 'The Development of Modern Management Structure in the US and UK', in L. Hannah, ed. *Management Strategy and Business Development.* London, Macmillan.

CHANDLER, A.D. (1980). 'The Growth of Transnational Industrial Firms in the United States and the United Kingdom: A Comparative Analysis', *Economic*

History Review, 33.

CHANDLER, A.D. (1990). *Scale and Scope: The Dynamics of Industrial Capitalism*. Cambridge, Mass., The Belknap Press of Harvard University Press.

CHANNON, D.F. (1973). *Strategy and Structure of British Enterprise*. London, Macmillan.

CHAPMAN, P. and TOOZE, M. (1987). *The Youth Training Scheme in the UK*. Aldershot, Gower.

CHILD, J. and PARTRIDGE, B. (1982). *Lost Managers: Supervisors in Industry and Society*. Cambridge, Cambridge University Press.

CHISHOLM, M. (1982). *Modern World Development*. London, Hutchinson.

CIPOLLA, C.M. (1969). *Literacy and Development in the West*. Harmondsworth, Penguin Books.

CLARE, J. (1986). 'The Victims of Comprehensive Education: Streamed for Failure in the Name of Equality and Socialism', *The Listener*, 5 June.

CLARK, D.G. (1966). *The Industrial Manager*. London, Businesss Publications.

CLARKE, J. and REES, A. (1989). 'Postgraduate Education and Training – Survey of 1980 Graduates and Diplomates', *Department of Employment Gazette*, 97, September.

CLEMENTS, R.V. (1958). *Managers: A Study of the Careers in Industry*. London, Allen & Unwin.

COCKCROFT COMMITTEE (1982). *Report of the Committee of Inquiry into the Teaching of Mathematics*. London, HMSO.

COLE, G.D.H. and M.I. (1937). *The Condition of Britain*. London, Gollancz.

COLEMAN, D.C. (1973). 'Gentlemen and Players', *Economic History Review*, 26.

COLEMAN, D.C. (1980). *Courtaulds: An Economic and Social History: Crisis and Change 1940–1965*. Oxford, Oxford University Press.

COLLINS, B. and ROBBINS, K., eds. (1990). *British Culture and Economic Decline*. London, Weidenfeld and Nicolson.

COMMAND PAPER (9703 1956). *Technical Education*. London, HMSO.

COMMAND PAPER (7368 1978). *Secondary School Examinations: A Single System at 16 Plus*. London, HMSO.

COMMAND PAPER (8455 1981) *A New Training Initiative: A Programme for Action*. London, HMSO.

COMMAND PAPER (8836 1983). *Teaching Quality*. London, HMSO.

COMMAND PAPER (9135 1984). *Training for Jobs*, London, HMSO.

COMMAND PAPER (9469 1985). *Better Schools*. London, HMSO.

COMMAND PAPER (9524 1985). *The Development of Higher Education into the 1990s*. London, HMSO.

COMMAND PAPER (9823 1986). *Working Together: Education and Training*. London, HMSO.

COMMAND PAPER (114 1987). *Higher Education: Meeting the Challenge*.

London, HMSO.

COMMITTEE OF VICE-CHANCELLORS AND PRINCIPALS (1986). *The Future of Universities*. London.

CONFEDERATION OF BRITISH INDUSTRIES (1989). *Towards a Skills Revolution*. London, CBI.

CONNELL, D. (1979). *The UK's Performance in Export Markets: Some Evidence from International Trade Data*. London, National Economic Development Office.

CONSTABLE, J. and McCORMICK, B. (1987). *The Making of British Managers: A Report for the BIM and CBI into Managemnet Training, Education and Development*. London, British Institute of Management.

COOPERS LYBRAND ASSOCIATES (1985). *A Challenge to Complacency: Changing Attitudes to Training. A Report to the Manpower Services Commission and the National Economic Development Office*. London, Manpower Services Commission and National Economic Development Office.

COPEMAN, G.H. (1955). *Leaders of British Industry*. London, Gee & Company.

COYLE, D. (1991). 'Why Is Britain So Bad At Exporting', *Investors Chronicle*, 8 March.

CROCKETT, G. and ELIAS, P. (1984). 'British Managers: A Study of Their Education, Training, Mobility and Earnings', *British Journal of Industrial Relations*, 22.

CROWTHER REPORT (1959). *Fifteen to Eighteen: Report of the Central Advisory Council for Education*. London, HMSO.

DAINTON REPORT (1968). *Enquiry into the Flow of Candidates in Science and Technology into Higher Education*. Cmnd. 3541. London, HMSO.

DALE, R. ed. (1981). *Schooling and the National Interest*. Sussex, The Falmer Press.

DALE, R. ed. (1985). *Education, Training and Employment*. Oxford, Pergamon Press.

DALY, A. (1981). 'Government Support for Innovation in the British Machine Tool Industry: A Case Study', in C. Carter, ed. *Industrial Policy and Innovation*. London, Heinemann Educational.

DALY, A. (1982). 'The Contribution of Education to Economic Growth in Britain: A Note on the Evidence', *National Institute Economic Review*, August.

DALY, A. (1984). 'Education, Training and Productivity in the United States and Great Britain', *National Institute of Economic and Social Research Discussion Paper*, No. 63.

DALY, A. and JONES, D.T. (1980). 'The Machine Tool Industry in Britain, Germany and the United States', *National Institute Economic Review*, May.

DALY, A. HITCHENS, D.M.W.N. and WAGNER, K. (1985). 'Productivity, Machinery and Skills in a Sample of British and German Manufacturing Plants', *National Institute Economic Review*, February.

DAVIES, S and CAVES, R.E. (1987). *Britain's Productivity Gap*. Cambridge, Cambridge University Press.

DE BETTIGNIES and EVANS, P.L. (1977). 'The Cultural Dimension of Top Executives' Careers: A Comparative Analysis', in T.D.Weinshall, ed. *Culture and Management*. Harmondsworth, Penguin.

DE JONQUIERES, G. (1987). 'Research and Development', *Financial Times Supplment*, 9 July.

DE VILLE, H.G. et. al. (1986). *Review of Vocational Qualfications in England and Wales*. London, HMSO.

DEAKIN, B.M. and PRATTEN, C.F. (1987). 'Economic Effects of YTS', *Department of Employment Gazette*, 95, October.

DEEKS, J. (1972). 'Educational and Occupational Histories of Owner-managers and Managers', *The Journal of Management Studies*, 9.

DENISON, E.F. (1967). *Why Growth Rates Differ*. Washington D.C., Brookings Institution.

DEPARTMENT OF EDUCATION AND SCIENCE (annual). *Education Statistics for the United Kingdom*. London, HMSO.

DEPARTMENT OF EDUCATION AND SCIENCE (1976). *Getting Ready for Work: 16–19*. London, HMSO.

DEPARTMENT OF EDUCATION AND SCIENCE (1978). *Higher Education into the 1990s: A Discussion Document*. London, Department of Education and Science.

DEPARTMENT OF EDUCATION AND SCIENCE (1986). *Education in the Federal Republic of Germany: Aspects of Curriculum and Assessment*. London, HMSO.

DEPARTMENT OF EDUCATION AND SCIENCE (1989a). *Selected National Education Systems: A Description of Six More Countries*. London, Department of Education and Science.

DEPARTMENT OF EDUCATION AND SCIENCE (1989b). *Standards of Education 1987–88: Annual Report of HM Chief Inspector of Schools*. London, HMSO.

DEPARTMENT OF EDUCATION AND SCIENCE (1991). *Aspects of Vocational Education and Training in the Federal Republic of Germany*. London, HMSO.

DEPARTMENT OF EMPLOYMENT (1974). *Unqualified, Untrained and Unemployed*. London, HMSO.

DEPARTMENT OF EMPLOYMENT (1990). *Training Statistics 1990*. London, HMSO.

DEPARTMENT OF INDUSTRY (1977). *Education, Industry and Management: A Discussion Paper*. London, HMSO.

DIVALL, C. (1990). 'A Measure of Agreement: Employers and Engineering Studies in the Universities of England and Wales, 1897–1939', *Social Studies of Science*, 20.

DIVALL, C. (1991). 'Fundamental Science Versus Design: Employers and Engineering Studies in British Universities, 1935–1976', *Minerva*, 29.

DIXON, M. (1987). 'Cosmetic Change in Education', *Financial Times*, 9 June.

DONOVAN REPORT (1968). *Report of the Royal Commission on Trade Unions and Employers Associations (1965–1968)*. Cmnd. 3623. London, HMSO.

DORE, R. (1973). *British Factory Japanese Factory: The Origins of National Diversity in Industrial Relations*. London, Allen & Unwin.

DORE, R. (1976). *The Diploma Disease*. London, Allen & Unwin.

DORE, R. and SAKO, M. (1989). *How the Japanese Learn to Work*. London, Routledge.

DUBIN, R. (1970). 'Management in Britain – Impressions of a Visiting Professor', *The Journal of Management Studies*, 7.

DUDLEY, N. (1977). 'Engineers' Concepts of Productive Efficiency', in C.Bowe, ed. *Industrial Efficiency and the Role of Government*. London, HMSO.

DUNDAS-GRANT, V. (1989). 'Vocational and Technical Education in France', *National Westminster Bank Quarterly Review*, February.

DUNNETT, P.J.S. (1980). *The Decline of the British Motor Industry: The Effect of Government Policy*. London, Croom Helm.

EASTERLIN, R.A. (1981). 'Why Isn't the Whole World Developed', *Journal of Economic History*, 41.

THE ECONOMIST (1981). 'Repairing Britain's Engineers', 21 February.

EDWARDES, M. (1983). *Back from the Brink*. London, Collins.

EHRLICH, E. (1985). 'Infrastructure', in M.C.Kaser and E.A.Radice, eds. *The Economic History of Eastern Europe 1919–1975. I: Economic Structure and Performance between the Two Wars*. Oxford, Oxford University Press.

EVANS, E.W. (1964). 'The British Machine Tool Industry', *The Three Banks Review*, 62, June.

EVANS E.W. and N.C. WISEMAN (1984). 'Education, Training and Economic Performance: British Economists' Views, 1868–1939', *Journal of European Economic History*, 13.

FAGERLIND, I. and SAHA, L.J. (1989). *Education and National Development: A Comparative Perspective*. Oxford, Pergamon Press.

FIDLER, J. (1981). *The British Business Elite: The Attitudes to Class, Status and Power*. London, Routledge & Kegan Paul.

FINEGOLD, D. and SOSKICE, D. (1988). 'The Failure of Training in Britain: Analysis and Perspective', *Oxford Review of Economic Policy*, 4.

FINNISTON COMMITTEE (1980). *Engineering Our Future: Report of the Committee of Inquiry into the Enginering Profession*. Cmnd. 7794. London, HMSO.

FISHLOCK, D. (1987). 'British Science Policy: Science Wakes Up to the Realities of a Changing World'. *Financial Times*, 9 June.

FONDA, N. and HAYES, C. (1988). 'Education, Training and Business Performance', *Oxford Review of Economic Policy*, 4.

FORES, M. and CLARK, D. (1975). 'Why Sweden Manages Better', *Management Today*, February.

FORES, M. and GLOVER, I., eds. (1978). *Manufacturing and Management*. London, HMSO.

FORES, M. and PRATT, J. (1980). 'Engineering: Our Last Chance', *Higher Education Review*, 12.

FORES, M. and SORGE, A. (1981). 'The Decline of the Manufacturing Ethic', *Journal of General Managament*, 7.

FORES, M., LAWRENCE, P. and SORGE, A. (1978). 'Germany's Front Line Force', *Management Today*, March.

FORES, M., SORGE, A. and LAWRENCE, P. (1978). 'Why Germany Produces Better', *Management Today*. November.

FRANKS REPORT (1963). *British Business Schools*. London, British Institute of Management.

FREEMAN, C. (1962). 'Research and Development: A Comparison Between British and American Industry', *National Institute Economic Review*, May.

FREEMAN, C. (1979). 'Technical Innovation and British Trade Performance', in F.Blackaby, ed. *Deindustrialisation*. London, Heinemann.

FREEMAN, C. (1980). 'Government Policy', in K.Pavitt, ed. *Technical Innovation and Economic Performance*. London, Macmillan.

FULTON, O. (1988). 'Elite Survivals? Entry Standards and Procedures for Higher Education Admissions', *Studies in Higher Education*, 13.

FULTON, O. (1990). 'Higher Education and Employment: Pressures and Responses since 1960', in P. Summerfield and E.J.Evans, eds. *Technical Education and the State since 1860*. Manchester, Manchester University Press.

FULTON, O., GORDON, A. and WILLIAMS, G. (1982). *Higher Education and Manpower Planning: A Comparative Study of Planned and Market Economies*. Geneva, ILO.

GAPPER, J. (1989). 'A Late Starter in the Race', *Financial Times*, 21 November.

GEORGE, K.D. and SHOREY, J. (1985). 'Manual Workers, Good Jobs amd Structured Internal Labour Markets', *British Journal of Industrial Relations*, 23.

GLEESON, D. (1987). *TVEI and Secondary Education: A Critical Appraisal*. Milton Keynes, Open University Press.

GLOVER, I. (1976). 'Executive Career Patterns: Britain, France, Germany and Sweden', *Energy World*, December.

GLOVER, I. (1978a). 'Executive Career Patterns: Britain, France, Germany and Sweden', in M. Fores and I. Glover, eds. *Manufacturing and Management*. London, HMSO.

GLOVER, I. (1978b). 'Professionalism and Manufacturing Industry', in M.Fores and I.Glover, eds. *Manufacturing and Management*. London, HMSO.

GLOVER, I.A. (1985). 'How the West Was Lost? Decline in Engineering and Manufacturing in Britain and the United States', *Higher Education Review*, 17.

GLOVER, I.A. and KELLY, M.P. (1987). *Engineers in Britain: A Sociological Study of the Engineering Dimension*. London, Allen & Unwin.

GOLDSMITH, W. and CLUTTERBUCK, D. (1985). *The Winning Streak*. Harmondsworth, Penguin.

GORDON, R.J. (1982). 'Why U.S. Wage and Employment Behaviour Differ from that in Britain and Japan', *Economic Journal*, 92.

GRANICK, D. (1962). *The European Executive*. New York, Doubleday & Co.

GRANICK, D. (1972). *Managerial Comparisons of Four Developed Countries: France, Britain, United States and Russia*. Cambridge, Mass., The MIT Press.

GRAYSON, L.P. (1983). 'Leadership or Stagnation? A Role for Technology in Mathematics, Science and Engineering Education', *Engineering Education*, February.

GRIFFITHS, J.G. (1989). 'The Illiteracy That Undermines Engineering Management', *Financial Times*, 23 August.

HADOW REPORT (1926). *Report of the Consultative Committee on the Education of the Adolescent*. London, Board of Education, HMSO.

HAGUE, H. (1991). 'Training a Workforce for a Competitive World', *The Independent on Sunday*, 24 March.

HANDY, M.C. (1987). *The Making of Managers: A Report on Management Education, Training and Development in the USA, West Germany, France, Japan and the UK*. London, National Economic Development Office.

HANDY, C. et al. (1988). *Making Managers*. London, Pitman.

HANNA, P.R. (1962). 'Education: An Instrument of National Purpose and Policy', in P.R.Hanna, ed. *Education: An Instrument of National Goals*. New York, McGraw-Hill Book Company.

HANNAH, L. (1976). *The Rise of the Corporate Economy*. London, Methuen.

HANNAH, L. (1980). 'Visible and Invisible Hands in Great Britain', in A.D.Chandler, jr. and H.Daems, eds. *Managerial Hierarchies: Comparative Perspectives on the Rise of the Modern Industrial Enterprise*. Cambridge, Mass., Harvard University Press.

HARBISON, F. and MYERS, C.A. (1964). *Education, Manpower and Economic Growth*. New York, McGraw-Hill Book Company.

HAYES, C. (1972). 'Manpower and Training Policies in Europe', *Personnel Review*, 1.

HAYES, R.H. and ABERNETHY, W.J. (1980). 'Managing Our Way to Economic Decline', *Harvard Business Review*, July–August.

HENNIKER-HEATON REPORT (1963). *Day Release*. London, HMSO.

HIGGINSON REPORT (1988). *Advancing A Levels*. London, HMSO.

HILL, J.M.M. and SCHARFF, D.E. (1976). *Between Two Worlds: Aspects of the Transition from School to Work*. London, Tavistock Institute.

HOLBERTON, S. (1990). 'A Social Revolution in the Boardroom', *Financial Times*, 3 November.

HOLLENSTEIN, H. (1982). 'Economic Performance and the Vocational Qualifications of the Swiss Labour Force Compared with Britain and Germany', National Institute of Economic and Social Research Discussion Paper, 54.

HOOPER, F. (1953). 'The Nation's Attitude to Industry', *The Manager*, January.

HOROVITZ, J.H. (1980). *Top Management Control in Europe*. London, Macmillan.

HOUGH, J.R. ed. (1984). *Educational Policy: An International Survey*. London, Croom Helm.

HOUGH, J.R. (1987). *Education and the National Economy*. London, Croom Helm.

HOUSE OF COMMONS (1976). *Report of the Select Committee on Science and Technology*. HC 680. London, HMSO.

HOUSE OF COMMONS (1976–7). *The Attainments of the School-leaver: Tenth Report from the Expenditure Committee*. HC 526-I. London, HMSO.

HOWARTH, J. (1987). 'Science Education in Late Victorian Oxford: A Curious Case of Failure?' *English Historical Review*, 102.

HUDSON INSTITUTE OF EUROPE (1974). *The United Kingdom in 1980: The Hudson Report*. London, Associated Business Programmes.

HUGHES, J.J. (1972). 'The Roles of Manpower Retraining Programmes: A Critical Look at Retraining in the United Kingdom', *British Journal of Industrial Relations*, 10.

HUSSEY, D.E. (1988). *Management Training and Corporate Strategy*. Oxford, Pergamon Press.

HUTTON, S.P. and LAWRENCE, P.A. (1980). *Production Management and Training: A Summary Report*. Southampton, Department of Mechanical Engineering, University of Southampton. Report 80/17.

HUTTON, S. and LAWRENCE, P. (1981). *German Engineers: The Anatomy of a Profession*. Oxford, Clarendon Press.

JAMES REPORT (1972). *Teacher Education and Training*. London HMSO.

JARVIS, V. and PRAIS, S.J. (1989). 'Two Nations of Shopkeepers: Training for Retailing in France and Britain', *National Institute Economic Review*, May.

JENKINS, D. (1980). 'The Real Skills Gap', *Management Today*, November.

JENNINGS, R.E. (1977). *Education and Politics: Policy Making in Local Education Authorities*. London, Batsford.

JOHNSON, C. (1990). 'Who Gets the Peace Dividend?' *Lloyds Bank Review*, April.

JOHNSON, P.S. (1971). 'The Economics of Training and the Industrial Training Boards', *Moorgate and Wall Street Journal*, autumn.

JOHNSTON, J. (1963). 'The Productivity of Management Consultants', *Journal of Royal Statistical Society*, A126, Part 2.

JONES, D.T. (1976). 'Output, Employment and Labour Productivity in Europe since 1955', *National Institute Economic Review*, August.

JONES, I. (1982). 'The New Training Initiative – An Evaluation', *National Institute Economic Review*, February.

JONES, I.S. (1984). 'Pay Relativities and the Provision of Training', *National Institute of Economic and Social Research Discussion Paper*, No. 77.

JONES, I. (1985). 'Skill Formation and Pay Relativities', in G.D.N.Worswick, ed. *Education and Economic Performance*. Aldershot, Gower.

JONES, I.S. (1986). 'Apprenticeship Training Costs in British Manufacturing Establishments: Some New Evidence', *British Journal of Industrial Relations*, November.

JONES, I. (1988). 'An Evaluation of YTS', *Oxford Review of Economic Policy*, 4.

JONES, I.S. and HOLLENSTEIN, H. (1983). 'Trainee Wages and Training Deficiences: An Economic Analysis of a British Problem', *National Institute of Economic and Social Research Discussion Paper*, No. 58.

JOWELL, R., WITHERSPOON, S. and BROOK, L., eds. (1986). *British Social Attitudes: The 1986 Report*. Aldershot, Gower.

KALDOR, M. SHARP, M. and WALKER W. (1986). 'Industrial Competitiveness and Britain's Defence', *Lloyds Bank Review*, October.

KATRAK, H. (1982). 'Labour Skills, R & D and Capital Requirements in International Trade and Investment of the United Kingdom, 1968–78', *National Institute Economic Review*, August.

KEEP, E. and MAYHEW, K. (1988). 'The Assessment: Education, Training amd Economic Performance', *Oxford Review of Economic Policy*, 4.

KEMPNER, T. (1983–4). 'Education for Management in Five Countries: Myth and Reality', *Journal of General Management*, 9.

KEOHANE REPORT (1979). *Proposals for a Certificate of Extended Education*. Cmnd. 7755. London, HMSO.

KINDLEBERGER, C.P. (1965). *Economic Development*. New York, McGraw-Hill Book Company.

KING, E.J. (1986). *Education and Social Change*. London, Pergamon.

KINGMAN COMMITTEE (1988). *Report of the Committee of Inquiry into the Teaching of the English Language*. London, HMSO.

KINMOUTH, E.H. (1986). 'Engineering Education and Its Rewards', *Comparative Education Review*, 30.

KNIGHT, C. (1990). *The Making of Tory Education Policy in Postwar Britain 1950–1986*. Sussex, The Falmer Press.

KOESTLER, A., ed. (1963). *Suicide of a Nation*. London, Hutchinson.

KOGAN, M. (1975). *Education Policy-Making: A Study of Interest Groups and Parliament*. London, Allen & Unwin.

KOGAN, M. (1978). *The Politics of Educational Change*. Manchester, Manchester University Press.

KOSTECKI, M. (1985). 'The Economic Foundations of Schooling', *Compare*, 15

KOVACEVIC, I. (1975). *Fact into Fiction: English Literature and the Industrial Scene 1750–1850.* Leicester, Leicester University Press.

KRUEGER, A.O. (1968). 'Factor Endowments and Per Capita Income Differences Among Countries', *Economic Journal*, 78.

LANDYMORE, P.J. (1985). 'Education and Industry since the War', in D.J.Morris, ed. *The Economic System in the UK.* Oxford, Oxford University Press.

LAUGLO, J. and LILLIS, K. (1988). *Vocationalising Education: An International Perspective.* Oxford, Pergamon.

LAWRENCE, P. (1980). *Managers and Management in West Germany.* London, Croom Helm.

LAYARD, P.R.R. et al. (1971). *Qualified Manpower and Economic Performance: An Inter-plant Study in the Electrical Engineering Industry.* London, Allen Lane.

LAYARD, R. and PRAIS, S. (1990). 'Employment Training: Time to Think About Compulsion', *Financial Times*, 15 March.

LAYARD, P.R. and SAIGAL, J.C. (1966). 'Educational and Occupational Characteristics of Manpower: An International Comparison', *British Journal of Industrial Relations*, 4.

LAYTON, D. (1984). *The Alternative Road: The Rehabilitation of the Practical.* Leeds, University of Leeds, Centre for Studies in Science and Mathematics Education.

LE GRAND, J. (1982). *The Strategy of Equality.* London, Allen & Unwin.

LEADBEATER, C. (1987a). 'The UK Skills Shortage: When It's Time to Stop Passing the Buck', *Financial Times*, 3 September.

LEADBEATER, C. (1987b). 'Managers' Apathy Threatens Jobs and Productivity', *Financial Times*, 4 September.

LEADBEATER, C. (1988a). 'Britain Badly Outpaced in Training Courses', *Financial Times*, 21 January.

LEADBEATER, C. (1988b). 'Risks Ahead on a Route Back to Work', *Financial Times*, 30 august.

LEADBEATER, C. (1988c). 'Time to Change the Culture', *Financial Times*, 5 December.

LEADBEATER, C. (1988d). 'The Crippling Shortage of Skills', *Financial Times*, 8 December.

LEADBEATER, C. (1991). 'No Chance of an Even Match', *Financial Times*, 18 June.

LEADBEATER, C. and GAPPER, J. (1988). 'Training White Paper – Employment for the 1990s', *Financial Times*, 6 December.

LEES, D. and CHIPLIN, B. (1970). 'The Economics of Industrial Training', *Lloyds Bank Review*, April.

LEGGATT. T. (1978). 'Managers in Industry – Their Background and Education', *Sociological Review*, 26.

LESTER, T. (1976). 'How the British Bikes Crashed', *Management Today*, May.

LEVITT, M.S. and JOYCE, M.A.S. (1987). *The Growth and Efficiency of Public Spending*. Cambridge, Cambridge University Press.

LEWCHUK, W. (1987). *American Technology and the British Vehicle Industry*. Cambridge, Cambridge University Press.

LEWIS, R. and STEWART, R. (1958). *The Managers: A New Examination of the English, German and American Executive*. New York, Mentor Books.

LEWIS, S. (1991). 'Cultural Shift Needed', *Investors Chronicle*, 5 April.

Liberal Industrial Inquiry (1928). *Britain's Industrial Future*. London, Ernest Benn.

LINDLEY, R. (1975). 'The Demand for Apprentice Recruits by the Engineering Industry', *Scottish Journal of Political Economy*, February.

LINDLEY, R. (1981). 'Education, Training and the Labour Market in Britain', *European Journal of Education*, 16.

LINDSAY, K. (1926). *Social Progress and Educational Waste*. London, Routledge.

LOCKE, M. and BLOOMFIELD, J. (1982). *Mapping and Reviewing the Pattern of 16–19 Education*. London, Schools Council.

LOCKE, M. and PRATT, J. (1979). *A Guide to Learning after School*. Harmondsworth, Penguin.

LOCKE, R.R. (1984). *The End of Practical Man: Entrepreneurship and Higher Education in Germany, France and Great Britain, 1880–1940*. Greenwich, Connecticut, JAI Press.

LOCKE, R.R. (1985a). 'Business Education in Germany: Past Systems and Current Practice', *Business History Review*, 59.

LOCKE, R.R. (1985b). 'The Relationship Between Educational and Managerial Cultures in Britain and West Germany: A Comparative Analysis of Higher Education from an Historical Perspective', in P.Joynt and M.Warner, eds. *Managing in Different Cultures*. Oslo, Universitetsforlaget.

LOCKE, R.R. (1988). 'Educational Traditions and the Development of Business Studies after 1945 (an Anglo-French-German Comparison)', *Business History*, 30.

LOCKE, R.R. (1989). *Management and Higher Education since 1940: The Influence of America and Japan on West Germany, Great Britain and France*. Cambridge, Cambridge University Press.

LOCKWOOD REPORT (1964). *Report of the Working Party on the Schools' Curricula and Examinations*. London, HMSO.

LOCKYER, K. (1976). 'The British Production Cinderalla. 2 – Facts', *Management Today*, June.

LODGE, D. (1988). *Nice Work*. London, Secker & Warburg.

LOMAX, D. (1989). 'Vocational Training', *National Westminster Bank Quarterly Review*, February.

LORENZ, C. (1982). 'Roots of the British Malaise', *Financial Times*, 15 September.

LORENZ, C. (1987). 'Management Education: Why Britain's Thirst Must Be Satisfied', *Financial Times*, 29 April.

LORRIMAN, J. (1986). 'Ichiban – the Japanese Approach to Engineering Education', *Electronics and Power*, August.

LYNN, R. (1988). *Educational Achievement in Japan: Lessons for the West*. London, Macmillan.

McCARTHY. S. (1990). 'Development Stalled: The Crisis in Africa: A Personal View', *European Investment Bank Papers*, December.

McCLELLAND, D.C. (1966). 'Does Education Accelerate Economic Growth?', *Economic Development and Cultural Change*, 14.

McCULLOCH, G. (1984). 'Views of the Alternative Road: the Crowther Concept', in D.Layton, ed. *The Alternative Road*. Leeds, University of Leeds Centre for Sudies in Science and Mathematics Education.

MACE, J. (1977). 'The Shortage of Engineers', *Higher Education Reveiw*, 10.

MACE, J. (1987). 'Education, the Labour Market and Government Policy', in H.Thomas and T.Simkins, eds. *Economics and the Management of Education: Emerging Themes*. Lewes, Sussex, The Falmer Press.

MACFARLANE REPORT (1981). *Education for 16–19 Year Olds: A Review Undertaken for the Government and the Local Authority Associations*. Middlesex, DES.

MACGREGOR, I. (1987). *The Enemies Within: The Story of the Miners' Strike 1984–5*. London, Fontana/Collins.

MADDISON, A. (1982). *Phases of Capitalist Development*. Oxford, Oxford University Press.

MADDISON, A. (1986). *Latin America, the Caribbean and the OECD*. Paris, OECD.

MADDISON, A. (1987). 'Growth and Slowdown in Advanced Capitalist Economies', *Journal of Economic Literature*, June.

MADDISON, A (1989). *The World Economy in the Twentieth Century*. Paris, OECD.

MALING, J.J. (1979). 'The Maling Theory of Management', *Investors Chronicle*, 31 August.

MALLIER, T., MORWOOD, S. and OLD, J. (1990). 'Assessment Methods and Economics Degrees', *Assessment and Evaluation in Higher Education*, 15.

MANGHAM, I.L. and SILVER, M.S. (1986). *Management Training: Context and Practice*. Bath, University of Bath School of Management.

MANPOWER SERVICES COMMISSION (1977). *Young People and Work. Report on the Feasibility of a New Programme of Opportunities for Unemployed Young People*. London, HMSO.

MANPOWER SERVICES COMMISSION (1987). *The Funding of Vocational Education and Training: Some Early Research Findings. Background Paper*. Sheffield, Manpower Services Commission.

MANT, A. (1977). *The Rise and Fall of the British Manager*. London, Macmillan.

MANT, A. (1978). 'Authority and Task in Manufacturing Operations of Multi-national Firms', in M.Fores and I.Glover, eds. *Manufacturing and Management.* London, HMSO.

MARSDEN, D., TRINDER, C. and WAGNER, K. (1986). 'Measures to Reduce Youth Unemployment in Britain, France and West Germany', *National Institute Economic Review*, August.

MATHIESON, M. and BERNBAUM, G. (1988). 'The British Disease: A British Tradition', *Journal of Educational Studies*, 36.

MATTHEWS, R.C.O., FEINSTEIN, C.H. and ODLING-SMEE, J.C. (1982). *British Economic Growth 1856–1973.* Stanford, Calif., Stanford University Press.

METCALFE, J.S. (1970). 'Diffusion of Innovation in the Lancashire Textile Industry', *Manchester School*, 38.

MILLAR, J. (1979). *British Management Versus German Management: A Comparison of Organisational Effectiveness in West German and UK Factories.* Westmead, Hampshire, Saxon House.

MILLS, C.T. (1925). *Technical Education: Its Development and Aims.* London, Edward Arnold.

MORGAN, K.O. (1990). *The People's Peace: British History 1945–1989.* Oxford, Oxford University Press.

MORRIS, V. (1973). 'Investment in Higher Education in England and Wales: the Human Capital Approach to Educational Planning', in G.Fowler, V.Morris and J.Ozga, eds. *Decision-Making in British Education.* London, Heinemann.

MORRIS, V. and ZIDERMAN, A. (1971). 'The Economic Return on Investment in Higher Education in England and Wales', *Economic Trends*, May.

MOWAT, C.L. (1955). *Britain Between the Wars 1918–1940.* London, Methuen.

MUELLER, A. (1977). 'Industrial Efficiency and UK Government Policy', in C.Bowe, ed. *Industrial Efficiency and the Role of Government.* London, HMSO.

MUSGRAVE, P.W. (1967). *Technical Change, the Labour Force and Education: A Study of the British and German Iron and Steel Industries, 1860–1964.* Oxford, Pergamon.

NATIONAL ECONOMIC DEVELOPMENT COUNCIL (1963). *Conditions Favourable to Faster Growth.* London, HMSO.

NATIONAL ECONOMIC DEVELOPMENT COUNCIL (1965). *Management Recruitment and Development.* London, HMSO.

NATIONAL ECONOMIC DEVELOPMENT COUNCIL (1970). *Management Education in the 1970s: Growth and Issues.* London, HMSO.

NATIONAL ECONOMIC DEVELOPMENT COUNCIL (1983). *Education and Industry.* London, HMSO.

NATIONAL ECONOMIC DEVELOPMENT COUNCIL (1984). *Competence and Competition: Training and Education in the Federal Republic of Germany, the United States and Japan.* London, HMSO.

NEW, C. and MYERS, A. (1986). *Managing Manufacturing Operations in the UK 1975–85*. London, Institute of Manpower Studies.

NEWSOM REPORT (1963). *Half Our Future: Report of the Central Advisory Council for Education*. London, HMSO.

NICHOLS, T. (1969). *Ownership, Control and Ideology*. London, Allen & Unwin.

NICHOLSON, A. (1976). 'The British Production Cinderalla. 1 – Causes', *Management Today*, June.

NORWOOD REPORT (1943). *Report of the Committee of the Secondary Schools Examinations Council on Curriculum and Examinations in Secondary Schools*. London, Board of Education, HMSO.

O'BRIEN, R. (1988). 'Training in the UK: Swedes Show How to Save Money by Spending It', *Financial Times*, 4 May.

ODAGIRI, H. (1981). *The Theory of Growth in a Corporate Economy: Management Preference, Research and Development and Economic Growth*. Cambridge, Cambridge University Press.

OECD (1974a). *The Educational Situation in OECD Countries*. Paris, OECD.

OECD (1974b). *Educational Statistics Yearbook. 1: International Tables*. Paris, OECD.

OECD (1979). *Policies for Apprenticeship*. Paris, OECD.

OECD (1980). *Report on Vocational Education*. Paris, OECD.

OECD (1981). *Educational Statistics in OECD Countries*. Paris, OECD.

OECD (1983a). *Compulsory Schooling in a Changing World*. Paris, OECD.

OECD (1983b). *The Future of Vocational Education and Training*. Paris, OECD.

OECD (1983c). *Policies for Higher Education in the 1980s*. Paris, OECD.

OECD (1984). *Educational Trends in the 1970s: A Quantitative Analysis*. Paris, OECD.

OECD (1985a). *Education in a Modern Society*. Paris, OECD.

OECD (1985b). *Education and Training after Basic Schooling*. Paris, OECD.

OECD (1989). *Education in OECD Countries 1986–87: A Compendium of Statistical Information*. Paris, OECD.

PAGE, R.M. (1991). 'Social Welfare since the War', in N.F.R.Crafts and N.W.C.Woodward, eds. *The British Economy since 1945*. Oxford, Oxford University Press.

PAVITT, K. (1980). *Technical Innovation and British Economic Performance*. London, Macmillan.

PERCY REPORT (1945). *Higher Technological Education*. London, HMSO.

PERLMAN, R. (1988). 'Education and Training: An American Perspective', *Oxford Review of Economic Policy*, 4.

PETERS, A.J. (1967). *British Further Education*. Oxford, Pergamon.

PISSARIDES, C. (1982). 'From School to University: The Demand for Post-Compulsory Education in Britain', *Economic Journal*, 92.

PLOWDEN REPORT (1967). *Children and Their Primary Schools: Report of the Central Advisory Council for Education (England)*. London, HMSO.

POLITICAL AND ECONOMIC PLANNING (1965). *Thrusters and Sleepers: A Study of Attitudes in Industrial Management*. London, Allen & Unwin.

POLLARD, S. (1989). *Britain's Prime and Britain's Decline: The British Economy 1870–1914*. London, Edward Arnold.

PORTER, M. (1990). *The Competitive Advantage of Nations*. London, Macmillan.

PRAIS, S.J. (1981a). *Productivity and Industrial Structure*. Cambridge, Cambridge University Press.

PRAIS, S.J. (1981b). 'Vocational Qualifications of the Labour Force in Britain and Germany', *National Institute Economic Review*, November.

PRAIS, S.J. (1986). 'Educating for Productivity: Comparisons of Japanese and English Schooling and Vocational Preparation', *Compare*, 16.

PRAIS, S.J. (1987). 'Educating for Productivity: Comparisons of Japanese and English Schooling and Vocational Preparation', *National Institute Economic Review*, February.

PRAIS, S.J. (1989a). 'Qualified Manpower in Engineering: Britain and Other Industrially Advanced Nations', *National Institute Economic Review*, February.

PRAIS, S.J. (1989b). 'How Europe Would See the New British Initiative for Standardising Vocational Qualifications', *National Institute Economic Review*, August.

PRAIS, S. (1990). 'Oiling the School System Machinery', *Financial Times*, 25 April.

PRAIS, S.J. and STEEDMAN, H. (1986). 'Vocational Training in France and Britain: the Building Trades', *National Institute Economic Review*, May.

PRAIS, S.J. and WAGNER, K. (1983). 'Some Practical Aspects of Human Capital Investment: Training Standards in Five Occupations in Britain and Germany', *National Institute Economic Review*, August.

PRAIS, S.J. and WAGNER, K. (1985). 'Schooling Standards in Britain and Germany: Some Summary Comparisons Bearing on Economic Efficiency', *National Institute Economic Review*, May.

PRAIS, S.J. and WAGNER, K. (1988). 'Productivity and Management: The Training of Foremen in Britain and Germany', *National Institute Economic Review*, February.

PRAIS, S.J., JARVIS, V. and WAGNER, K. (1989). 'Producivity and Vocational Skills in Britain and Germany: Hotels', *National Institute Economic Review*, November.

PRATTEN, C.F. (1976). *Labour Productivity Differences Within International Companies*. Cambridge, Cambridge University Press.

PROWSE, M. (1986). 'When Paying Workers Less Doesn't Help', *Financial Times*, 13 March.

PROWSE, M. (1989a). 'The Need to Stay the Course', *Financial Times*, 29 November.

PROWSE, M. (1989b). 'A Nation That Can't Count', *Financial Times*, 8 December.

PSACHAROPOULOS, G. (1973). *Returns to Education: An International Comparison*. Amsterdam, Elsevier Scientific Publishing Company.

PSACHAROPOULOS, G. (1985). 'Returns to Education: A Further International Update and Implications', *Journal of Human Resources*, 20.

RAE, J. (1981). *The Public School Revolution: Britain's Independent Schools 1964–1979*. London, Faber & Faber.

READER, D. (1979). 'A Recurring Debate: Education and Industry', in G.Bernbaum, ed. *Schooling in Decline*, London, Macmillan.

READERS' DIGEST (1987). 'State Schools', September.

ROBBINS REPORT (1963). *Higher Education: Report of the Committee on Higher Education*. Cmd. 2154. London, HMSO.

ROBERTSON, P.L.(1981). 'Employers and Engineering Education in Britain and the United States, 1890–1914', *Business History*, 23.

RODERICK, G.W. and STEPHENS, M.D.(1978). *Education and Industry in the Nineteenth Century: The English Disease?* London, Longman.

RODERICK, G.W. and STEPHENS, M.D., eds. (1981). *Where Did We Go Wrong? Industry, Education and Economy of Victorian Britain*. Lewes, Sussex, The Falmer Press.

RODERICK, G.W. and STEPHENS, M.D., eds. (1982). *The British Malaise: Industrial Performance, Education and Training in Britain Today*. Lewes, Sussex, The Falmer Press.

ROGALY, J. (1988). 'Another Great British Muddle', *Financial Times*, 12 February.

ROTHWELL, R. (1977). 'The Characteristics of Successful Innovators and Technically Progressive Firms (with Some Comments on Innovation Research)', *R & D Management*, 7.

ROTHWELL, R. (1978). 'Where Britain Lags Behind', *Management Today*, November.

ROTHWELL, R. (1980). 'Policies in Industry', in K. Pavitt, ed. *Technical Innovation and British Economic Performance*. London, Macmillan.

ROTHWELL, R. and ZEGVELD, W. (1979). *Technical Change and Employment*. Oxford, Frances Pinter.

ROWTHORN, R.E. and WELLS, J.R. (1987). *De-industrialisation and Foreign Trade*. Cambridge, Cambridge University Press.

RYAN, P. (1980). 'The Costs of Job Training for a Transferable Skill', *British Journal of Industrial Relations*, November.

RYAN, P. (1984). 'The New Training Initiative after Two Years', *Lloyds Bank Review*, April.

RYAN, P. (1987). 'The Cost Disease and Educational Finance: The Adverse Effects of Cash Limits', in H.Thomas and T.Simkins, eds. *Economics and the Management of Education: Emerging Themes*. Lewes, Sussex, The Falmer Press.

SAKO, M and DORE, R. (1988). 'Teaching and Testing: the Role of the State in Japan', *Oxford Review of Economic Policy*, 4.

SAMUELSON REPORTS (1882–4). *Reports of the Royal Commission on Technical Instruction*. C. 1371, C. 3981. London, HMSO.

SANDBERG, L.G. (1982). 'Ignorance, Poverty and Economic Backwardness in the Early Stages of European Industrialisation: Variations on Alexander Gerschenkron's Grand Theme', *Journal of European Economic History*, 11.

SANDERSON, M. (1969). 'The Universities and Industry in England 1919–1939', *Yorkshire Bulletin of Economic and Social Research*, 21.

SANDERSON, M. (1972). *The Universities and British Industry 1850–1970*. London, Routledge & Kegan Paul.

SANDERSON, M. (1987). *Educational Opportunity and Social Change in England*. London, Faber & Faber.

SANDERSON, M. (1988) 'Education and Economic Decline, 1890–1980s', *Oxford Review of Economic Policy*, 4.

SANDERSON, M. (1990). 'The Missing Stratum: the Problem of Technical School Education in England, 1900–1960s', in G.Tortella, ed. *Education and Economic Development since the Industrial Revolution*. Valencia, Generalitat Valenciana.

SCASE, R. and GOFFEE, R. (1982). *The Entrepreneurial Middle Class*. London, Croom Helm.

SCHOBER, K. (1984). 'The Educational System, Vocational Training and Youth Unemployment in West Germany', *Compare*, 14.

SCHOOLS COUNCIL (1966). *Closer Links between Teachers and Industry and Commerce*. London, HMSO.

SCHOTT, K. (1981). *Industrial Innovation in the United Kingdom, Canada and the United States*. London, The British–North American Committee.

SCHULTZ, T.W. (1961). 'Investment in Human Capital', *American Economic Review*, 51.

SELBY-SMITH, C. (1962). 'Benefits to British Employers from Post-secondary Education', *Journal of Royal Statistical Society*, A132, Part 2.

SELBY-SMITH, C. (1970a). 'Costs and Benefits in Further Education: Some Evidence from a Pilot Study', *Economic Journal*, 80.

SELBY-SMITH, C. (1970b). *The Costs of Further Education: A British Analysis*. Oxford, Pergamon.

SHADWELL, A. (1906). *Industrial Efficiency*, Vol. II. London, Longmans Green & Co.

SHARPLES, S. and CARTY, V. (1987). *Vocational Training in the United Kingdom*. Berlin, European Centre for the Development of Vocational Training.

SHELDRAKE, J. and VICKERSTAFF, S. (1987). *The History of Industrial Training in Britain*. Aldershot, Gower.

SHIPMAN, M. (1984). 'The United Kingdom', in J.R. Hough, ed. *Educational Policy: An International Survey*. London, Croom Helm.

SIEDENTOP, L. (1986). 'British Education: Fostering an Instinct for the Marketplace', *Financial Times*, 30 July.

SILBERSTON, A. (1955). *Education and Training for Industrial Management*. London, Management Publications Ltd.

SIMMONS, J. (1979). 'Education for Development, Reconsidered', *World Development*, 7.

SIMON, B. (1991). *Education and the Social Order 1940–1990*. New York, St. Martin's Press.

SKAPINKER, M. (1987). 'Management Education: Why Britain's Thirst Must Be Satisfied', *Financial Times*, 29 April.

SKED, A. (1987). *Britain's Decline: Problems and Perspectives*. Oxford, Blackwell.

SMITH, A. (1776). *An Inquiry into the Nature and Causes of the Wealth of Nations*. London.

SMITH, A.D., HITCHENS, D.M.W.N. and DAVIES, S.W. (1982). *International Industrial Productivity: A Comparison of Britain, America and Germany*. Cambridge, Cambridge University Press.

SMITH, B.P. (1977). 'Managing for Productivity', *Management Today*, October.

SMITH, D. (1983). 'Britain's Recovery; the Bottleneck Factor', *Financial Weekly*, 3 June.

SMITH, K. (1986). *The British Economic Crisis: Its Past and Future*. Harmondsworth, Penguin.

SORGE, A. (1978). 'The Management Tradition: A Continental View', in M.Fores and I.Glover, eds. *Manufacturing and Management*. London, HMSO.

SORGE, A. (1979a). 'Engineers in Management: A Study of British, German and French Traditions', *Journal of General Management*, 5.

SORGE, A. (1979b). 'Technical Education and Training as a Public Concern in Britain, France and Germany', *Management Research News*, 2.

SORGE, A. and WARNER, M. (1980). 'Manpower Training, Manufacturing Organisation and Workplace Relations in Great Britain and West Germany', *British Journal of Industrial Relations*, 18.

SORGE, A. and WARNER, M. (1986). *Comparative Factory Organisation: An Anglo-German Comparison of Manufacturing, Management and Manpower*. Aldershot, Gower.

SPENS REPORT (1938). *Report of the Consultative Committee on Secondary Education with Special Reference to Grammar Schools and Technical High Schools*. London, Board of Education, HMSO.

STANDING, G. (1988). 'Training, Flexibility and Swedish Full Employment', *Oxford Review of Economic Policy*, 4.

STANWORTH, P. and GIDDENS, A. (1974). 'An Economic Elite: A Demographic Profile of Company Chairmen', in P. Stanworth and A. Giddens, eds. *Elites and Power in British Industry*. Cambridge, Cambridge University Press.

STEEDMAN, H. (1984). 'Running to Stay in the Same Place: Quantitative Comparison of Provision for Technical Education and the Training of Young People in France, England and Wales', *Compare*, 14.

STEEDMAN, H. (1987). 'Vocational Training in France and Britain: Office Work', *National Institute Economic Review*, May.

STEEDMAN, H. (1988). 'Vocational Training in France and Britain: Mechanical and Electrical Craftsmen', *National Institute Economic Review*, November.

STEEDMAN, H. (1990). 'Improvements in Workforce Qualifications: Britain and France', *National Institute Economic Review*, August.

STEEDMAN, H. and WAGNER, K. (1987). 'A Second Look at Productivity: Machinery Skills in Britain and Germany', *National Institute Economic Review*, November.

STEEDMAN, H. and WAGNER, K. (1989). 'Productivity, Machinery and Skills: Clothing Manufacture in Britain and Germany', *National Institute Economic Review*, May.

STEVENSON, J. (1984). *British Society 1914–45*. Harmondsworth, Penguin Books.

STEWART, R. and DUNCAN-JONES, P. (1956). 'Educational Background and Career History of British Managers, with Some American Comparisons', *Explorations in Entrepreneurial History*, 9.

STONEMAN, P. (1984). 'Technological Change and Economic Performance', in *Out of Work: Perspectives of Mass Unemployment*. Coventry, Department of Economics, University of Warwick.

STOREY, D.J. (1982). *Entrepreneurship and the New Firm*. London, Croom Helm.

STOUT, D.K. (1977). *International Price Competitiveness: Non-Price Factors and Export Performance*, London, National Economic Development Office.

SUMMERFIELD, P. and EVANS, E.J., eds. (1990). *Technical Education and the State since 1850: Historical and Contemporary Perspectives*. Manchester, Manchester University Press.

SWANN REPORT (1968). *The Flow into Employment of Scientists, Engineers and Technologists*. Cmnd. 2760. London, HMSO.

SWORDS-ISHERWOOD, N. (1980). 'British Management Compared', in K.Pavitt, ed. *Technical Innovation and British Economic Performance*. London, Macmillan.

TARSH, J. (1987). 'Higher Education and the Labour Market: A View of the Debate', in H.Thomas and T.Simkins, eds. *Economics and the Management of Education: Emerging Themes*. Lewes, Sussex, The Falmer Press.

TAUNTON REPORT (1868). *Report of the Schools Inquiry Commission*, Vol. I. London, HMSO.

TAYLOR, R. (1980). *The Fifth Estate: Britain's Unions in the Modern World*. London, Pan Books.

TAYLOR REPORT (1977). *A New Partnership for Our Schools*. London, HMSO.

THOMAS, D. (1989). 'The Battle Over the Secret Garden', *Financial Times*, 2 September.

THOMAS, H. and SIMKINS, T. (1987). *Economics and the Management of Education : Emerging Themes*. Lewes, Sussex, The Falmer Press.

THUROW, L. (1982). 'America in the 1980s: Thurow's Third Way', *The Economist*, 23 January.

TIPTON, B. (1982). 'The Quality of Training and the Design of Work', *Industrial Relations Journal*, spring.

TISDELL, C.H. (1981). *Science and Technology Policy: Priorities of Governments*. London, Chapman & Hall.

TORTELLA, G. ed. (1990). *Education and Economic Development since the Industrial Revolution*. Valencia, Generalitat Valenciana.

TRAINING AGENCY (1989). *Training in Britain: A Study of Funding, Activity and Attitudes*. London, HMSO.

TURNER, G. (1971). *Business in Britain*. Harmondsworth, Penguin.

TWISS, B.C. (1974). *Managing Technological Innovation*. London, Longman.

TYLECOTE, A. (1977). *Managers, Owners and Bankers in British and German Industry: Causes of German Industrial Superiority*. Sheffield, University of Sheffield, Division of Economic Studies Working Paper.

TYLECOTE, A. (1981). *The Causes of the Present Inflation: An Interdisciplinary Explanation of Inflation in Britain, Germany and the United States*. London, Macmillan.

UNESCO (annual). *Statistical Yearbooks*.

URWICK, L. and BRECH, E.F.L. (1953). *The Making of Scientific Management. Vol II: Management in British Industry*. London, Pitman.

UTTON, M.A. (1982). *The Political Economy of Big Business*. Oxford, Martin Robertson.

VAN DER WEE, H. (1986). *Prosperity and Upheaval: The World Economy 1945–1980*. Harmondsworth, Penguin Books.

VENABLES, E. (1974). *Apprentices Out of Their Time: A Follow-up Study* London, Faber & Faber.

WADDELL REPORTS (1978). *School Examinations*. Cmnd. 7281-I-II. London, HMSO.

WALFORD, G., PURVIS, J. and POLLARD, A., eds. (1988). *Education, Training and the New Vocationalism: Experience and Policy*. Milton Keynes, Open University Press.

WARD, D. (1967). 'The Public Schools and Industry in Britain after 1870', *Journal of Contemporary History*, 2.

WARNER, M. (1987). 'Industrialisation, Management Education and Training Systems: A Comparative Analysis', *Journal of Management Studies*, 24.

WEAVER REPORT (1966). *Report of the Study Group on the Government of Colleges of Education*. London, HMSO.

WHITE, M. (1988). 'Educational Policy and Economic Goals', *Oxford Review of Economic Policy*, 4.

WHITE, M. and TREVOR, M. (1983). *Under Japanese Management: The Experience of British Workers*. London, Heinemann.

WHITLEY, R. THOMAS, A. and MARCEAU, J. (1981). *Masters of Business?* London, Tavistock Publications.

WIENER, M.J. (1981). *English Culture and the Decline of the Industrial Spirit 1850–1980*. Cambridge, Cambridge University Press.

WILKINSON, M. (1977). *Lessons from Europe: A Comparison of British and West European Schooling*. London, Centre for Policy Studies.

WILLIAMS, G. (1957). *Recruitment to Skilled Trades*. London, Routledge & Kegan Paul.

WILLIAMS, G. (1963). *Apprenticeship in Europe: The Lesson for Britain*. London, Chapman Hall.

WILLIAMS, G. and BLACKSTONE, T. (1983). *Response to Adversity: Higher Education in a Harsh Climate*. Guildford, Surrey, Society for Research into Higher Education.

WILLIAMS, G.L. and GORDON, A.G. (1981). 'Perceived Earnings Functions and *ex ante* Rates of Return to Higher Education', *Higher Education*, 10.

WILLIAMS, K., WILLIAMS, J. and THOMAS, D. (1983). *Why Are the British Bad at Manufacturing?* London, Routledge & Kegan Paul.

WILSON, R.A. (1989). *Review of the Economy and Employment 1988–89. Vol. I: Occupational Assessment*. Coventry, University of Warwick, Institute of Employment Research.

WOODS, L. (1990a). 'Counting the Cost of Training Provision', *Financial Times*, 9 May.

WOODS, L. (1990b). 'Setting Standards for All Occupations', *Financial Times*, 24 July.

WORLD BANK (1990). *World Development Report 1990*. Oxford, Oxford University Press.

WORSWICK, G.D.N. (1985). *Education and Economic Performance*. Aldershot, Gower.

WRAGG, R. and ROBERTSON, J. (1978). 'Britain's Industrial Performance since the War', *Department of Employment Gazette*, May.

INDEX